**JEFFERSON
HACK
THE
SYSTEM**

First published in the United States of America in 2016 by
Rizzoli International Publications, Inc.
300 Park Avenue South
New York, NY 10010
www.rizzoliusa.com

Publisher: Charles Miers
Managing Editor: Anthony Petrillose
Production: Rebecca Ambrose
Editorial Assistant: Gisela Aguilar
Text Editors: Kelli Rae Patton and Elizabeth Smith

© 2016 Dazed Media

100% INDIVIDUAL
Each individually-designed cover has been created using the **Kodak Prosper** 6000 inkjet web press. Covers printed in Dayton, OH, USA. Made with Kodak.

All rights reserved. No part of this publication may be reproduced, stored in retrieval systems, or transmitted in any form or by any means, electronic, mechanical, photocopying, recording, or otherwise, without prior consent by the publishers.

Distributed in the U.S. trade by Random House, New York.

Printed in China.

ISBN: 978-0-8478-4743-3
Library of Congress Control Number: 2015952518

2016 2017 2018 2019 / 10 9 8 7 6 5 4 3 2 1

WE CAN'T DO THIS ALONE

JEFFERSON HACK THE SYSTEM

Art Directed and Designed by
Ferdinando Verderi

Edited by
Ferdinando Verderi and John Paul Pryor

Produced by
Felicity Shaw

"We are in science fiction now. All the revolutions and old methods for changing consciousness are bankrupt. We're back to magic, to psychic life . . . all public reality is a script, anyone can write the script the way he wants. The warfare is psychic now. Whoever controls the language, the images, controls the race."
— "Allen Ginsberg in America", *The New Yorker*, 1968

I used to call them flashbacks; now they seem more like flash-forwards. I have a kind of persistent memory jog where I remember fiction as if it's fact, remember a scene from a movie as if it were a scene from real life, or bring to my mind an image rendered on a screen as if it were an image I'd witnessed with my own eyes. It began when I was a child and I would replace the Super 8 movies of my childhood as real memories. But then, the distinction between the real and unreal remained in the flicker of film and in the patina of Kodachrome. Now I Skype my daughter on holiday and she uploads her memories in real time into a feed. For her generation, who have a different relationship to time and memory, if there's no documentation, no posting of the event, then it's as if the event might never have happened—so acutely has the representation of reality replaced reality itself, so acutely has the high-definition quality of our digitised memories come to be more real than real.

Like Joaquin Phoenix in the movie *Her* (2013), I am in love with an operating system. It's as if we are married. I exist through her/it. The pronoun for machine love is unclear. All I know is that she/it knows more about me than I can imagine. She/it knows what I will do next and even think next, before I do. She/it makes me feel incredibly intelligent as she/it delivers me into universes previously unknown. While technically the media and communications landscape that has been built around us is wondrously brilliant, as conceptually magnificent to behold as Diller and Scofidio's "Blur Building", the output, the creativity in media feels, in comparison to the technological brilliance that abounds, intrinsically banal. It feels and behaves as clumsily as its popular adage: "content." A first wave of technology is partly to blame, where "search" and intuitive recommendations have narrowed the filters for newness or the unexpected to humdrum clichés. Cultural "Non"ness—sounds like numbness—a sort of manicured, perfected, synthetic new non-world is what pop culture is steeped in. It is described by what it is not. Like living in Heathrow Terminal 5 or, say, Googleplex in Mountain View. These are the future laboratories for how life may become. The industrialisation of storytelling financed by the speculative content-farm mentality of corporate media giants has sucked the soul out of the machine. The digital-media landscape is a map in search of territories where the race for scale obfuscates emotional realities. The philosopher Jean Baudrillard predicted what he called the "simulacra" or "hyper-reality," which was a postmodern term for the moment when it became absolutely impossible to distinguish between the real and unreal. The simulacra is the suspension of reality for new media that "protects us" from what it thinks we don't need to know and orders us to consume more of the same to propagate the illusion. Like a Jenny Holzer artwork it screams unironically: "Protect Me From What I Want."

The hybridisation of art, advertising, fashion, politics, terror, war, technology, and science has been one of the most incredible things to witness in my time building the editorial ethos of *Dazed & Confused* and *AnOther*. The pop psychology of modern life had a violent seizure in September 2001 and woke up to a new world order. This was the new beginning: a technologically enabled terrorism, the start of cyber-espionage, drone strikes, zero privacy, zero tolerance, and barbaric staged beheadings posted on social media. I feel hyperalert in it; mostly I feel a sense of extreme anxiety and fear but somewhere underlying that there is also a degree of hope and what I refer to as "punk positivism." The generation of digital natives born in a world at war with terror have been born into a world with cultural fear on red alert. It's a very different set of cultural conditions than the one I was born into.

We live virtually. Our data trails live as mirror images of ourselves in the cloud. We can find digital footprints of our emotional profiles etched into code. The codification of life. Yet aren't we all machines of some description? Is not all life, from animal to plant life from distant stars to sound and light waves that emit from mobile phones in designer handbags all part of a complex, interconnected magical system of metadata? I met the *Generation X* author and artist in residence at the Google Cultural Institute Douglas Coupland at a conference recently and I asked him about his theory of the "cloudganger." It has long been an obsession in fiction that we all have a doppelgänger in real life, someone out there who looks just like us, who shares our behaviour, our soul. Coupland suggests our cloudganger is our virtual self, who behaves and thinks just like us. But it will far outlive us. Standing next to him at this conference was a young tech genius who happened to be in charge of operating the cloud for one of those giant corps. I wanted to know if it was a possibility that I would live forever in the cloud and if my cloudganger would continue to consume, create, or possibly even procreate beyond my years on the planet. "Yes, it's possible," the genius tells me, "but not only for you, but for you and all your multiple selves."

The idea of a singular Internet already feels like a linear, old-fashioned concept. We are now curating multiple Internets for our multiple selves. In *The Fabric of Reality* (1997) David Deutsch reveals new quantum dimensions and suggests the concept of a multiverse—the idea of many worlds existing simultaneously. The idea that everything that ever exists or happens at any place or time is as seriously real as the contents of what we are able to experience here and now. He takes a transhuman, or posthuman, approach and calls the brain "a virtual-reality-generating computer," which he sees as capable of rendering humanly experienceable environments.

Para is the ancient Greek word meaning "beside," "next to," or "contrary to." It both suggests being on top of or underneath something else. The concept of our lives being many parallel realities, all equally as real as the other, feels to me to be an incredibly relevant concept—a mix of sub- and superconscious reality operating at once.

"Para-real" may be the moment we recognise that the artificial is the new norm and that there in the multiplicity of causality is where "I" becomes pluralised. Perhaps the title of this book, *We Can't Do This Alone*, is an affirmation of that. The "We" is in many ways a reference to our many selves. In a para-real world of multiplicity, one of me is clearly not enough.

In terms of our hyper-atomised individuality this may come as a relief or as a shock to the system. Maybe it will produce the same kind of sensation that Douglas Coupland described when walking along Clerkenwell Road and seeing a billboard featuring an advertisement for Gap jeans which said "Be Normal"—"I was like, 'What! What the fuck was that, seriously?'—it was a real moment." When normcore is no longer ironic then hyperreality is already in full mainstream swing. In hyperreality, the causal instruction, the slogan of indifference, is "be normal"—like acting normal during a tsunami or keeping cool during a hijack, it's the mainstream's new calm face, masking extreme fear under pressure.

This social passivity, dismissiveness, blandness, a certain monotony and monotone EDM beat is the normcore reaction to hyperreality—a Prozac of consciousness. In this newer para-real time, the multiplicity of fictional universes has created a greater sense of friction and juxtaposition. I see a return to anger, frustration, and impatience in the voices of young artists in the transgender movement, in the pro-choice, gay marriage, climate change, pro-equality, pro-legalisation groundswell. It's a protest against indifference—a new emergent, emergency movement.

Timothy Leary's slogan "Tune In, Turn On, Drop Out" was about resistance against the Man, the faceless corporations running America's sociopolitical status quo in the late 1960s. It was something to do with creating an alternative "countercultural" society and sparking a revolution where the hippy search for meaning in ancient cultures inspired a spiritual togetherness that would triumph over individualism, where the underdogs would crawl over the mad dogs who were running and ruining everything. To have been a part of that time always looked amazing to me. The Civil Rights marches and victories, the Sexual Revolution, Woodstock, May '68, independent politicised cinema, environmental activist movements, the Beat Generation, flower power, first-wave feminism—everyone looked sexy and cool and had hip sunglasses and quoted philosophical and political text. I buy the retro-fetishism of it. Looking back there's rarely been a better time for literature—photography, graphic design, and magazines flourished. I loved collecting the worn and fragile old issues of *OZ*, *International Times*, *Avant Garde*, *Playboy*, *Interview*, *Nova*, and *Evergreen* magazines, the underground, social media of their time. It was a time of such fundamental, monumental change that it seems almost unrepeatable. The failed communes and failed utopias of the 1970s may echo the failure of the Arab Spring but they don't stop successive cultures or generations wanting to tear down the power structures to erect their own. The "Twitter Revolution" attempted to bring democracy and designer sunglasses to the political systems of Iran, Egypt, Libya, Syria, Bahrain, and Tunisia. The ecology of social resistance is hugely liberated by technology, but humanity is still playing out its dark self globally, and the reality is that many die and sacrifice their liberty while utopias appear glacially slow in emerging. Perhaps the very notion of them as utopic, replacing one extreme with another, an idea with an ideal is the inherent flaw. In many places democracy, civil liberty, human rights are like the global ice caps actually in full-blown retreat. Advances that we in the West can all be grateful for, such as racial and gender equality and improved drugs for managing diseases such as HIV/AIDS and polio have made respectable gains on the surface of some areas of our society. But you only need to look at the incarceration statistics in US jails to get a perspective on a new, more silent form of racial segregation, or look at the statistics for female filmmakers in Hollywood, female CEOs in the San Francisco tech community, or the number of female political leaders to see how wide the gap still is in racial and gender equality. The surface of Western society masks a thin veneer of anxiety, patriarchal control, mistrust, and—one of the most infectious barriers to positive change—a sense of spiritual hopelessness.

In the 1970s there were faceless corporations that ran the world but that was when most Western middle-class kids like me were guaranteed a job, and if we didn't want a job, at least a future. Now the middle class has been hollowed out and the odds of getting a job or having a future that the generation before you enjoyed are stacked wildly against you.

Kids are not kids anymore. The rite of passage is filled with new rebel myths and mystique. Technology is the new discriminator. The algorithm automates the new tabloid headline. The data cloud is the new prison. Are you shut out or shut in? Douglas Coupland's essay title "Shopping in Jail" (2014) describes technology as the new paradigm for social advancement. What happens when the majority of China's millennial population gets access to high-speed connectivity, one hundred times faster than anything currently in use in San Francisco? What happens to our morality when a tech giant can predict, like the movie *Minority Report* (2002), within ninety-five per cent accuracy, exactly when you are genetically predisposed to die?

Like all communications systems and feedback loops the ecology or management of technology is really in the hands of the very few—the one per cent of the one per cent, but that's a top-down view; looking at it from the bottom up, where everyone is now the media, there is an alternate perception. There is more transparency, more authorship, more evidence, more relevance, more diversity, more power to the people, to the individual voice.

The system is flawed when serious news organisations and genuine investigative journalism are in decline. The true accountability to society is society's right of self-investigation. Yet self-expression is the new news. The system follows your innermost codes and desires so it can better understand you. It rewards you for subscribing and following and sharing and accumulating followers and it invites you to post, retouch, edit, shoot, upload, download, and internally busy yourself feeding the machine. It wants you to be so busy expressing yourself that you no longer care about what really matters other than that cycle, that loop of narcissism, that addiction, that sense of self-worth that this projection of desire gives you. "Do we continually have to prove to ourselves that we exist?" asks Baudrillard in *America* (1986). He saw it as a flaw in humanity and describes it as "a strange sign of weakness, harbinger of a new fanaticism for a faceless performance, endlessly self-evident."

As Coupland revealed to me in our conversation for this introduction, "I want to create as much data as I possibly can by being alive. The question is how do we even do that? And I got to thinking that maybe in the future we can look at . . . things like frequent flyer points. The frequent flyer points of the future are going to be data—the more data you generate, the more mileage points you get to fly, or something like that."

And that really sums up the way the relationship between the individual and the machines are playing out. You are rewarded for feeding the machine. The more you feed it, the more rewards you accumulate. The true revolutionary figures in all of this are the ghosts in the machine: Edward Snowden, Alan Rusbridger, Julian Assange (who was interviewed in *AnOther Magazine*, Issue 21, 2011), and Aaron Swartz. These are some of the freedom fighters who have risked everything to bring truth and accountability into public consciousness. These are the ones who risked life, liberty, and all the rewards. The fact that technology is getting the bad rap is to some extent counterintuitive. It's too obvious. It's humanity that has always had the potential to be its best solution or its own worst enemy. Yet the very essence of who we are is more acutely rendered in real-time HD, in VR, in AI, in all of these new portals into our understanding of ourselves than it ever has been in any moment of our existence. It's beautiful and harrowing, fear inducing and liberating, horrific and beatific all at the same time.

I remember in a very early issue of *Dazed & Confused* talking to one of my first mentors, Tibor Kalman, and he said, "Extreme acts of individuality are what propel the world forward, but it takes individual people and passion to make things happen and you have to be unpopular and you have to risk everything. It's almost a cliché but advertising is the complete opposite of that because those producing it need to have security."

Every action is a political action even if we don't recognise it as such. It's the individual and individual action, not society, that will make counteraction and real change possible. Society is too slow, too fragmented, too crippled with nostalgia to know how to adapt to change. It has got to be an inside job.

Hans-Ulrich Obrist, co-author of *The Age of Earthquakes* (2015) with Douglas Coupland, reinforces this idea of a protest against indifference with his "protest against homogenised globalisation." He explains, "The forces of globalisations are at work and are a risk to the world—erasure of difference is the danger of homogenising forces. Can we protest against homogenising forces and impose global dialogues that are not nationalistic, which are not refusing to engage, which are generous?"

Artists and storytellers are our dreamers but they are also our creators of new realities, without whose artistic endeavour the public cannot imagine stepping into territories mapped by technology or modern philosophies. That's why I am excited about promoting and participating in the new narratives and counter-narratives that emerge as we system-hack between the hyper- and para-real, between truth and fiction. From new quantum understandings of space and time we can view stories from territories that were impossible to fathom previously.

We Can't Do This Alone is for and about storytellers who transcend their borders, their age, their genres, their identities—people who live simultaneously in between them all, criss-crossing like ice-skaters on the cool flat surface of digital screens. Shifting identities within this shifting landscape is a surreal game of simultaneous camouflage and exposure. Some storytellers, such as Rem Koolhaas (yes, you can tell stories with buildings), stand out in contrast to the backdrop, an elevated position in relief to the landscape, while others, like Miuccia Prada or Björk, seem to assimilate it and wrap themselves up in its paradox—the high/low of consumer culture brought to bear in the characterisation of the feminine: fashion as art, as social and political metaphor.

It was Tilda Swinton who really helped me understand that we were not alone, but part of a much wider cultural resistance movement. I first collaborated with her for *AnOther Magazine*, when she generously guest-edited the literary section, "AnOther Document." It was the beginning of many creative adventures that have resulted in covers, interviews, and happenings, both on and off the page. I have enormous gratitude for her generosity and her spirit of collaboration. For this book, we discussed the notion of resistance, the sense of scale in which it's possible to exist as an artist if we take the wider view, a perspective that allows us to belong to a tradition of resistance, "a continuum" as she calls it. There are few artists who traverse pop culture with as much plurality as Swinton. She is a true artist-chameleon, a polymath on a perpetual voyage of discovery—she is a Moonage Daydream, an action painting, a futurist manifesto, a Dadaist discoball of the imagination. Talking to her is like tripping naked through a culture field—she makes me feel that vulnerable, that inconsequential, that human, that connected to others, that real.

Fashion is the ultimate dream factory. I had the privilege of working with Alexander McQueen, who, very early on in the history of *Dazed & Confused*, taught me the power of fashion to convey ideas, of clothing to be a canvas for storytelling—the catwalk a stage set for transcendental wonder, where he would synthesise music, art, fashion, and technology to trigger all the senses into a state of suspension in which an almost ritualistic desire for belonging was evoked. It was cathartic, quasi-religious, like so much of the early 1990s in London—it was tribal, outsider, and it created an extreme sense of spiritual connection as fashion transcended its boundaries. It was the coming of age of high fashion as a new globalised industry dominating the ideal of what is beautiful, desirable, and seductive, with an aesthetic that evokes power and ultimately cultural, economic, social, and political advancement. The genesis of a paradigm in which logos are an international language understood from Lagos to Shanghai—the goods, easily distributed, globally tradeable, and quickly copied. Our times are defined by the acceleration of this industry as it broadens. Brands recode their products to target the various richly individuated lifestyles from the Jet Set to the Art Set, from the Gyp Set to the Boyz-N-the-Hood Set. Different parallel realities have begun to exist within brands that switch storylines between product lines, that exert paradox as a marketing strategy, that utilise duality or para-reality as a way to broaden desire and reach within a narrowing of time, surfing the fourth dimension in the slipstream of the extreme.

When Marc Jacobs collaborated with Richard Prince for Louis Vuitton in the mid-2000s, it felt as though fashion was an appropriated art form. Art needed a bigger stage and fashion needed a metaphor for authenticity and they found it in each other. But fashion is now established as pop. Karl Lagerfeld is the new Andy Warhol and the "Chanel Supermarket" shows the ultimate expression of high-fashion consumerism, as bold as a Kanye West lyric sheet and as self-referential. I see a few welcome exceptions in the pages of *Dazed & Confused* with designers like Eckhaus Latta, Hood By Air, Simone Rocha, Iris van Herpen, and Grace Wales Bonner, designers, image-makers and stylists who are inventing new narratives. It's still on the fringes that we find experimentation. There is a new generation who are living and identifying our times, but it's still a minority voice hemmed in by a constant barrage of mediocrity, where successful formulas for sales and not invention are encouraged.

Perhaps the true new form of revolution or individual subversion is coming not so much from the decoration of the body but from the DNA of the body itself. A pro-diversity movement is in full swing and it is redefining sexual stereotypes and archetypes across all aspects of culture. The orientation of a society across gender binarism is in flux—we have a multiplicity of choice and all the traditional codes of references, what we knew about man and woman, what we were taught in school, what we learnt from the morality and sensibilities of our social codes seem so old-fashioned, so quaint, and so oppressive. Anyone who stands in the way of cultural diversity is pro–cultural oppression. Anyone who stands in the way of gender diversity and equality is by definition gender stereotyping.

The landscape of the body and personal identity as a canvas for storytelling is now more potent, more popular, and more empowered than ever before. It will be what reshapes fashion, media, and communication in the next decade more than any other cultural movement. *Dazed & Confused* in name and intent was always waiting for this moment to connect to those brave enough to stand apart from the system's status quo and take individual and collective responsibility to effect change on their terms. It was David Bowie who told me, "The moment you feel safe, move on"; it's the most unnatural emotion in the world for creativity to feel "safe."

I met practically everyone I worked with in nightclubs, and I mean everyone. Long before the social-media explosion, nightclubs were the physical manifestation of where youth cults existed. In London these clubs were salons of creative dialect, laboratories of fashion, the pop-up homes of radical free expression—places of ecstasy, experimentation, and performance. From Acid House, Psych Rock, Northern Soul, Punk, Techno, Hard House, Dub, Jungle, Dubstep, and Trip Hop, from the Colony Club to *Dazed & Confused*'s own "Been There Seen It Done It," from the Brain club in the early 1990s to BoomBox almost two decades later, London club culture was where I grew up, where I learnt what it meant to synthesise the subcultural codes of nightlife, where music, fashion, performance art, and sexual adventure manifested. Where ideas and individuals that would change the future of pop culture were born. As my friend Malcolm McLaren once said, "I am obsessed with the look of music and the sound of fashion." There was never a more authentic catwalk or social network displayed than through club culture.

I am certain my brain has been rewired by more than just psychedelics and the shocking displays of exhibitionism I witnessed through living mostly in nightclubs in the 1990s and 2000s. We know from brain scientists that neuroplasticity from digital media causes a natural reengineering of our memories and our ability to multitask and concentrate on many things simultaneously and nothing specific for any length of time, the same could probably be said for club culture.

It's always been an unrealised ambition of mine to interview Björk under clinical hypnosis. Apparently the neural pathways open in unexpected ways under a deep, trance-like state and I find that fascinating—not least because she is someone who explores her own interior as an artist, the innermost workings of the heart and mind. What new memories will come to light? What connections between her emotions and her work could be exposed and explored and a deeper and more profound understanding of her as an artist revealed? I've always distrusted the classic interview format and have tried to subvert it wherever possible. For this book, Björk suggested we try something new and chat through emails. I couldn't imagine a more generous, eventful, and surprising collaboration. It's published here, completely raw and un-edited, a transparent facsimile copy of our correspondence and a view into a brilliant mind; dancing across subjects, emotions, interests and speculative theory—"just like a musical."

This post-symbolic interview, or meta-interview, is about inventing new rules of the game with certain willing subjects; Thom Yorke's self-interview for *Dazed & Confused* (Issue 19, 1996) was my first attempt. Yorke also shared a healthy distrust of media and disliked the fake feeling of being interviewed by a journalist for the obligatory sixty minutes and that interview somehow becoming a genuine profile of his ideas and work. So I asked him to interview himself. It sounds almost ridiculous but you can read more about the process later in this book. The process of undoing—that brings new realities and truths to the page.

I recently came across a lecture that William S. Burroughs gave at the City College of New York in 1974, where he considers writing "a magical operation." He talks about the ceremonial and magical qualities of writing and sculpture and how when it's separated from the ceremonial it loses its magical quality and becomes like a tribe selling dolls to tourists. "It may make money but it isn't magical," he continues. "Journalism is closer to the magical origins of writing than most fiction, and the technology is the technology of magic." In the wrong hands he describes it as "black-magic."

The independent way is a way of keeping the magic alive, because as soon as publishing becomes solely in the aid of commerce and power, then creativity and decision-making becomes about the formulas of success and not invention. The process becomes a means to an end. Burroughs said that art was about "qualitative magic" and journalism is about "quantitative magic"; one asks the big questions about life and death, the other reports on them looking for a bigger splash.

This "magical operation" to bring art to publishing and journalism, to try to transcend the form and function of magazines in the curious pursuit of new cultural territories, through new encounters and with new visual horizons—this was my naive world view at eighteen years old when I met my future partner in misadventure, John "Rankin" Waddell, at the London College of Printing sometime in 1990. It is still my naive world view today, some twenty-five years later. I am still anti-rules, anti-corporate, anti-Facebook, anti-self . . . For me, it's about "we" over "I," about creating a meaningful connection to people, not personal footprints in the sand.

We Can't Do This Alone: Jefferson Hack The System lists me as the author. But I am not an artist or author. I have made nothing. I feel like a fake. If anything, I am an observer of artists who, to my mind, are truly listening to the future and galvanising it in the present. I'm an encourager of their ideas, perhaps even a collector of their ideas and therefore a channeller of their cultural energies. My pattern of enquiry has always been to search for who is provoking, who is challenging the culture, and to go where the real energy is flowing and start a conversation there.

As much as editing this book has been a flashback over the twenty-five years of my editorial life observing culture close-up, it has also triggered many flash-forwards. I relish these déjà vu moments, described by Richard Prince as "tight spots," as they are possible imaginings for me of what's to come. I believe in the magical operation, the magical possibility that this book may fall into the hands of someone for whom it will be useful—a toolkit perhaps to unlock a way of thinking or behaving. I hold a high degree of hope for the cultural diversity movement and for a better future for all of humanity, not just the ones who can afford a book like this. We live in extraordinary times, extraordinarily dark and indifferent as well as extraordinarily vulnerable and therefore observant times. The status quo distrusts any positive change. We are in para-real science fiction now. We are all media. We can rewrite the rules together. We have the power to construct our own language and distribute our own images. We have and will continue to break the control of the status quo by refusing to be indifferent to change, by replacing old habits with new positive behaviours and maintaining a sense of collective responsibility for each other and the future of our planet with an open mind. The independent way is to never secede control—remember as Allen Ginsberg said, "Whoever controls the language, the images, controls the race." Time to take control of that system.

— *Jefferson Hack*

HACK THE SYSTEM

NOSTALGIA OF NOW

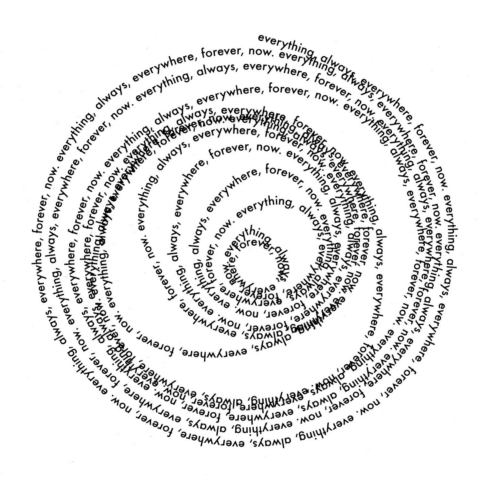

IF YOU CAN'T AFFORD IT, STEAL IT

A CONSPIRACY OF IDEAS

indifference, indifference,

the best
~~the~~ IS best

way
w~~a~~y NOT

to make

money
m~~o~~n~~e~~y ANY

DELUSIONS

of

GRANDEUR

_WE CAN'T DO THIS ALONE

Tilda Swinton: States of Being

Jefferson Hack: I watched *Ways of Listening* (2013) and you used a phrase in your interview with John Berger, I think it was a "continuation." You talked with him about the idea of our lives being transient within a bigger framework. That concept has really touched me, because it's the idea that your output is not only all about you but from and for others.
Tilda Swinton: The idea that the buck stops with oneself, with myself, is too much for me. I can't do it—it just doesn't work. It's not true for a start, but just the sensation of that idea gives me claustrophobia. The only way in which it's possible to feel capable of doing anything is to link oneself up to that generational through line. It's like hanging onto a galloping horse—you're just hanging on to the reins; the horse has got all the power. You are just being pulled along. That's the feeling, somehow.

JH: Everything is a continuation, isn't it?
TS: That's one of the great things about life, that there are these—not exactly repetitions—but these revisitations from generation to generation. It goes on and on. That's one of the things I love about reading the diaries, the letters, and the biographies of artists—it's very often the same territory from century to century.

JH: When did you meet John Berger?
TS: I met him when he asked me to be in a film called *Play Me Something* in 1989, which was based on a story by him. It was directed by Timothy Neat and is about a group of people who land on this island in the Hebrides called Barra. They are stranded in the airport terminal because the airplane can't land and can't take off. John Berger plays a mysterious storyteller who starts telling us a story to pass the time about some lovers in Venice. It's a beautiful, beautiful film, and I play a sort of island girl. He is unique, and what he brought into my life is unique.

JH: He was a generation before Derek Jarman, wasn't he?
TS: Yeah, he is the same age as my father. And he is the same generation as my great teachers Margot Heinemann and Raymond Williams, who were these great socialist writers I knew at Cambridge. He was another foster father for me. I had read *Ways of Seeing* (1972) when I was at school. It just blew my mind, as it blew most people's minds. He feels like a witness to an invaluable experience.

JH: "Witness" is a good word.
TS: He is from the generation of our parents but he feels like an ally in a different way, in a quiet, original way. One of the reasons that I wanted to make *Harvest* (2016)—which is the last of our four films together—is because the first film became about the two of us talking about our fathers, and I wanted the last film to be about our children. I wanted to share how interested he is in their ideas. He always claims that what he is doing as a storyteller is listening. He is listening to other people's lives. He wrote letters for illiterate soldiers during the war. When someone would say, "I want to write to say how much I love her but I can't find the words," he would say, "Would you maybe like to say it like this?" It was an amazing training for a storyteller.

JH: I guess that's sort of what we are talking about when we discuss continuation; this through line where we are all interpreting the work of those that have gone before us and maybe adding a little something to it.

TS: I think his attitude of attention to the world outside of him has been incredibly supportive to me. I mean, certainly, when you are a young artist you're given to understand sometimes that you're supposed to have a lot more interest in yourself than you might have. And he—for me, anyway—he validated: "No, you're not as interesting as anything out there. Go look. It's fine not to be caught up in yourself." Which is really a great thing. I want more of John Berger than I fear the universe is going to give us.

JH: When you look on YouTube, you see a lot of clips from him in the 1970s, then there's a little bit in the early 1980s, and then he sort of disappears. It's incredibly urgent to get him today, with the perspective of time. It seems he's even more relevant in this post-digital age. We believed the Internet would expand our view of time and space and our relational connectivity but actually it's reduced communications to a very small, narrow bandwidth. Tell me about the "cultural resistance movement" because this is something that I've held on to a long time, but I want to understand what that term means to you.
TS: I have to really think when it started to mean something to me. Because practically speaking, the idea of resistance, or feeling oneself swimming upstream, or just feeling slightly out of kilter with those around one was something I was familiar with from a very early age. But when did I start to feel there might be other people who were also swimming the same way? I feel like it was late in my life. When I left school and went to South Africa as a volunteer, I was aware that I was swimming against the political current there. One of the things I'm very, very moved by with my own children is that they have the good fortune to be living through a different education than I did. They know their life has begun and they would have said that when they were eleven or eight. I didn't feel that my life had begun at their age. I was sitting it out through my childhood—well, between about ten and eighteen, when I left school.

JH: What I got from the notion of a cultural resistance movement was this idea of being in opposition to things like inequalities in cultures, so when Derek was fighting for gay rights, when there was class war and Thatcher was in power and there was so much nationalist pride—these kinds of reductive notions were pervasive and dominant in culture, and the idea of being a cultural resistance movement was saying, "No, we're not agreeing to that. We have our own codes and practises."
TS: But the first step even before saying that is to turn and face someone else and say, "Hey, we're in this together." So even before you get your message together and turn to the rest of the world and say, "We're saying this," there is this amazing, exhilarating moment when you realise you're not the only one and there is somebody else. And if you feel alienated as a child or as a young person and are slightly led to believe that you are in the minority, that the world thinks one thing and you think another, then when you start to make alliances and recognise fellow travellers it is *beyond*. It's a wonderful, wonderful thing. I suppose I started doing that properly when I met Derek. That was when I realised that there were people who felt so many of the things I had felt… It was like going through the looking glass. I can't put it more simply than that. "Right, there is a universe there and other people exist, too," and that was amazing. I first met Derek in 1985, when he asked me to be in *Caravaggio*. He was already a very visible figure on the cultural landscape of this country.

JH: Yeah, *Jubilee* had already come out. He was one of the first people to be very vocal about being HIV-positive, wasn't he?
TS: I honestly believe that when Derek became aware that he was HIV-positive and when he owned it publicly, it was a real grounding for him in the way in which we were talking earlier about the idea of being linked up to some kind of force that goes through you. It was as if he was—I won't say he was removed previously—but he was plugged in at that point more than he had ever been. There was something that had plugged him in as a cultural activist, beyond being an artist. I mean, he became HIV-positive in '89 and he quite quickly publicly declared it. At that time many people were terrified and silent about their HIV status. I hate to say this, but it's not that hard to imagine now because people are still saying ridiculous things in some parts of the world—people were talking about HIV-positive people being shipped away and put on some kind of plague islands, and not being able to get insurance or not being able to get mortgages or losing their jobs or their homes.

JH: He was doing it for everyone else. He was doing it for the hundreds of thousands of people who were living with the stigma but unable to tell their friends and family that they were positive.
TS: It was a sort of penny drop for him in terms of his service.

JH: It was heroic.
TS: It was, but at the same time he couldn't have done anything else, and it did cause him a lot of grief. That doesn't mean to say that it wasn't a selfless act, but it served him, too, like all the best selfless acts.

JH: When you met him in that creative underground scene in London, of experimental filmmaking, theatre, performance, art, photography, club culture—that sense of a creative milieu must have been so rich, so much came from that period that it must have felt like a cultural resistance movement; no one was doing it for money, no one had any money. Today, that seems increasingly rare.
TS: It's phenomenal to think that only twenty-five to thirty years ago, someone like Leigh Bowery was living and working in the way that he was. You look at that work, look at those performances, look at those costumes, you look at those looks—beyond looks, those artworks—and you realise that he made them very often for one time only. Not for film, but for the people who happened to go to that party that night. It was a completely different, existential thing. Process not product. Unique, original, authentic experience not reproducible units for widespread, impersonal sale.

JH: It was a really interesting thing to feel that what we were doing at *Dazed & Confused* and *AnOther Magazine* was in this tradition of independent creativity—a resistance movement that was also against pop culture, or a popular culture that had a political agenda.
TS: It occurs to me to look at this term "cultural resistance," because although I completely accept and support it—I'm not nitpicking about it—I do want to say that there's an alternative to thinking about oneself as a resistance, which is thinking of oneself, or realising, that one is at the centre. That one's not peripheral, one's not alternative, that one is at the centre. There isn't one mainstream and the rest are some twiddly little burns just running down the hills and sort of dribbling into a puddle, but that there are many, many mainstreams, and one man's mainstream is another man's puddle, and one man's puddle is another man's mainstream.

JH: Many streams in a delta.
TS: Many streams in a delta! And that feeling of being excluded somehow ties up with the idea of being a resistance, because one needs a certain force to resist something.

JH: There was a lot of that in the 1980s; there was a lot of violence, a lot more tribal identity and commonality—with the multiplicity of options today do you think the power or force of opposition is perhaps lessened?
TS: It brings with it its own problems—it brings with it a potential lack of focus. I don't want for a second to sound nostalgic but there's no question that in the 1980s and early 1990s when times were really dark politically in this country and when very sinister things were being put forward, it was clearly a choice to be, as you say, in resistance.

JH: What were you fighting for—Derek and your tribe?
TS: We were fighting just to be our own mainstream, not to be excluded or marginalised or dismissed or disenfranchised. And to dignify our audience by the fellowship of the company we keep with them.

JH: Did you seek validation from the establishment, or was that not part of the agenda?
TS: One of the things that was really true about Derek, and I'm sure he'd agree if he was sitting here at the table—so I'm sure he is giggling somewhere as I say this—is that he had this great indignation because he was from a privileged background, very well educated, and he saw himself as this sort of heir to a classical trajectory, and yet he felt himself marginalised because he was a gay man and was completely out as a gay man. He was really indignant that he was not placed at the centre of the culture. So he would absolutely support this idea of resistance, because he did—he resisted the fact that he was being marginalised, dismissed.

JH: What is your cultural resistance movement? What does it mean to you to do the Ballerina Ballroom Cinema of Dreams [a pop-up cinema in Nairn], to do *The Maybe* [a sleep project in art institutions]? What does it mean to you to make the films you make, to spend years developing independent movies?
TS: For me, it's a question of being a witness. I mean, I don't carry with me that sense of having been persecuted the same way as Derek did, but I am the witness to those who do carry that sense, and I am really enlivened to do what I can to bear witness and do whatever I can to represent and keep company with them. If I am creative at all it's because of my ability to have conversations with people and to connect with other people.

JH: This whole thing about collaboration is such a part of this book and my work, and what I relate to is this ability of yours to work within a family of creators but also to extend that to be constantly bringing in new influences, constant new participants to challenge your own way of thinking. Do you see collaboration as a compromise, or do you see it as a gift?
TS: I don't know. I do occasionally work alone. I work as a writer by myself, of course, and a few times made pieces of work that are conceived and articulated as pieces of work by myself.

JH: How do you do it? What's your process?
TS: Well, I keep thinking during this conversation of this example Jonah Lehrer gave in his book *Imagine* (2012)—he was talking about a study people have made about creativity but they had taken the example of the Broadway musicals. They had taken the most successful Broadway musicals and they realised that there was a correlation between a string of very successful productions. The ones that worked consistently were the ones that were made by a core of the same people, but always with the inclusion of a little something extra, an element of change. And it just kept pushing the form. And all the way through this conversation between you and me, I keep thinking of this because that really speaks to me. I think the reason it speaks to me is because when you ask me the question, "How does collaboration work for you?" I just picture myself in a state of curiosity about the conversation, and that's why I've been very thoughtful. I've started with Derek and it's kind of extraordinary that I've been able to make these other collaborations after that very long, very thoughtful collaboration. And I keep going on finding more collaborations, and it's amazing to me. And now I've worked several times with Jim Jarmusch, several times with Olivier Saillard, with Bong Joon-Ho, with Luca Guadagnino—and that's just only from the past four years! And when I think back about the Jonah Lehrer example, it's all about a new strand of a familiar and compelling conversation, it's a new chemical reaction, it's a new set of synapses, and for whatever reason, it makes me tick. Without it, I would run aground.

JH: And how important is play in creativity?
TS: It's everything, absolutely everything. And what I mean by "play," if this is what you mean, is a sense of spontaneous connection, making it up as you go along. Which I know is a cause dear to your heart, because I was looking at evidence of it yesterday morning: I was moving some books onto a shelf and I saw the *Dazed* book, and I thought it's such a great title, because that's how I feel about life in general and making work in particular.

JH: The title of this one is *We Can't Do This Alone.* The idea that we are part of a tradition—that we wouldn't be doing this now if it weren't for those who had come before us. Also, we can't do this alone physically because I am a product of the people I collaborate with; it's very much about their input, and also "we" as to who it is for—the work is not for me, it's for others . . . It's really interesting because everything you have talked about has echoed the search that I'm on for understanding why I am attracted to those kinds of storytellers.
TS: Absolutely. And my sense of how you work is that you feel yourself deeply connected to your audience. And that is incredibly important as a creative input as well. It's not all done in a vacuum; it's done with that force field that one's there to be in dialogue.

JH: I'm the fan. I take the point of view of the audience.
TS: Exactly. There are all these myths abound that we are all very different; that life is incredibly long and that we can get out of it alive and that we can get away without experiencing pain and heartbreak and joy and miracles. And that myth is a real obstacle, so it feels to me that one of the things we can do, in the movement of cultural resistance, is to dissolve as much as we can the bonds of that myth, to encourage people to recognise and acknowledge how short life is, and how worthwhile it is getting real and honest about all of the wonderful things and difficult things, and sharing and feeling a sense of trust and engagement with each other before it's too late! It feels to me that that's what the force of the resistance movement is about. It's about disillusioning people that they can usefully be distracted from the real stuff. Some of it is really tough and difficult, but at the same time, the really miraculous stuff resides in it as well.

JH: What I am trying to do with the book is provide the reader with a toolkit of ideas to unlock the future possibilities, and say that everything is possible.
TS: I believe that's a really responsible thing to do. It's not just an exciting thing. I think it is responsible exactly because of all the things we have been talking about—the line, the torchbearers, all the way back to William Blake. It is possible for that thread to be lost if one doesn't bear witness to it. It's a point of responsibility and point of record to bear witness to the line, to the baton, the race . . .

JH: It's always been key to me to empower youth. What do you think we can learn from them?
TS: What can youth teach us? One word: illusionment.

Tilda Swinton in conversation with Jefferson Hack, June 16, 2015

We Can't Do This Alone
Jefferson Hack: *Introduction*
4

Slogan Posters
9

Tilda Swinton: *States of Being*
21

EVERYTHING ALWAYS STARTS WITH A QUESTION.
ALTERED PERSPECTIVES.
THOUGHT MAPS.
LYRICAL MIND-BOMBS.
DON'T READ IT, FEEL IT.
33

1.

DAZED & CONFUSED ISSUE ONE
Always Be Defiant and Never Be Defined
37

FOAM
Living in the Screen-Age of Photography
41

THOM YORKE
The Self Interview: In Conversation with the Psyche
47

FELDMAN
The Best Conversations Are Beyond Words
55

NOWNESS
Welcome to the Perpetual Conversation
63

MANTRA
Cut it Up: The Magical Operation of Language
67

NECESSARY PROVOCATION.
WHY MISTAKES ARE BEAUTIFUL.
THE RIGHT TIME. THE RIGHT PLACE. THE RIGHT ENERGY.
COLLECTIVE ACTION.
71

2.

DOLLAR BILL
Inspiring Political and Artistic Provocation
75

CORINNE DAY
Trusting in the Power of Instinct
85

NATURAL BEAUTY
Reversing the Beauty Myth
91

THE DIGITAL EDITION
Futuring: the Right Time, the Right Place, the Right Energy

95

3. ART DIRECTING REALITY. REAL VERSUS UNREAL. THE BEAUTY OF THE INVISIBLE. WE ARE ENDLESS... NOW... THE FUTURE IS A VERB.

99

SCARLETT JOHANSSON
Fact or Fiction? The Post-Symbolic Interview

103

NICK WAPLINGTON
Shoot Everything: Capturing the Mood of the Zeitgeist

111

KM3D-1
Three-Dimensional Fashion: Being Everywhere at Once

117

SX70
Music as Conversation

121

MAKING IT UP AS WE GO ALONG
Celebrating Twenty Years of Cultural Disruption

125

4. THE TRIUMPH OF OPTIMISM. DEFIANT NOT DEFINED. PUNK POSITIVISM. THE ONLY CHANGE IS SOCIAL. ANTI-NOSTALGIA.

131

U2 SONGS OF INNOCENCE
Retro-Minimalism and the Eternal Dialogue of Reflection

135

SKATEISTAN
The Short Film That Became a Movement

139

STUDIO AFRICA
Fuelling the Fire of Positive Change

143

BARBARA KRUGER   DAMIEN HIRST
Kicking Against the Pricks

147

PATTI SMITH
Cultural Provocation and Questions in Bed

151

PROJECT RED
A Network for Social Change

159

NO CODE: RECODE.
THE RULES ARE BROKEN.
RE-WRITE THE RULES.
MEDIA OUTLAWS.
ILLUSION OF FREEDOM.
THE POWER OF PARADOX.
165

5.

AI WEIWEI
Defining the Age of Craziness
169

BARBARA KRUGER
Decoding the Magazine
179

DAZED VS. WARHOL
How Upstarts Took the Mantle
185

MOVEMENT
Where Fashion, Dance and Film Unite
189

DRESS ART
Fashion Collides with Art: Transdisciplinary Style
193

FILMS OF INNOCENCE
Anti Retro Futurism
197

PRINT EMPOWERMENT.
THE INDEPENDENT WAY.
VALUING THE INTANGIBLE.
TRUST IN THE YOU OF IT.
201

6.

ANOTHER MAGAZINE
Going Global: The Emergence of Another Point of View
205

ANOTHER 13 PERFUME
The Sweet Scent of Print Addiction
209

BLOW UP
A Live Magazine Exhibition and the Art of Not Giving Up
213

THE FIRST COVER STAR
The Patron Saint of Dazed & Confused
217

DECADE IN STYLE
Growing Up: Ten Years of AnOther Magazine
223

DROP DEAD LETTER CLUB
Inspiring the Art of Letter Writing
231

CHANEL
No Expense Spared: Reflecting on History
235

RAG & BONE
Keeping it Real: Documentary as Fashion Advertising
239

7.

**MULTIPLE SELVES.
SHIFTING PERSPECTIVES.
SEX & IDENTITY.
WHO DO YOU THINK YOU ARE?
CONVERSATION IS CREATION.
243**

MCQUEEN BOWIE
The Synergy of Radical Creativity
247

RENEGADE TV
Bringing the Magazine into the Living Room
253

MASQUERADE
Scary Monsters / Super Creeps
257

GWYNETH PALTROW
Imagining New Interview Formats
261

FASHION ABLE
The Inimitable Beauty of Otherness
267

Björk: *Just Like a Musical*
272

Slogan Posters
277

Acknowledgements
290

Credits
292

Slogan Posters Overview
296

Outro
301

EVERY

Jefferson Hack: "Did you become the magazine or did the magazine become you?"
Hugh Hefner: "Both. I used the magazine without question as a stage for reinventing myself."

Another Man, 2007

STARTS

What do you most dislike about contemporary culture?
"That uninformed and bitter opinions can live in the same spheres as smart and thoughtful ones."

James Franco, *Anothermag.com*, 2012

A
QUEST

"Sometimes I feel like I'm tuning into a real wanker. Do you know what I mean? It's a question of identity and the loss of it among young people in today's wildly commercial, youth-marketing world. Like a line of cocaine, the fantasy of youth culture involuntarily fuses the synapses, causing repetitive talking and egomania, eliciting a flammable personality instinctively believing itself to be intellectually stimulating and more attractive than it really is. Like cocaine, the fantasy of youth culture can easily turn people into floundering tossers."

Jefferson Hack, *Dazed & Confused*, 1996

ALTER
PER

THING ALWAYS

1

"The contents of this issue are defined by our thoughts. Sometimes we plan and the thoughts become realised but most of the time it's the space between the thoughts that fill the pages. Nothing is ever really planned; the elements that combine to make up the issue are decided by the thoughts that escaped us as much as by the thoughts that were remembered... Don't read it, feel it."

Jefferson Hack, *Dazed & Confused*, 1995

WITH

"I like escapism, I like fantasy, I like drugs, but when a lifestyle buys them all wholesale, any initial explorative, liberating, life-changing properties are quickly used and it turns into a repressive, self destructive regime. Magazines, technology, advertising and chemical compounds can all add up to another form of long-term social control, one sure fire way of keeping young people in a permanent state of wankerdom. There are few answers, only questions."

Jefferson Hack, *Dazed & Confused*, 1996

ION.

ED SPECTIVES.

What do you most dislike about contemporary culture?
"I have some kind of magnetism that interferes with all of the electrical appliances and cell phones...
I am an analogue in a digital age."

Jean-Paul Gaultier, *Anothermag.com*, 2014

THOU

"Put it this way: Live fast, die young, always have fun, be wild, go mad, spend, spend, spend, get high, fly, drink more lager, party 'til you drop, fuck up but still look cool. These are the artificial dreams, designed for mass escapism. The foreign holidays of perpetual leisure time that allow us to lie on our backs and float on the surface of the ocean of our popular culture, carried by the tide of consumerism. Walk into the cartoon world of a megastore on Oxford Street and you see fantasy interaction has reached dangerously new levels of sophistication. Just appropriate that catchy jingle in the TV commercial for Duty-free goods. Why pay for reality? When you can spend money with me?"

Jefferson Hack, *Dazed & Confused,* 1996

LYRICAL MIND-

DON'T

At what points do life and work intersect?
"As a writer of fiction, I write about real life—stuff that's actually happened, but the act of writing removes me from it. So I guess they intersect in the past and then hopefully again in the future."

Harland Miller, *Anothermag.com,* 2010

FEEL IT.

GHT MAPS.

BOMBS.

"I don't have an 'if you can't beat them join them' philosophy, but I also don't have the 'if you can't beat them, curl up in a ball' philosophy. If you can't beat them, just do your work. And as I like to put it, it becomes a thorn in their side—just keep pricking them and pricking them and pricking them until they bleed."

Patti Smith, *AnOther Magazine*, 2006

READ IT,

"I should've had a plan, but I didn't. And I still don't."

Mia Farrow, *AnOther Magazine*, 2007

ISSUE 1 DAZED & CONF

EDITORIAL

This is not a magazine. *This is not a conspiracy to force opinion into the subconscious of stylish young people. A synthetic leisure culture is developing - plastic people force fed on canned entertainment and designer food. Are you ready to be* Dazed & Confused? *Get high on oxygen! This is urban ideas for creative people. People who want to read - something else.*

This issue of Dazed & Confused is sponsored by Black Bush Irish whiskey

BLACK BUSH

DAZED & CONFUSED ISSUE ONE

Issue one of *Dazed & Confused* was created in a poster format with three different A3 pages that folded into an A4 cover. It was done that way simply because it was the only thing we could afford – it was the most inexpensive way to create something that behaved like a magazine. Retrospectively, what is interesting is that certain elements, like the cover copy, were beginning to show that kernel of provocation and participation; there is a strong sense that comes through of rebellious dissatisfaction with the cultural paradigm. We were pushing an aesthetic that was totally DIY and unstudied, and looking back on it now, it was pretty ugly and raw, kind of wilfully unattractive really. It has a sense of idealism mixed with arrogance, which has really carried through our whole journey in publishing. It's all in the title: I mean, it's called *Dazed & Confused* because it's about not accepting one's place, so it's a brief for a mindset that feels naturally disengaged, dissatisfied, alienated, and disillusioned.

Always   Be   Defiant   and   Never   Be   Defined

Rankin On the cover of the first issue we stated that *Dazed & Confused* was an open access magazine, and we really were. We were both inspired by the punk movement, by this idea that anybody can do anything—you can be a photographer, you can be anything you just have to give it a go. That was what it was about for us. It was very much about giving people a voice and a pre-Internet way to communicate their ideas. I mean, very early on we created the first mirror cover, and that is like a "fuck you!" to all the other magazines. For me, putting a mirror on the cover defines what the Internet was going to become. I think we were ahead of the curve on the shifting of traditional fashion and style magazines—telling you what to wear, how to wear it, what to read—like the idea of the "Style Bible." Who needs a fucking Bible? Write your own Bible; write your own history, your own autobiography. That's what we were about.

FOAM

Living in the Screen-Age of Photography

FOAM is the contemporary photography museum in Amsterdam and they invited me to curate a show for their tenth anniversary. I wanted to only show photography on screens, so the frame for each image was the form of the screen and the exhibition became a dialogue with the audience about new observations of photography. The final room was an interactive auto-portrait room devised by Hellicar & Lewis.

Rise Sculpture
by Jefferson Hack

What's Next exhibition, FOAM

Marcel Feil: Jefferson, please tell us something about the origin of your proposal.
Jefferson Hack: I am very interested in the relationship between the viewer and photography through the screen. In this new digital era screens are omnipresent and this has changed our relationship with photography dramatically, especially compared to the times when photography was primarily seen as a print-based medium. I wanted to explore this new paradigm. Also given the restrictions with the space and the contributions of the other curators, I felt it to be a very natural, dislodging thing to explore the screen and the future technologies.

MF: In your proposal there is clear distinction between what you call the *Mother Sculpture* and the *Rise Sculpture*. Can you explain the first piece the audience encounters, the *Mother Sculpture*?
JH: Yes, I wanted to do something that was respectful to some of the traditional notions of photography that was about looking at the work of established photographers. The idea for the *Mother Sculpture* was to work with what I like to call the *Dazed & Confused* family of photographers. These photographers are all part of the current group of photographers who represent the visual language of the magazine across different genres. These genres may vary from fashion, portraiture, and reportage to art photography.

MF: All those different genres will be mixed in the presentation?
JH: I think we have to use the word "mixed" quite carefully. What I am not interested in doing with the established photographers is remixing, re-editing, or even reinterpreting their work. It is about presenting it onto a screen and having the viewer presenting themselves to photography that is in a digital format. In that sense, the main question was how am I going to do that and still be respectful of the photography?

MF: Also because most of the images in the *Mother Sculpture* were perhaps originally analogue and meant to be published as prints?
JH: No. I have purposely tried not to show too much archive. I have briefed all the photographers to supply images that are either unpublished but have been taken recently or new work made in the last four months. So it is also about the current visual language of the magazine as it is on the shelves now. All images are shot within our current time and therefore the photographer is influenced by the contemporary time we are living in. They are not photographs taken ten or twenty years ago.

MF: Obviously the audience has a comparable visual framework. They are also living in this digital, screen-based era in which photography is presented primarily on screens. How do you see the relationship between the viewer and the screen?
JH: That's the thing I really wanted to explore. The presentation shouldn't be a step-back experience, in that people are looking at the entire thing as a single form of entertainment, as multiple screens simply bombarding you with images. That is the exact opposite of what I am trying to do with the *Mother Sculpture*. The idea for that is much more about drawing people into the image, to establish a lean-forward experience. The image that catches the eye should have a certain focal point, so the audience can choose their position and look at the picture as an image of itself in respect to everything else that is going on in the space. What happens then is a more meditative experience. It is not so much about the relationship with the screen. It's about the relationship between the viewer and the photograph via the screen.

It's quite interesting, I spoke with Ingrid Sischy about this just recently and she told me a story about the first show of William Eggleston's colour images at MoMA. It was a sensational show for many reasons but also because the images were very, very small. She said she remembered wiping the glass of all the images everyday and telling the curator that the Eggleston images had more spit on them than all other images. She ended by saying that sometimes the small bombs are the most powerful bombs. It made me rethink how big I wanted the screens to be. I thought it to be really nice if the screens were something like nineteen or twenty inches, comparable with an average laptop. So it would become about a personal relationship with the image. I want people to get close and see their spit on the screen.

MF: That requires a really focused, concentrated way of looking.
JH: The overall impression I wanted to convey is a kind of minimal feeling, more meditative and personal. I mean, in a digital culture there is already the over-bombardment of images we are all subject to, the over-accessibility, which results in a kind of visual junkyard. That's not what I wanted the audience to experience. It should feel edited and curated.

MF: The *Rise Sculpture* requires a less meditative relationship.
JH: Totally. The *Rise Sculpture* has many more and larger screens and is about a different question. It is about using technology and about our relationship with photography via technology. For the *Rise Sculpture* we are using the Internet, social media and other new media to allow young and semi-professional photographers who maybe aren't shooting for *Dazed & Confused* yet, but are developing their own work in their own way, to submit work to the show. It is a submissions project about the future, but it is not real-time and it is not a free-for-all. The idea is that the photographer will send us the work and we choose and edit based on the *Dazed & Confused* spirit. The best work will be put into the *Rise Sculpture*.

One of the interesting aspects of this method was to have an exhibition that builds over time. New submissions will continually be added to the screens that will build from an initial 150 images to perhaps more than 300 or 400 images towards the end of the show. It is a living, growing exhibition that's never the same thing from day to day. The images will be presented pretty close to each other, resulting in a feeling like scattering images over a desktop. The other thing we are looking at is to create generative groupings of images by employing specific software. In a way, it is about looking for technology that allows different curatorial schemes to be employed by me on a whim, wherever I am in the world. It is much more of an experimental room.

MF: There is a third part as well, a room with a work by Hellicar & Lewis.
JH: This is really interesting because this is about interactive digital art. Hellicar & Lewis are long-time collaborators and friends of *Dazed & Confused*. They have made incredible work with different musicians and different exhibition spaces involving the public in real-time manipulations of recorded images. The idea is that portraits of the public will be taken by video cameras and then, based on the movement of the public picked up by sensors, the images will be manipulated in real time. If the first room is about the relationship of the viewer with photography via screens, the second room is of the viewer with photography via technology, and this third room is about the relationship with photography via the self-portrait. It's like a post-photographic meltdown of the idea of the portrait, with a real sense of engagement, interaction, and fun.

Interview originally published in FOAM *magazine, Issue 29, 2011*

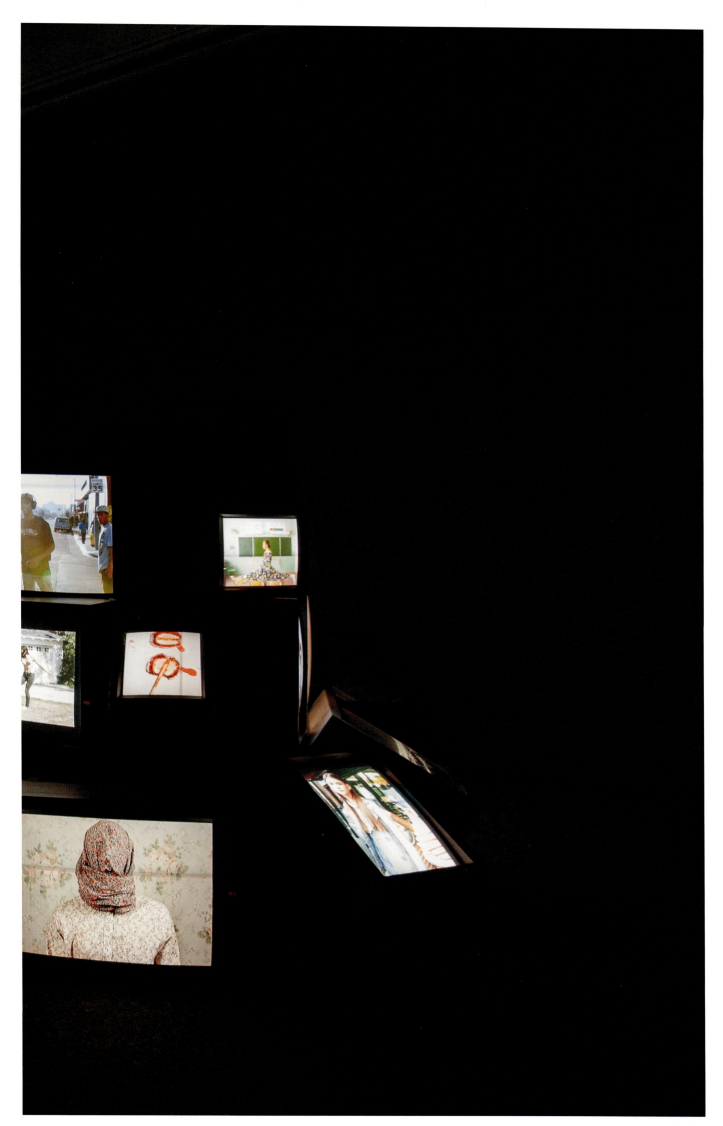

Rise Sculpture
by Jefferson Hack

THOM YORKE

I asked Thom to do a self-interview because he has always distrusted the press. He thought that the whole process was a fabrication and that no one could present an accurate portrait of an individual in a two-hour meeting. I just wish I still had the original cassette tape. I remember it arriving in a brown envelope like some kind of message in a bottle. He'd recorded it in a very private situation and it was extremely moving. He tried to do it in two different voices at first, but it merged into one voice halfway through. He went through all kinds of emotions — there was rage, there was anger, sadness, self-investigation, there was a lot of truth-seeking going on that would never be achieved via the traditional interview format and it put goosebumps on my neck playing it back. One day the audio will resurface, it's got to exist somewhere.

The Self Interview: In Conversation with the Psyche

You Do It To Yourself

THOM: This is a quote, and I think this is you. "The history of our times calls to mind those Walt Disney characters who rush madly over the edge of a cliff without seeing it. The power of their imagination keeps them suspended in mid-air, but as soon as they look down and see where they are, they fall."
THOM: Well, am I looking down? I don't think I'm looking down. I sort of understand the Walt Disney bit, though. The cartoon character bit. I understand running off the edge of a cliff, the expression on the face as they look down. I suppose it means something about the suspension of disbelief, and I suppose what you are trying to ask me, is "What are you doing?" I can understand that, but it's better than working in advertising, which is what my dad wanted me to do. And I'm looking down and I'm not falling.

T: No, but other people in your position do. Why should you be any different?
T: I don't say I'm any different at all. I just worry about losing it, you know? I spend most of every fucking day worrying about losing it. I've got to stop swearing as well, because some woman just wrote me a letter saying she really likes my music, but she's fifty years old; our music (*laughs*) and she doesn't like the swearing. (*laughs*)

T: Really? That's really interesting that you'd actually get worried about that. It's pretty pathetic, isn't it? You're really "Be nice to everybody, nice big grin, shake hands, worry about wasteful packaging, worry whether people are going to break into your home while you're asleep." You worry about not having written back to fan mail. You worry about what to say to important people. You worry about what to say onstage in front of people. You're just a worrier. You're about as intuitive as a brick. You spend half your life worrying, more than half your life. You should fucking get a life, you should be enjoying what you're doing. Get on with it, enjoy it. Suck it up. All those lovely people being nice to you. It's what you always wanted.
T: I didn't know what I wanted. I don't think anybody knows what they want. We did a show in Los Angeles. It's a Christmas radio show; they have these every year and everybody does it who wants to be liked by the radio station that year, and we did it. And we thought we were going to hate it, but we turned up and everybody there, like Lenny Kravitz and people like Oasis, were talking to us and saying, "Hi, you know, I really liked that song" or something and you're going, "Er, thanks very much." And that was great, and it was like being at your own birthday party, but you don't know anybody, but they know it's your birthday and I don't know. No, that's bullshit. Anyway it got a bit out of hand because all the people there—except for a few like Oasis and Lenny Kravitz who we have respect for—were just fucking clinging on, you know? And they got this crazy look in their eye, and apparently a lot of them were on coke. I didn't know that; they said it's the coke paranoia thing.
There was one particular famous ex-celebrity who I can't name who was really ready to punch me and was giving me a lecture about not behaving in the correct manner towards him because he came up to me and says: "Hey man, you, I really love you, man, you know, your album's great, you know, we want to make music like you" and I'm talking to somebody else and I'm thinking, "Well, I'm not impressed", and it's not like I'm having a fucking go or anything, I'm just not into talking to him simply because he's another famous person, ex-famous person in this business. I'm sorry, but I didn't get into this to sort of go to the parties and fucking talk to other famous people. I got into this because I really love what we did and I really love the other blokes in the band and that's why I got into this and get out of my face, you know? But I didn't say any of these things, I just sort of said nothing.
And there was this famous model there and I snubbed her because I was a bit out of my head at the time and I was a bit stoned. Anyway, I couldn't do it, you know? I wasn't really able to communicate with anyone except for the people I really knew. I suppose the novelty of these people has worn off and I just sound like this sulky kid who has had a big birthday party but didn't get the present he wanted and, you know, someone should just slap him around the face. And this guy was prepared to do that.

T: Okay, this is an obvious question. Why did you want to be famous then?
T: Because I wanted to meet REM and Elvis Costello (*laughs*) and now I have. But really we just started making tapes when we were younger. First me on my own, and then me and Jonny, and then with the others. And we'd play them to people, and they'd really like them and they'd take them home and they'd actually play them at home and I was really into this. Or I'd be at a party or something and someone would give me a guitar and I'd play a song. I mean this is all when we were sort of fifteen, sixteen and it was the first time that I found something I really loved and I suppose that I just loved the attention, so I wanted to be famous, I wanted the attention. What's wrong with that? But there is also something really seriously fucking unhealthy about it.

T: You haven't really answered the question. You've said, "Oh, I want to be loved." And that's not the real fucking reason, is it? I think you're a bit of a fucking prat.
T: Yeah, I agree. Um... other reasons to be famous. I think this discussion is so fucking lame. There's no point in continuing it, really. My favourite answer is: "Because that way more people get to hear what we do," but that would be a lie, because I'm sure if you asked other members of the band they would agree, but it isn't the only reason.
I just get really wound up because I think that when we got involved in what we do, we were so naive. I still think we are naive and I used to sort of want to hide it and now I'm proud of it because I think the most offensive thing about the media in general, is the level of cynicism and the fact that people really believe that they can pawn off endlessly recycled bullshit with no heart and people will buy it. And people do buy it, so I'm wrong and they're right.
Just to end this one; whenever I get lost about this, then the others always pull me up. And this is not just about me; I mean I'm doing this interview on my own because I think it's a good idea because I'm not very good at dealing with day-to-day press interviews. I'm not that precious about the way people think about me, but I am precious about offensive stuff that people write and I am precious about headlines like the one that was put in the *NME*, "Thom's Temper Tantrum".
This was a while ago, before Christmas. As they put it, I threw a tantrum in Germany and left the stage and nobody could understand what had happened and everyone was really pissed off and the whole audience were really angry and wanted the money back or whatever. The article was run like that and it was sort of second or third-hand. What actually happened on that night was that I'd been really, really ill for quite some time and I didn't know whether I would be able to do it or not and it's very difficult to tell but after a while, if you're doing a tour, there is a point where you have to just carry on. It doesn't matter how ill you are,

you still have to get onstage, and that really fucking does something to your head after a while. When I tried the sound track I got really worried because I couldn't sing anything. And when the show came round, people had driven hundreds of miles to come and it was snowing and it was like three or four foot deep and I just thought, "There is no way I'm not doing the show because these people have travelled so far". So I go up onstage and I thought it would be alright, but after three songs I lost my voice completely and I was croaking and I just got really fucking freaked out. I got tunnel vision and I don't really know what happened. I threw stuff around and threw my amp around and drum kit and ended up with blood all over my face and things. I cried for about two hours afterwards. I want people to know what happened that night. I'm sure no one gives a fuck and I'm sure the NME don't give a fuck, but what they wrote in that piece hurt me more than anything else anyone has written about me.

T: I think you've said enough about your fucking precious bullshit. It seems that you're a graduate of the Sinead O'Connor school of media handling and don't you feel it's about time you grew up a little? Stamping your little feet comes across as rather laughable under the circumstances, don't you think?
T: I think that has a lot to do with the expression that's on my face. People are born with certain faces, like my father was born with a face that people want to hit. (laughs) I do stamp my feet out of frustration really, but I don't do it as much now because I feel that we're in more control of what's happening.

T: Do you think that people who read this find this level of agonising pretty offensive?
T: I think the only reason that I'm able to think like this is because we've been off the wheel long enough and I've been at home long enough to start to see a lot of things for what they are. What worries me more than anything else is the whole notion that I'm who people focus on, like it's of significance, you know? People look at me and think it's a complete existence. What really fucks me up in the head is that basically I'm supposed to be endorsing this sort of pop star, "Wow, lucky bastard, he's got it all" existence. What frightens me is the idea that what Radiohead do is basically packaged back to people in the form of entertainment, to play in their car stereos on their way to work. And that's not why I started this but then I should shut the fuck up because it's pop music and it's not anything more than that.
But I got into music because I naively thought that pop music was basically the only viable art form left, because the art world is run by a few very extremely, um, privileged people and is ultimately corrupt and barren of any context. And I thought that the pop music industry was different and I was fucking wrong, because I went to the Brits and I saw it everywhere and it's the same thing. It's a lot of women who couldn't fit in their cocktail dresses and lots of men in black ties who essentially didn't want to be there, but were. And I was there and we were all committing the same offence. All my favourite artists are people who never seem to be involved in the industry and I found myself getting involved in it, and I felt really ashamed to be there.

T: It sounds to me like you're going around in ever-decreasing circles.
T: Yeah, I agree. I don't know if anybody else has this feeling. When you're walking down the street and you catch your reflection in something like a car window or a shop window and you see your face and you think, "Who's that?" You know: "That's not me, that doesn't represent who I am". And I think I've recently discovered what the problem is and it's a feeling that essentially you're just in a room full of mirrors. You can shoot at all the reflections, but basically it's all meaningless because you're just trapped and you put yourself there.
I've realised that it's actually worrying about it that's the fucking problem. It's actually saying, 'No, this is me, that's not me', and being precious about who you are, because I believe now that everyone changes all the time. I think the most unhealthy thing for a human being is to feel that they have to behave in a certain way because other people expect them to behave like that, or to feel they have to think a certain way because what happens then is basically your mind goes around in circles.
I was getting really freaked out the other day because I was talking to Jonny when we were in the studio, and I woke up one morning and discovered that during the night, as a dream or something, my mind was going round in a trap. Like, it was going round and round and round and round. It's like four or five words just going round in my head and it went on for about an hour and I couldn't stop it. And Jonny said he had the same thing. He went to Israel with his wife after a tour and he'd just got out of the bath, and picked up a towel to dry himself. Then once he put the towel down on the floor, he stood there completely freaked out for a half an hour because there were so many different places to put the towel. He'd become paralysed and got really really scared, because his mind had gone into a lock and wouldn't stop.
So I get scared about my mind going round in circles but I think that's only because I'm constantly aware of my own reflection and I feel that's an extremely unhealthy thing. And I feel sorry for anyone who actually starts to believe their own reflection because I've done it. What a wanker!

T: Well, I think you're being very dishonest. I think that you're a little shit like every other narcissistic little boy in a pop band. Your particular angle in life is being the tortured artist, which frankly is already appearing fairly tired. It's about time you lightened up.
T: You're right. I'll lighten up. At the moment I'm really excited about what we could do, but just as much, like fifty percent of the time, I'm thinking how close it is to being completely banal. I guess that's what's supposed to happen. The best thing for us is to just keep turning stuff out and not worrying about what people think. The thing that paralysed us for the first two or three months of recording The Bends was the fact that we were paralysed about what people would think. We were paralysed about who we were supposed to be. We were paralysed about how we were supposed to be.
It's pretty difficult not to love the attention. And I kind of went through a phase of going to London a lot and going to parties and things. Part of me really wanted to do that, wanted to go out and sort of soak up this beaming fucking sunshine coming out of my bottom or whatever it was, but you know . . . Maybe I should have done it, but it's not my thing, that's all. I'm not good at taking compliments, but I do it. I think it's more that people have put this level of significance into it, to the point where it's really taking the piss. The reason I'm proud of the fact that people have jumped to The Bends now is because I know how difficult it was to make. The record is a document of a period of time and that was a difficult period of time and the fact that people really like it makes me very proud. I don't really care who wins Brit awards because nobody else does.

T: It sounds to me like you're desperately trying to find something to fight against.
T: I didn't come here to be attacked by you. Just fucking lay off, alright? (laughs).

T: No wonder you don't talk too much: you don't seem to have much to say, Thom.
T: I don't think I have.

T: Do you enjoy getting drunk on your own, then, Thom?
T: Stuff comes out, and I like it because there's sort of comfort in it. Being pissed out of your head and on your own, but it's a bit softer. I think that I should ask you some questions now. You're the one that's been trying to pick a fight with me. Why do you follow me around everywhere?

T: What do you mean, "follow you around"? I'm just another voice in the tape recorder, part of the interview. What do you mean, "follow you around"?
T: You know what I mean. Why do you make me do that stuff? Why do you make me hurt people?

T: You sound like some dodgy John Hurt serial killer character.
T: I don't mean "hurt people"; people say I get in a state, and I think it's because you're around.

T: I think you're just creating this as part of a convenient excuse for your bad behaviour.
T: You've always got a fucking answer, haven't you? You've always got a fucking answer.

T: I think this sounds a little bit too much like a very bad '80s thriller, or something. You're trying to create some sort of persona thing. Anyway I don't think this is really for the public domain. Do you?
T: No, but this is the first time I've ever talked to you.

T: No it's not. That's bullshit.
T: Everyone has different sides, and at least I don't go and harm anybody. Except maybe the fish in the pond. I think maybe this house is haunted. I'll tell you about the fish. It was during a Christmas and I bought this house and there were these two beautiful oriental fish that lived in a pond at the bottom of the garden and my other half went away for a few days and one of the things that was left on a note was "look after the fish" because at that time there was ice and snow covering the ground. It was like two foot deep or something ridiculous. Now, I let these fish die because I couldn't even be fucking bothered to get my shit together to go down to the bottom of the garden and knock a little hole in the ice to keep these fish alive. So when I eventually remembered that they were there, I saw them belly-up in the ice and one of them was, his little mouth was right next to the last hole that had been made there in the pond. A last gasp for breath of air and I couldn't even fucking manage that.

T: Poor little Thom.
T: You're the wanker that wants me to sleep with all these women. But I haven't done it, and I won't.

T: But you know they're still there.
T: I don't think it's any of your business

T: Of course it's my business.
T: Okay then, but I don't think it's anybody else's business.

T: Everything is their business. That's the whole point, Thom. This tape's running out. Have you got anything else you want to say in this somewhat random interview that we've been doing?
T: I want to say that I did this for a reason. It was a good idea because I wanted to just take a different photograph. You know, a different reflection in a different shop window. But maybe I just kind of forgot what it was I wanted to do. I wanted it to be some sort of deep psychological experience. I wanted to be locked in a room for a day, but my life being what it is, I couldn't do that.

T: So let's find you a cheery question to end this, shall we? After all, this is the media. Do you think you'll ever get to heaven, Thom? Or maybe just the top of the charts?
T: Only if I get rid of you.

T: Absolutely no chance whatsoever.

Interview originally appeared in Dazed & Confused, *Volume I, Issue 19, 1995*

What are your favourite newpapers and magazines?

FELDMAN

Hans-Peter Feldman is notorious for never talking to the press. He is known for his collaborations with Hans-Ulrich Obrist, so Obrist and I invited Feldman to answer a question with an image. Obrist created the rules of the game by making it temporal and sending a question a day which Feldman had to respond to. Over time, they collected all the answers and made it into a book and an exhibition. It exemplifies the power of placing the conversation at the axis of creation and using the magazine as an exhibition space—it went so far beyond the page as they became more and more addicted to the process; the project took on a life of its own.

The Best Conversations Are Beyond Words

Could you give me a definition of the present?

What is your favourite image?

What is the moment we are all waiting for?

What is your favourite sound?

What job have you hated most?

Can you tell me about your unrealised projects?

What city do you like most?

Is there a way to avoid banality?

Do books furnish a room?

Is art making life better than art?

What is subjective?

What is memory visually?

What irritates you more than anything in the world?

What is your favourite food?

What is you favourite word?

Are you fearless?

What is your least favourite image?

What is objective?

NOWNESS

NOWNESS was named in a session where I invited people who use language in an interesting way—artists, writers, poets and copywriters—to participate in a naming salon at Milk Studios in New York. At that point, we were on deadline to name this new channel that was designed to premiere the very best in visual culture, and we were going to push the button within twenty-four hours, but we still didn't have a name. The salon was the last-ditch attempt, and it involved a lot of whiskey—at some point, after hours of discussion, the artist Rashid Johnson began telling this story about the notion of a long perpetual moment, a kind of "long now," and he described it as "Nowness"—it was perfect, and it was that wonderful eureka moment when you are down to the wire and out of nowhere, inspiration comes.

Welcome to the Perpetual Conversation

NOW

NESS

AnOtherM[a]

ISSUE 1 AUTUMN/WINTER 2005 UK £ 4.95 IT € 13.00 US $ 14.99 CAN $ 15.95   JOAQUIN PHOENIX PHOTOGRA[PHED]

HaNDLE WIth CA[re]
JOAQUIN PHOENIX ON JOHNNY [CASH]

KATE MOSS DRESSES UP IN DIOR HOMME, **RICHARD PRINCE** AND **GLENN O'BRIEN** TAKE ON OUTSIDER AMER[ICA]
REVEALS HER SWEET SIDE. EXCLUSIVE ESSAYS TACKLING GLOBAL ECONOMIC MELTDOWN, SEXUAL DEVIA[NCE]
NEW ART REVOLUTION. SOVIET MODERNIST ARCHITECTURE, PLUS THE ESSENTIAL FASHION FOR MEN THIS S[EASON]
BY THE PUBLISHERS OF DAZED & CONFUSED AND ANOTHER MAGAZINE.

MEN'S FASHION

MANTRA

Cut it Up: The Magical Operation of Language

The idea of the Another Man mantras has its genesis in the William S. Burroughs and Brion Gysin cut-up techniques, and the idea of a cacophony of voices coming together in a random way to create a new feeling and a new tonality. I tend to think of a magazine as a party, and all of the people invited are the voices or personalities in the room. I just loved the idea of taking a sentence from each story and putting it back-to-back as a form of reconstructed poetry—it's a form of hybridisation and it's about consolidating the myriad themes of the entire issue into one page. When you read it, it reads very much as though it has a rhythm and a cadence to it. To me, it feels almost magical, in that Burroughs' sense of language as magical operation. I called it the mantra because it has that metaphysical, Eastern philosophical beat-poet vibe at its heart, but essentially, it's an alternative contents page, the sound of the party between the pages of the magazine.

ANOTHER MANTRA

THAT SEARCH IS WHAT GIVES MEANING TO ART AND TO LIFE... POLITICS IS MORE AND MORE THE POLITICS OF JOUISSANCE... IT WILL CHANGE EVERYTHING ABOUT THE WAY WE LIVE... IT IS TRUE THAT WARHOL CREATED A NEW ART/FAME EQUATION... ONE MINUTE YOU CAN BE HAVING A ROMANTIC KISS, AND A FEW STROKES LATER YOU'RE IN THE WOODS BEING FUCKED BY A GANG OF VIKINGS AND THEIR DOGS... THE INITIALLED HANDKERCHIEF CAME OUT OF ELVIS'S BEDSIDE TABLE... HIGH TIMES UP IN THE GYPSY CAMPS OF THE CARPATHIAN MOUNTAINS: IMPOSING WOMEN AND STOUT MIDDLE-AGED MEN POSING PROUDLY... EVERY HUMAN CREATURE IS CONSTITUTED TO BE THAT PROFOUND SECRET AND MYSTERY TO EVERY OTHER... EXPLORE THE EXISTENTIAL DIMENSION OF THIS NEW WORLD... A STRANGE MIX OF SPONTANEITY AND UNEASE... WITH ALL THE FEEL OF AN ENGLISH GENTLEMEN'S CLUB... COMBINE CATCHY INSTRUMENTAL LOOPING WITH RAW AND HONEST LYRICISM... BORN FOR SOCCER, AS BEETHOVEN WAS BORN FOR MUSIC... THOSE PEOPLE ARE ALL IN ME WHEN I LOOK AT THE WORLD, THEIR PHOTOS WERE MY REFERENCE BOOK... A FORWARD THINKING APPROACH TO THE FUTURE... THE WORLD IS INTOLERABLY DREARY. YOU ESCAPE IT BY SEEING + NAMING WHAT HAD HERETOFORE BEEN UNSPEAKABLE... THINKING SMART BUT ACTING LOOSE... SOMETIMES I THINK ABOUT THINGS TOO MUCH. I LOVE TO FUCKING THINK... WE ALL DRESS UP EVERY DAY. EVERYTHING WE WEAR IS A REPRESENTATION OF OURSELVES... IT COULD BE INTERESTING TO DO SOMETHING ABSOLUTELY TINY... I FIND TEACHING SOMETHING AND DOING THE OPPOSITE VERY HARD TO TAKE... TO WRITE WELL YOU HAVE TO CARE ABOUT SOMETHING... I JUST WANTED TO EXPLAIN HOW AN AVERAGE PERSON FEELS WHEN THEY DO EXTREME THINGS... THE WHOLE CULTURAL REVOLUTION IS OVER AND WE HAVE WON. THEN WHO ARE "WE" AND WHAT HAVE WE WON... A FASCINATING WORLD REMAINS TO BE DISCOVERED...

Ben Cobb Another Man is about that crossroads—rather than just commenting on what is going on in the fashion industry and culture, it's part of the fabric of what's going on; rather than an outsider voice, we're in the middle of the conversation. The Creative Director Alister Mackie has got a very unique vision. He talks a lot about a kind of counterculture archetype that appears and re-appears throughout history, so it's Byron, Rimbaud, Mick Jagger… He's a genius at identifying that character in each era, and everything in the magazine is extrapolated from that. I think the great success of Another Man is that each season we have one thing to say, and every single shoot, every article, is just ramming that home, so you get a very singular point of view each season. Within the present media culture that kind of filter is really important. The way the younger generation consumes culture is all at the same time in a constant stream—it's Punk straight to Renaissance. That's how they consume reality. I think Another Man has always been about pulling all these disparate elements together with purpose.

That search is what gives meaning to art and to life… politics is more and more the politics of jouissance… it will change everything about the way we live… it is true that Warhol created a new art/fame equation… one minute you can be having a romantic kiss, and a few strokes later you're in the woods being fucked by a gang of Vikings and their dogs… the initialled handkerchief came out of Elvis's bedside table… high times up in the gypsy camps of the Carpathian Mountains: imposing women and stout middle-aged men posing proudly… every human creature is constituted to be that profound secret and mystery to every other… explore the existential dimension of this new world… a strange mix of spontaneity and unease… with all the feel of an English gentlemen's club… combine catchy instrumental looping with raw and honest lyricism… born for soccer as Beethoven was born for music… those people are all in me when I look at the world, their photos were my reference book… a forward thinking approach to the the future… the world is intolerably dreary. You escape it by seeing + naming what had heretofore been unspeakable… thinking smart but acting loose… sometimes I think about things too much. I love to fucking think.. we all dress up every day. Everything we wear is a representation of ourselves… it could be interesting to do something absolutely tiny… I find teaching something and doing the opposite very hard to take… to write well you have to care about something… I just wanted to explain how an average person feels when they do extreme things… the whole cultural revolution is over and we have won. Then who are "we" and what have we won… a fascinating world remains to be discovered…

Originally published in Another Man, *Issue 1, 2005*

NECES
PRO

"I think when you put an image that upsets people in a magazine it can make them think, and that's always a good thing."

Corinne Day, *Dazed & Confused*, 2000

"I've spent most of my life being on the edge! It's not a good way to live and yet, if you believe in what you are doing, and you feel you have to do it, what choice do you have?"

Lou Reed, *Dazed & Confused*, 1996

WHY
MIS

"Do you think this can be a form of ballet, this new transdisciplinary dance in print? That maybe through all the energy and networking and conversation that's going on it could actually have a real-life component. Could that work?"

Jefferson Hack, *AnOther Art Book*, 2010

SARY
VOCATION.

2

"Showing the truth is often the focus of moralistic criticism. Yet, what is often considered 'controversial' is that which comes closest to reality and has the greatest chance to incite change . . . More and more people are now willing to question self-censorship: to question what it means to be alive, and express how they truly feel. It's happening in music, art, film, literature and fashion, and spontaneously—in small towns, cul-de-sacs, bare-brick, boarded-up estates, self expression is at the very heart of society and no amount of political and corporate scrubbing will ever remove the messages from the walls."

Jefferson Hack, *Dazed & Confused*, 1995

"A lifestyle magazine shouldn't be just about turning pages and flicking through dreams. It should be about inspiring change, destroying myths, being ambitious, adventurous, making mistakes, growing up in public, bringing new ideas to light, being silly and serious at the same time, not buying into the hype and above all believing in its readers as well as itself."

Jefferson Hack, *Dazed & Confused*, 1996

TAKES
ARE
BEAUTIFUL.

"We need a new Diaghilev moment, when the arts all come together."

Hans-Ulrich Obrist, *AnOther Art Book*, 2011

THE

"Put the idea out there first and don't wait for someone to come to you, just get out and do something, whichever way you physically can."

Jefferson Hack, *RCA Open Lecture Series*, 2004

THE
PLACE.
THE
ENERGY.

If you could wish for one change in the world what would it be?
"I don't profess to know better—it is all an evolutionary miracle that seems to balance out despite collapse and glory."

Rick Owens, *Anothermag.com*, 2014

CO
ACTION.

RIGHT TIME. RIGHT

If you could wish for one change in the world what would it be?
"To find a new human race."

Gore Vidal, *Anothermag.com*, 2010

RIGHT

LLECTIVE

Dario Robleto
Our Sixties Radicals Forgot to Stay Suspicious
Home-made paper (pulp made from US one dollar bills, cotton and bone dust from every bone in the body), collage elements from one dollar bills and glue.

DOLLAR BILL

I have this vague, perhaps unreal, memory of reading that the American government were going to redesign the dollar bill. I think there was this sense at that time that it urgently needed to evolve from the post-war green-back. The design hadn't changed, so it got Mark Sanders and me wondering how artists would deal with it and that created a premise for the group show.

"We always wanted to open the magazine up as a platform for the people who were trying to do the same things that we were trying to do, and we were lucky, because the whole British art world was exploding at that time, and there was a synergy in the way we were trying to explode the two-dimensional format of a magazine and rethink what media could be. I think the AnOther Dollar Project was the first big international art project that we really got off the ground, and it coincided with the bloating of the contemporary art market, so there was a definite subtext about money and art. It was incredible to have so many great people involved, such as John Baldessari, KAWs and Richard Louderback, and the coming together of them all helped us pose an important question about commercial elements in art in an ironic way. My favourite is one of the dollar designs by Jim Shaw in the style of Jackson Pollock—it's this sort of abstract expressionist dollar bill, and it's really intelligent because in the 1950s the American government used expressionist art and promoted it all over Europe as a sign of cultural freedom and advancement. It is, of course, totally illegal for legal tender to be changed in any shape or form, but that's what cultural provocation is." —Mark Sanders

Inspiring   Political   and   Artistic   Provocation

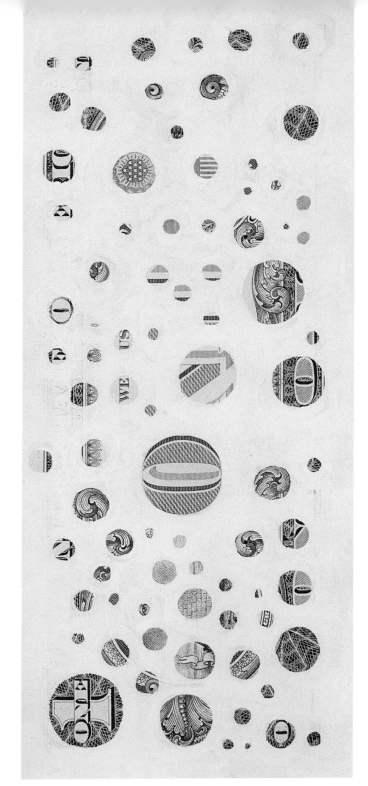

Hanna von Goeler
The Optimum Quantity of Money and Other Essays
(part of a series)

Bill Saylor
Diamond Fed Motor Heads

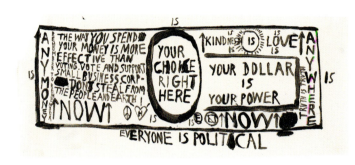

Chris Johanson
Your Choice Right Here

Brian Degraw
One Mess

Banks Violette
*Dollar Bill Proposal Model
(W.R Hearst/ Pabst Blue Ribbon/ATF Inverted)*

Richard Louderback
Cash

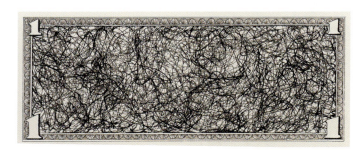

Jim Shaw
0ist Dollar

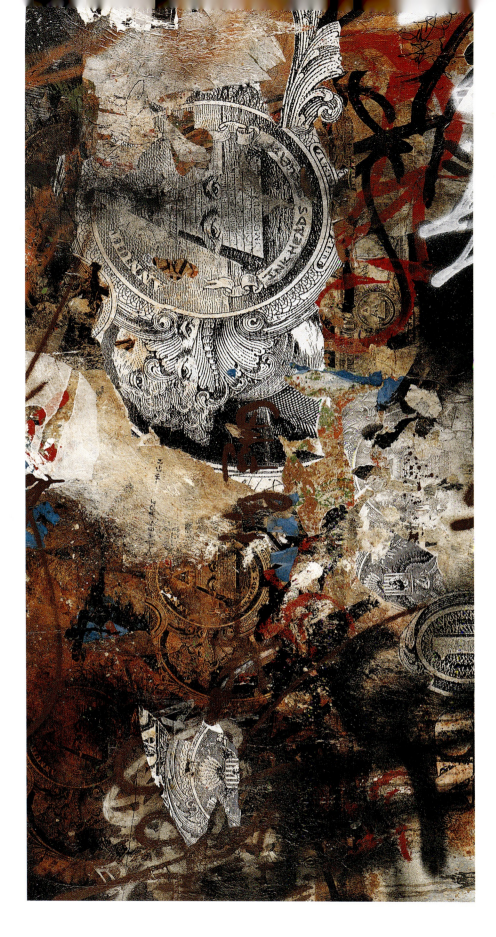

José Parlá
Masquerade Stakes of America

Jason Meadows
Washington

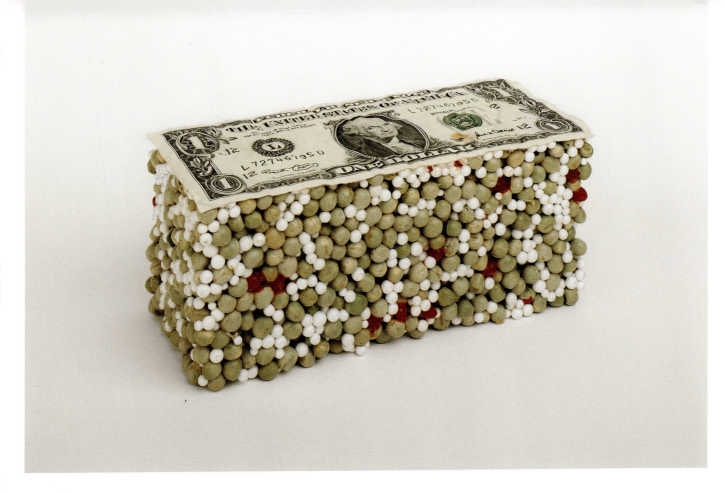

Jason Rhoades
PeaRoeFoam Nubuck (Dollar sized)
Whole green peas, bait style salmon eggs, white virgin foam bead.

Barry McGee
Gank Dollar
Used by streetwise American kids to cheat the system,
the customised tail means that the dollar can be yanked out of vending machines
after both change and product have been received.

Brad Kahlhamer
The States of Almost American

Tara Donovan
Money Disappears
A single dollar perforated with hundreds of pin pricks to emanate light and aid disintegration.

Tom Friedman
Untitled
36 dollar bills cut up and pieced together to make one giant dollar.

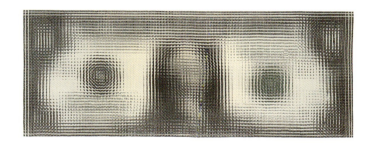

Christopher Taggart
Another (Three) Dollar(s)
A dollar bill cut into 2,048 pieces and reconfigured to make two separate dollars, front and back, out of one original.

John Baldessari
The Bogie

Peter Coffin
Untitled (Out-View Moneta)

KAWS
Companion

Carrie Moyer
Resistance Currency

Jeremy Blake
An Everyday Story of Country Folk

Meg Cranston
The Magic Disappearing Twenty
Alluding to that never-to-be-returned $20 loaned to druggie friends.

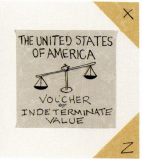

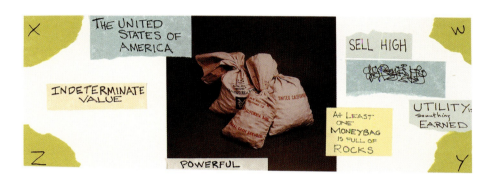

T. Kelly Mason
Another Dollar Value(s)

CORINNE DAY

Trusting the Power of Instinct

The relationship with Corinne began when we started renting a flat underneath hers in Brewer Street as an office for Dazed & Confused. We would meet often and soon found ourselves spending a lot of time talking about photography and how she saw the world. Corinne taught me a lot about photography, and she taught me a lot about being authentic and true to yourself – she taught me about the importance of not caring what anyone else thinks about your point of view; she was so strong in that way, it was like, you either like what I do, or you don't. Corinne was an inspiring cultural provocateur because she was so self-confident and uncompromising in her way of looking at the world.

georgina 1993

1993

Thursday 22.5.97

George said hed met loads of weirdos before he met me. thats ok next time he comes round for a haircut well see who looks like a weirdo! We known george about five years. He was into techno music then twas into psychedelic rock now im into techno, hes into nirvana. were both into suicide - the band.

We taken a lot of photographs of George over the years. some of them are published in youth culture magazines. thats how we make a living. Last night we went to the opening of the new Vivienne Westwood shop. Our friend Barry, who works as a tree surgeon, had surgically embossed and polished a tree that was standing in the middle of the shop. so we went to have a look. It was the most beautiful thing in the room. We drank some champagne, had an unusual conversation with the editor of penthouse magazine and were staped on the way out by a lady with a mike and camera wanting to know who made our jeans and T shirts. then we left.

On the way home I saw Rose, a friend of mine, not in person. She was standing seven feet tall in a shop window. Rose looked very glamorous. We first met in mcdonalds in afford street.

day hair nell moodie

Vinca drives a truck and travels around Europe with friends they have a sound system and paron free techno parties. Vinca has been partyin for two years and only comes home when shes ill. she is ill with a virus, Hepatitis it has been living in Italy, and recently got caught nicking scrap metal from a junk yard, she spent the night in jail apart from her skin turning yellow she feels ok.

Vinca asked if I had seen the newspaper today, they had used a photograph of Rose without my permission in an article about president clinton criticising fashion magazines for glamorising drugs. Youth culture magazines write articles nearly every month about drug culture, most people we know smoke Maryjuana, the photographs I have reflect the world around me.

Vinca said shes leaving in two weeks, I wouldn't mind leaving with her. I need a change. She said, change your supermarket.

I said ill see ya to marieval. Vinca has asked me to help edit her holiday photographs that she has taken of techno parties and her life. Over the last two years, I suggested she should publish that

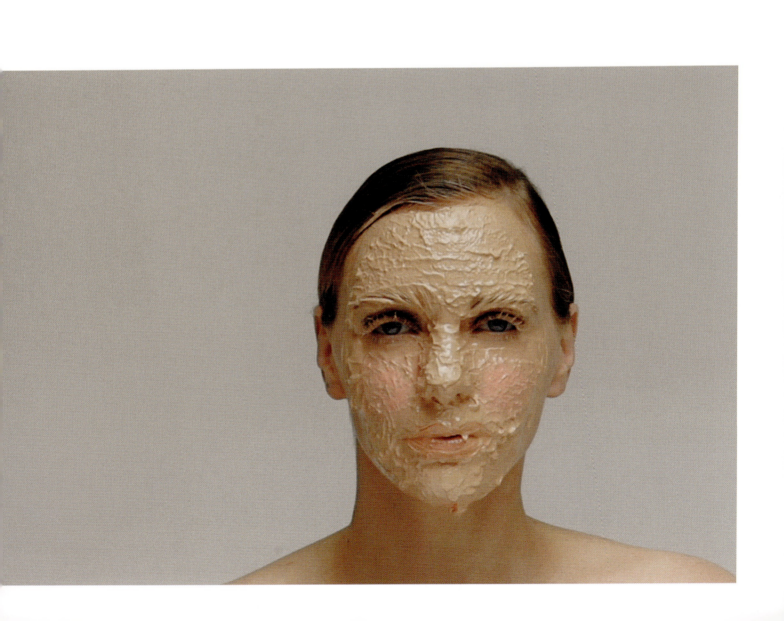

NATURAL BEAUTY

NOWNESS has had countless incredible moments but one of my favourites is possibly *Natural Beauty* as it's a stunning deconstruction of the beauty myth. Hannelore Knuts the model becomes caked in 365 days of make-up in the space of a few minutes. The make-up is applied to her face and there is a reveal at the end of the film where we are witness to the totality of one year's application. It's one of the most viewed films on NOWNESS and certainly the most commented upon film. It was also one of the first films that we premiered, so it's had this incredible viral and social impact after being launched. It's a profound comment on the beauty myth, identity, and femininity.

Reversing the Beauty Myth

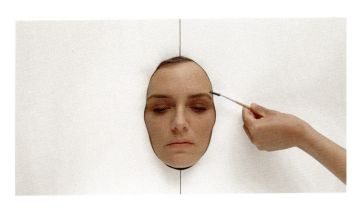

Lernert & Sander We tend to always go the opposite way from the platform we have been invited to do something for, and we wanted to do something subversive for NOWNESS, which is all about beauty. I think it's a tragedy when a girl feels like she has to put too much make-up on. I'm not a girl, obviously, and I've never been forced into that situation, but for me it is always very off-putting. I mean, you have day and night make-up, and the supposed trick is to not show that you have makeup on at all—for some girls it all becomes a blur. It's just a tragedy. Our film starts off with natural beauty, and then we put 365 days of "natural beauty" make-up on the model. It was fantastic that it premiered on NOWNESS and that they gave us the money to make the film based on the idea. If you don't dare to say something on those kind of platforms, then what are you doing, really? Sometimes people don't even notice that it is really subversive, and that is the ultimate subversion, I think.

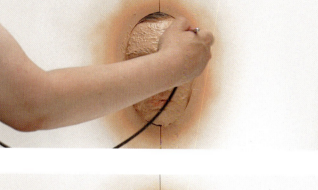

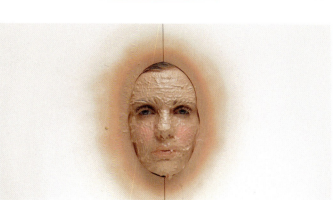
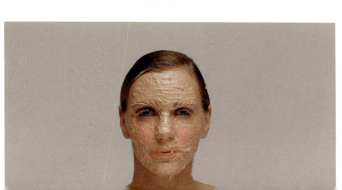

THE DIGITAL EDITION

The idea of putting a full LED screen as a moving cover has long been an ambition of mine. This edition was thematically linked to the *Savage Beauty* exhibition at the V&A. The crux, conceptually, was "Alexander McQueen: Past, Present, Future," so we wanted three covers, with three female cover stars exploring each temporal element. It was already a very expansive idea, but I really wanted our "the future" archetype Rihanna to be realised in a format that represented my idea of the future, and it had to be super high-definition; it had to look amazing, and it had to move.

I tried to find a way to make this for nine months and that process of constant research, trial and failure is a whole other story. I was really broken — defeated — as it seemed impossible technically to realise this dream. I met Liam Casey, by chance, at a Founders Dinner in Dublin. I'd just read an article on him in *Wired* and David Rowan had called him "Silicon Valley's Go To Guy for Hardware". It was a case of right time, right place, right energy to meet the man whose company slogan is "If It Can Be Imagined, It Can Be Made." I showed him a rendering we had put together on my iPhone and he started rapid firing questions at me, trouble-shooting the concept. A week later, he was at our office and we shook hands on it — that was in mid-November, and by early January we had our first prototype; his process is so fast, it's unbelievable.

Futuring: Right the Time, Right the Place, Right the Energy

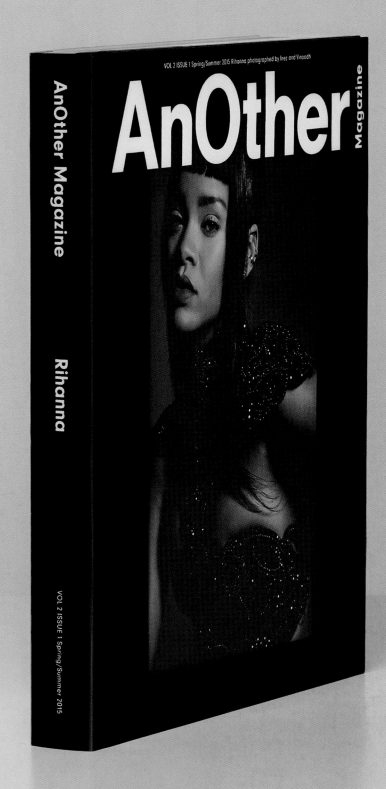

Jefferson Hack What was important to me about the project was that it was a fully realised hybrid; a digital and analogue "future" package. So there was a moving image cover, and there was also a forty-five minute album soundtrack composed by John Gosling, Alexander McQueen's sound designer—so, when you buy it, you buy a completely immersive audio and visual experience, as well as the print edition of course. The cover was shot in slow motion, so the movement is unexpected, and creates a sense of wonder. It's almost as if the magazine comes to life, evolving from a two-dimensional time capsule into a multi-dimensional interactive time machine.

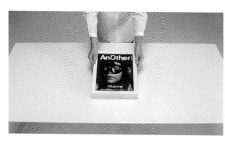

ART DIRECT

"In order to be stimulated or moved in the future, we probably have to go into space and look at our world from there."

Rei Kawakubo, *AnOther Magazine*, 2011

REAL VERSUS

"I have attention deficit disorder. But I also have obsessive compulsive disorder, so they balance each other out very well."

Mia Farrow, *AnOther Magazine*, 2007

THE OF THE INVI

"It's interesting to see the order and disorder that's been present in history non-chronologically. It's important to witness."

Jefferson Hack, *AnOther Art Book*, 2010

ING REALITY.

"Nothing should be considered outside the scope of interest. High art, low culture, politics, decadence, history, the latest technology, drugs, disabilities, bloody knickers—late night parties—everything is up for grabs."

Jefferson Hack, *RCA Open Lecture Series*, 2004

UNREAL.

BEAUTY

What do you most dislike about contemporary culture?
"It's too fast."

Juergen Teller, *Anothermag.com*, 2013

SIBLE.

WE END

"These are our protagonists, producing images you will want to rip out and stick on your wall. They have come together to fire inspiration and action, style and reflection into the ether; to kick through our daily realities and fuel the fantasies of a generation caught in the slipstream of the extreme."

Jefferson Hack, *AnOther Fashion Book*, 2009

THE

"Putting things off is the biggest waste of life. It snatches away the present by promising the future. The greatest obstacle to living is expectancy, which hangs upon tomorrow and loses today. You are arranging what happens in fortune's control and abandoning what lies in yours. What are you looking at? To what goal are you straining? The whole future lies in uncertainty, so live immediately."

Seneca, *On the Shortness of Life*, c. 1st century, as quoted by Jefferson Hack in *AnOther Magazine*, 2005

IS

ARE LESS... NOW...

"The future is overrated because it is predetermined by the choices you make today. If you consider the present then the future will naturally sort itself out. It's a great relief to find myself back at square one because now at least I know where I am."

Jefferson Hack, *Dazed & Confused*, 1996

FUTURE A VERB.

"Because of entertainment, culture has become a caricature. I call it the Springfield Effect: people become so much of a caricature they exist in a Simpsons-like context. Their iconography lives on forever in Springfield. The greatest minds of our generation live on in beautiful episodes of *The Simpsons*."

Jefferson Hack, *Purple Fashion Magazine*, 2010

SCARLETT JOHANSSON

I wanted to create a fictional interview where Scarlett appeared as a character in a short story. The story is authored by A.M. Homes, who thought that I was insane when I commissioned her because she didn't believe that Scarlett or her publicist would go for it—we didn't yet have permission and she figured the publicist would freak out. A.M. sat with Scarlett for an hour-and-a-half in New York and then turned the meeting into a fictionalised road trip. In this non-reality she brings out a lot of Scarlett's real character—you actually do learn about her backstory, and the different personality traits that A.M. observed. It's what Hans-Ulrich Obrist coined a "post-symbolic interview"—situations are exaggerated and fictionalised, completely invented even. It illustrates the importance of the real versus the unreal, and the power of that relationship in journalism and celebrity mythology. Scarlett was cool enough to okay it in the end and let us print it. Phew!

Fact or Fiction? The Post-Symbolic Interview

Scarlett Johansson

As one of America's most daring and original novelists, A.M. Homes knows a thing or two about the fine line between real life and fairy tales. So when we asked her to take a very special road trip with Scarlett Johansson, one of the most charming and enigmatic actresses we know, we knew she would be up for the ride. They were both soon to discover that fiction, myth, and magic would never be far behind for them.

Where does this all begin?
Let's just say it was Jefferson's idea. Jefferson Hack, the wily wizard behind the curtain of this whole operation. He cooks up this idea that Scarlett Johansson and I should go on a road trip—it's an American tradition, a rite of passage, think Kerouac's On the Road. With barely an arm twist, he gets us both to agree—he sends us an email, "Start your engines", and "call if you get lost along the way." Within seconds Scarlett emails back, "I thought the whole point was we're supposed to get lost." An hour later Scarlett sends me a Web link for a youth hostel near Niagara Falls, New York. I click the link, all the while wondering—is she kidding? The HI-Buffalo Niagara at 667 Main Street advertises: twenty-four hour hot showers, no curfew, lockers in dorms, washing machines.

There are photos of the communal kitchen and rooms of multiple wooden bunk beds. The romance of sleeping on bunk beds in a room of strangers is something I left behind at summer camp. But what about Scarlett; how do I tell if she's serious? Do celebrities have a sense of humour? I email back—"Scarlett, I'm really busy on Niagara Falls day, what comes next?" She sends a photo of herself snapped in the garden of the Bel Air hotel in Beverly Hills in a beautiful white silk dress feeding the hotel swans. I like the Bel-Air, they make a good Arnold Palmer (a combination of iced tea and lemonade). "Okay," I write back, "But we need a plan." "I have maps," she says. When I ask how long she thinks we'll be gone she says, "Let's play it by ear." I'm a little nervous, this is all a kind of a construction, something we're doing so I can write this article, but we're not really going cross-country, are we? I express my anxiety to Jefferson, who says, "Be easy going, the more relaxed you are the more open she'll be." "Fine," I lie. Maybe Scarlett and I can just take a taxi and drive around Manhattan; she can show me where she grew up, where she went to school, and tell me how she became Scarlett Johansson, an ever-rising icon co-starring in the latest Woody Allen film, a singer with a disc of Tom Waits covers, David Bowie singing back-up and Salman Rushdie burrowing into her neck in a music video. (The album produced by Dave Sitek of TV on the Radio also features an original composition "Song for Jo".)

When did I first notice Scarlett? It goes back to The Horse Whisperer, when she was engaging at fourteen under Robert Redford's direction. Then there was Terry Zwigoff's alienated adolescent in Ghost World at sixteen. But it was Lost in Translation at nineteen for which she got the gold.

Her performance was about a young girl coming to consciousness, changing from a child into a woman, and in the end it also clearly marked the transition between Johansson being an up-and-coming actress to her being a star. And then there was Girl with the Pearl Earring where her features with their genetic Dutch/Jewish roots added a certain something, and where her performance was entirely about performance, about a kind of stillness and surrender—Scarlett in the role of Griet, a young woman living in the Netherlands in the 1660s, maid and then muse to the painter Johannes Vermeer. And from there on to becoming a regular in Woody Allen's odd ensemble, and so it goes. I am thinking about Scarlett when I am home packing—pillow for my bad back, snacks, car charger for the phone, tape recorder, tapes, batteries, note book, pyjamas—is the magazine paying for the two hotel rooms or are we sharing?

As I pack the contents of my apartment into a suitcase, Scarlett leaves a message on my cellphone: "I'm at Whole Foods picking up snacks—you're not vegan are you? See you in twenty minutes." I wonder what kind of car she has; a Honda or some kind of eco-friendly hybrid? Or maybe it's an enormous mini van with a third row of seats and we'll be throwing all our candy wrappers in the back, or maybe she doesn't really drive at all and she'll arrive in a long black limo with a man at the wheel. Scarlett pulls up in a red Mini Cooper. She looks normal for a movie star. "Oh sorry," she says moving her mega purse from what's about to become my seat. I close the door and buckle up. "I like your car," I say. "It's not my car. It's a rental," she says, stepping on the gas, giving me momentary whiplash. How do I do this? Do I turn on a tape recorder, do I record the sound of wheels on the highway? "So," I say, "Where are we going?" "How about leaving that to me," she says. How about, I hate surprises, and despite the fact that she's a movie star, I suddenly feel kidnapped. "I'm thinking Nyack," I offer. "It's thirty minutes from NYC, we could get a coffee, talk for an hour and then head home?" She shakes her head. "Bennington, Vermont—there's a good cheeseburger place?" She shakes her head. "Okay, the Eastern Shore of Maryland, Chesapeake Bay?" "Nope," she says, laughing.

I look over at Scarlett and think, this is odd, but I'm doing a magazine profile and there she is in profile—she can't really turn her head to talk as she's got to keep her eyes on the road. In profile she's the young woman other young women want to be, and she's the kind of girl a guy might think he'd have a chance with because she's not a "perfect" beauty, but she is very much a natural beauty. The late afternoon light sweeps across her face and her skin picks it up; there's a translucence about Scarlett, a subtlety which is what acting is all about, the flicker of her eye, the deft turn of the head, and the fact that she's got a great speaking voice, a curvy body, and at just twenty-three, she exudes an assured self-confidence. While she's driving, I'm dashboarding—writing while in the car—and I think of Nabokov's notes on index cards, Sam Shepard writing plays while at the wheel. I am taking notes, my laptop heating my knees while Scarlett appears to be drag-racing tractor trailers on the New York State Thruway. So we start talking, and somehow I begin with Scarlett's grandmother, who I had recently read was performing for a concert for seniors. I'm a sucker for grandmother stories—my own died recently at ninety-nine. I click the record button.

Scarlett Johansson: My grandmother's parents were from New York, so I'm from a long line of New York, row housing. She moved to Denmark in the 1970s because it was liberal, clean and they had great social programmes.

A.M. Homes: Did your mom move with her?
SJ: Yeah, she married my father when she was twenty and they lived in Denmark for a couple of years, and then moved back to New York. My father was from Copenhagen—born and raised there.

AMH: So, a very different persona than . . .
SJ: Than my Jewish mother from Brooklyn?

AMH: Don't you think?
SJ: Yeah, totally different, although there are certain similarities as far as the ironic sense of humour goes; Scandinavian humour is extremely dry. My parents got divorced, well they separated about ten years ago, but I think humour is what brought them together. My grandmother is like a little firecracker, she's so cute. It's an interesting perspective to be friends or have an older person in your life. It's wonderful. I treasure my relationship with her. It's incredible to think about what she has actually lived through. She must've been born around 1922 and then when you think how much has changed, what she's lived through, it's incredible. I wonder sometimes if years from now when I'm talking to my grandchildren I'll be like, "Everything's pretty much the same, just worse."

AMH: The technological and scientific progress happening now is a lot like it was at the turn of the century...
SJ: Yeah, so why are we socially disintegrating?

AMH: When you think about change what do you think about?
SJ: I'm really inspired when I watch Barack Obama speak. I think the kind of change that he's talking about isn't like, "Let's get those Republicans out of there, take over, and polarise this society." He's talking about a change that's from the bottom up: where the people are proactive, proud, and excited, and can do well for themselves, and can start small businesses, and support their families, and follow their dreams. Really create a land of opportunity for people.

AMH: Do you feel a sense of social responsibility? That we are all supposed to be doing something in our communities?
SJ: I think that it's hard for people to be active in their community and politically active when they are so freaked out about how they are going to feed their children or take care of a sick parent—problems that are completely all-consuming. I really feel that, yes, of course, it's important for people to be part of the community, it's personally fulfilling as well, but people are freaked out and really it just feels like a depressing time. What do I feel when I watch Obama speak? That he is incredibly intelligent, which unfortunately has been misconstrued by certain media sources as being elitist.

AMH: Can a person who has a public career have a private life?
SJ: I think you can. I certainly have a private life.

AMH: How?
SJ: I've been working in the industry for fifteen years, so I feel in a sense that's allowed me time to adjust to it, and also I don't live a crazy, sensational life. I'm fortunate to have a very supportive family. My family's very normal and not fazed by it all.

AMH: Where do you like to go when you're not at home?
SJ: I like to travel around the country. I love driving and I love travelling around the States and seeing the terrain change. We live in such a beautiful country. Sometimes you forget somehow. You're all wrapped up in the things we've been talking about, and you don't realise that there's all these incredible national parks, so many places to see. It's great; I drive as much as I possibly can.

AMH: What do you like about driving?
SJ: I like to listen to music, and I like to get out when I feel like it and go, "Oh look it says it's the best hot chocolate in America."

Scarlett's cell phone rings, I put the recorder on pause and pretend I'm not here, hard to do in a Mini Cooper. She keeps driving while she's talking and even though I don't know where we're going, I'm betting we're a little lost. She takes us on to a secondary road and then we pull up to a diner, "I'll call you later," she says to her friend, and I assume we're making a pit stop. Before we go in, she puts a wide-brimmed baseball hat on—I'm never sure if this draws more or less attention to someone. In a truck-stop diner somewhere in upstate New York, Scarlett orders the veggie burger deluxe, lettuce, tomato, pickle on top. And once again I push the record button.

AMH: So let's go back for a second, why Tom Waits?
SJ: I'll start with how long I've been singing. One of the main reasons I started acting was because I wanted to be in musical theatre when I was little. I loved musicals. *Oklahoma!*, all those Rodgers and Hammerstein musicals, and everything on Broadway. My mom took me to a lot of Broadway when we were young, she's a big Broadway fan.

AMH: Are you quite shy?
SJ: I got incredibly, cripplingly shy. I just didn't want to go onstage. But I always sang. And then a couple of years ago my friend, who's a vocal coach, did a benefit album for Music Matters, which is a wonderful organisation. He did an album with actors singing lullabies, and I sang "Summertime," a song my grandma used to sing me. The label really responded to it. They said, "Hey if you ever want to record an album . . ." It was no strings attached. I couldn't really pass it up. The only song I really wanted to do was this duet that Tom Waits did with Bette Midler called "I Never Talk to Strangers," it's on *Foreign Affairs*. I thought of doing some old standards and a Cole Porter song, but eventually I figured if I did all Tom Waits songs and I could reimagine them, it would be more inspired in a way.

AMH: So how did you come to that sound?
SJ: I wanted a sound that was ambient, a massive, almost cinematic sound, like Kevin Shields from My Bloody Valentine. And then somebody suggested Dave Sitek from TV on the Radio, so I spoke to Dave, and we completely had the same vision for the project. We decided to record it in Louisiana, because I always associated Waits with that humidity.

AMH: Like a really big Eggleston photograph . . .
SJ: Exactly. I wanted space, I wanted swampy air, that ambient sound, to tie everything together. It is a very coherent thing.

AMH: Who do you turn to for advice?
SJ: In regards to what? What kind of advice?

AMH: When you're thinking about what to do next?
SJ: I would say usually my mom. The really great thing about working with my mom, other than she's wonderful, is she's always encouraged me to follow my interests, to follow what excites me and see what lies there.

Scarlett eats half a burger and six French fries and it's only at the moment when she smiles up at the waitress with ketchup on her lip like make-up that our cover is almost blown. "You look like someone," the waitress says. Scarlett wipes her lip and swallows. "Thank you," she says and asks for the cheque. I decide for the purposes of public conversation to change her name to Charlotte or sometimes Charlie—which would be confusing in a *Boys Don't Cry* kind of a way, but she gets it. As the sky is beginning to get dark, and the battery on my laptop is fading, we pull into a rather random-looking motel. "I know this isn't exactly what you were thinking," she says. "But I swear it'll be fun, we'll watch movies and talk." The sign just outside the motel says "cancy" (the VA has fallen off the word "vacancy"), phone in room and free cable TV. How is it possible that I am being more of a diva than Scarlett? "Okay," I say, thinking about bed bugs. Despite being a "transgressive writer" I'm a hotel snob; anything less than five stars makes me nervous. In Stockholm syndrome affected hostages develop sympathy for their abductor, and with the Lima syndrome abductors begin to sympathise with their hostages. I think we've got a little bit of both going on here, and it's not clear which is which and who is who. I come out of the bathroom, where admittedly I've been hiding out, having a whispery conversation with my agent about the fact that this particular profile is starting to seem slightly more "involved" than what was originally discussed. The room smells like popcorn and there's Scarlett in her jimmies on the bed with a bag of microwave popcorn. "The guy in the front office made it for us," she says, holding out the bag. I try to smile, "Oh was that a mouse?" she says, jumping from her bed to mine. I must have looked especially startled. "Just kidding," she says jumping back to her own bed and then back to mine. "Come on," she says, "you're not that old," and suddenly we are both jumping back and forth on the beds, which are so decrepit that this is probably all they're good for.

AMH: When you look at a script for the first time do you think more about the movie, or who the director will be?
SJ: The script has to be solid. I've turned down projects with amazing auteurs before because the script was not right.

AMH: The script for *Lost in Translation* was very much an evolution.
SJ: Yes, that script was very short, but its complex simplicity was very moving. I felt it had a lot of potential to be really powerful.

AMH: With Woody Allen, what is that process like?
SJ: Never obvious. Every time I read one of Woody's scripts I never have any idea how the hell it's going to turn out. The only film that I have done with him that I could clearly see was *Scoop*.

AMH: Because the script was clearer?
SJ: Right. I knew exactly how he was writing it, who he was writing it for, and what he had in mind—there was a particular impersonation I'd done of somebody he was really into. So that was much clearer for me. I think that Woody looks at casting his films . . . looking at specifics. Age—can this person play a young woman? Okay, I like this young woman. He's not precious about everything, I mean he is in some ways and isn't in others, it's very strange. He's very precious about strange things like the clothing that you wear in the film, which is always t-shirt and jeans. But it's always that particular t-shirt and jeans. It's very strange. It's a really particular aesthetic. But in other regards you feel interchangeable somehow—if I couldn't do it another actor that is my age could come and do it.

AMH: I think Woody Allen puts a person into a particular role and then projects the film on the actor.
SJ: Right, which is how it should be for an actor, you hope it's like that. My character in *Match Point* couldn't have been any more different than my character in *Scoop*, but you know how he sees different sides of me and that's exciting to me. This is going to sound completely ridiculous, but when I was eight years old I did this movie called *Just Cause*. I was Sean Connery's daughter and it was with Blair Underwood and Laurence Fishburne, and I really took a shine to Laurence—he was wonderful. I remember going to visit him in the first class we did, I was like "Hi" and he was like, "Let me ask you something Scarlett, do you want to be an actor or do you want to be a star?" And I said, "Well, why can't I be both, I want to be both." He was like, "No, you can only pick one. You can be an actor or you can be a star." At the time I didn't know what he was talking about, but looking back on it, he's right, it's quite valid.

AMH: What about the difference between being a movie star and being a celebrity?
SJ: I think a lot of it has to do with a person's passion for film in a way. I mean, I still walk through the set at lunch when the whole crew has gone and I look around; I look how things are built and the equipment, it's magic to me. I love making movies, I love seeing 150 people getting together for this one frame, this one shot, this moment, and capturing it, and why? Just for entertainment and human connection, and I just think it's magical. It's like watching *The Wizard of Oz*—it's just incredible. I saw *The Wizard of Oz* recently, I've seen it eight thousand times, but it was on TNT. I was watching it on mute because I was doing something, and every once in a while I'd look over at Judy Garland. Those facial expressions and the way that they shot her in glitter, it could make you weep, it's so beautiful.

AMH: It was movie magic.
SJ: It was, it is. It's always about trying to find a project that's going to inspire you in that way. When you get that tingly feeling—you sob or you laugh or you get completely involved in the story.

AMH: When you were a kid, who were your idols?
SJ: I loved Judy Garland. Who else did I love? Natalie Wood, I loved her, I thought she was so beautiful. I loved Rosalind Russell, Jack Lemmon, and Walter Matthau. But it was hard for me to disassociate Rosalind Russell from *His Girl Friday*—it was hard of me to think of that as a performance, like seeing Betty Davis in *All About Eve*. There were movies that I loved, and I loved musicals, of course, but as far as people that I idolised, I mean, god I wanted to sing like Frank Sinatra. I guess when I say it like that I sound like I was some kind of dorky kid. I loved all the stuff that my mom loved, all the stuff she showed us. I had a really great grounding in a sense as an actor because my mother was a movie buff.

AMH: Are there people who are inspirational to you, or people whose work you follow closely because you think that person's doing something interesting and you want to understand what they're doing . . .
SJ: Sure, there's a lot of interesting people. Philip Seymour Hoffman, for instance, even if the movie is not that great, his performance is totally worth it. I love Zooey Deschanel—I think she's adorable, and certain directors will always be interesting like Spike Jonze, like my friend Bennett Miller. Johnny Depp always, and I love Tim Burton, his work is so good.

AMH: How tall are you?
SJ: How short am I? I'm 5"3. People don't immediately look at me and go, there she is.

AMH: They have to find you first.
SJ: How tall are you?

AMH: 5"10. Just kidding, I'm 5"6, I'm regular.
SJ: It's not even nine o'clock, we've finished the popcorn and the acrobatic and the TV only gets about four channels. I have a bottle of nail polish, so if worse comes to worse we can play beauty parlour.

Scarlett picks up the phone, calls the front desk, and gets the name of a place down the road, a bar where we can go hear some music. Soon we're there, having a beer, getting local, talking to people. "Where are you from?" someone asks her. "Minneapolis," she says, and I am reminded that she's an actress. And then like a scene in a movie, the band begins to play a song, it's an old Patsy Cline song and Scarlett snaps to attention and starts moving towards to the stage like she's being magnetically pulled. It's like the sum of all of America's parts, one guy gives her his cowboy hat and she climbs up on the stage, takes the microphone, and turns to the band, "I hope you don't mind if I help you out with this song." The boys in the band smile, and she starts right in with "Walking After Midnight". It's smoky and wild and the folks in the bar are loving it. The roadside rodeo are sucking it up, when she wants to come down from the stage two of the men in the audience lift her off it and half carry, half fly her around the room. She lands and someone hands her a fresh beer and one of the guys has got his arm around her waist and she seems comfortable with all the physical language. I overhear her say to another man, "Oh baby, that's sweet, but I'm spoken for." And when it starts to get a little too intense, she catches my eye and it's like a Thelma and Louise moment, and we're out of there, tyres spinning out of the parking lot and heading back towards the motel.

AMH: One of the things that gets written about you is "Scarlett Johansson is so sexy". Which is a funny thing to be, a woman who is categorised as "sexy".
SJ: I think a lot of that is just because I have breasts and an ass. Is it because I'm curvy and most people in this business are thin? I don't know what it is. I think I'm just very comfortable in my body.

AMH: Was that always okay with you?
SJ: Yeah. I think because my mom was very beautiful and wore red lipstick and make-up and dresses and was very feminine and my sister and I were always really feminine, I guess I just never thought to use this to my advantage. I was just like this is who I am, and maybe that's what people are attracted to.

As we're parking, the desk clerk is running out to the car, "I figured it out," the desk clerk says. "Cool," Scarlett says. "I figured out who you remind me of, that girl, what's her name," He snaps his fingers, "You know . . ." "Give me a clue," Scarlett says. "Is she a singer? Is she on TV?" "Is she a movie star?" I ask and Scarlett glares at me. "Oh god," the guy says, hitting himself on the forehead, "What is her name?" "When you think of it again, let me know," Scarlett says, and we lock ourselves in our room and push the dresser in front of the door, just in case. And just before we go to sleep, I pop in another tape and like some stream of consciousness interview we both lie back on our beds—and the interview game continues.

AMH: Are there designers you really want to wear?
SJ: I have a lot of friends who are in the fashion industry, so I have an idea in my head of what I want to wear and find the dress out of that idea. For this last event, the Metropolitan Museum ball, I wanted it to be feminine. I like the idea of wearing something nude, timeless—the dress was sort of Marilyn Monroe-y. I wanted that sort of whimsical look. The dress was designed around that idea—it's exciting to be able to create that. It's like getting into character—the movie-star character that all of us actors play when we go to the Academy Awards and all that, and when we get to see each other at 5.30 in the morning for work, it's totally different. I have

my own style on the street—part of that is a style that's casual and not wanting to stand out, and I try to not dress in a flashy way. If I wasn't as recognisable I would have a more bright and expressive way of dressing. I try to dress in an understated way so that I blend in.

AMH: Any specific designers?
SJ: Dolce & Gabbana cut well for me—womanly. It's funny, a lot of clothing has become more androgynous, kind of tulip-shaped. I love to look at it, but I could never wear it—I'm petite and curvy. Dolce & Gabbana cut for a heroine—a 1950s physique.

AMH: Do you collect anything—design objects, paintings?
SJ: I don't collect too many things—I don't like clutter. I grew up in a house with six people so it was cluttered. I collect Victorian jewellery and other Victorian things, like locket chains, snuff boxes. In the immediacy of text messages, emails, and cell phones we've lost this very romantic sense of keepsakes and handwritten letters, or making things that remind you of someone—keeping a locket of hair, friendship rings, promise rings, and various charms. It's never going to be that way again. My dad once got me a pair of Victorian gold cuffs and I fell in love with them. I went with him to the shop where he'd bought them and they had all kinds of fascinating things.

AMH: Going back to music—can you talk about music you like?
SJ: I'm listening to a lot of Bob Dylan lately. His songs are such beautiful poetry, and you discover new things every time—even when you know all the words. They mean different things to you as you go along. I always listen to TV on the Radio. Peggy Lee, I don't know why, maybe it's the rain in the spring, I love to listen to her when it's raining, and Tammy Wynette.

AMH: So what's coming up for you?
SJ: I have *He's Just Not That Into You* coming out soon, a project based on that book, an anti-how-to-keep-a-man book. I was attracted to the film because it wasn't about the romance of the geeky guy who turns out to be the prince charming, but about women supporting each other and friendships and strong women. All the characters in it are independent and very different from each other. It's got an all-star cast—a lot of the reason I wanted to do the project was so I could get to know Drew [Barrymore]. She's a fantastic role model. She's fun, she's an avid reader, a real bookworm—it's fascinating to meet people who read that much and know all kinds of strange random things. I also just finished Frank Miller's *The Spirit*, based on the Will Eisner graphic novel. It was a lot of fun, I got to play a lot with Sam Jackson. I am such a huge fan of Frank, I think he's so talented. When I heard he was casting for a new film I was desperate to find out about it, and when I met him I just fell completely in love with him. There was not a part for me in the script, but we had lunch for three hours and he ended up writing the part. That was out of fan worship for Frank.

AMH: Okay, here's an A.M. Homes question. How would you describe yourself to a police sketch artist either physically or psychologically? You looking at yourself is very different from others looking at you—what do you see?
SJ: I have such a lame perspective on myself—I know who I am, I feel very comfortable with myself, I guess so comfortable that I hardly ever self-analyse. I'm determined, curious, interested, passionate, sensitive, and impatient. And I think that more than anything, I'm fascinated by human nature and social behaviours . . . and I'm 5"3, blonde, and curvy.

AMH: Are you excited about getting married?
SJ: I never had any foresight as to what was going to happen in my life. I knew eventually marriage and kids seemed like something . . . I knew I wanted children, and as far as marriage goes I never thought that much about it. I'm so comfortable where I am in my life, I feel like everything is falling into place.

And the tape clicks off, like that's just the perfect stopping point. I'm too tired to get up and put a fresh one in and we keep talking for a bit and I'm not sure who falls asleep first, but when I wake up at two am, she's fast asleep, looking young and incredibly angelic and I turn off the room lights and make sure the chain is on the door. In the morning when we get up there's a note under the door, "Don't worry I'm not spying on you," it says in big uneven letters. "I just wanted to say I figured out who you were. All night I kept thinking, I know that girl from somewhere, junior high, summer jobs, and then I realised, in fact, I don't know you, I only feel like I do. Anyway, I just wanted to tell you . . ." And then it trails off to nothing. Scarlett puts the letter in her pocket. She steps on the gas, the speedometer is hovering at around eighty. We're hurtling down the highway and I'm feeling a little bit bad for her, and she must know it. "Isn't this great?" she says. I nod and look at her in profile, she means what she says. And despite seeming to be just a little bit lost, we're back in New York in an hour. She pulls up in front of my building: "Hey thanks," I say. "That was fun." "Are you sure?" she asks. "Yeah, I think so," I say. I'm tempted to say we'll do it again sometime, but stop short. After all, we're not really friends, but did a good job of pretending. And I like her; she is someone I'd be friends with if such a thing were possible, if one could ever be friends with a movie star.

So what really happened? What if I told the truth? I would tell you that we never left New York, that we met for tea at a hotel in New York City and that I had a horrible cold, a plague of sorts, and I spent the three hours we talked blowing my nose constantly.

And that Scarlett was gracious and normal and not at all movie-star like, though she does seem more mature than your average twenty-three year-old girl. And to her credit she didn't seem grossed out to be sitting with drippy me, and later reported she didn't even get the voracious bug that kept me home for the three weeks that followed. She is thoroughly appealing and engaging, someone who really would be great to take a road trip with.

The interview between A.M. Homes and Scarlett Johansson contained in this story took place in New York City in June 2008, as described by the end of the piece. The road trip is purely fictional, a fabrication by the author in response to the interview.

Interview originally published in AnOther Magazine, Issue 15, 2008

CONTINUING REVOLUTION OF THE MIND

NICK WAPLINGTON

Nick Waplington was well known on the art photography scene through his book *Living Room* and the idea for this project was to explore the notion of using the magazine as a platform for casting. *Safety in Numbers* was pitched as a global survey of youth culture, and we advertised the casting call in the pages of *Dazed & Confused*. It was a truly global project and in every city he went to Nick would kind of sofa-surf and take pictures, networking all the clubs and the different communities that he came across. It became this incredible survey of youth culture and the dark side of club culture. You get a sense that when he finally returns to London at the end of the book the party is well and truly coming to an end. *Nothing* was a follow-up commission for BBC 2. I was really into this idea of using television as a canvas, and it was the perfect brief because we had carte blanche to do whatever we wanted. Nick travelled around the world filming with his assistant and friend Nick Clegg, and Orbital recorded an original sound track to complement the work. Essentially, it was about creating a moving version of Nick's photography—a visual collage of his worldview. The work was amazing because Nick wasn't afraid to take risks, and he always wound up in the most unusual situations. I remember getting a phone-call from him from Peru or Bolivia at one point, and he said: "Please wire me $2,000, I've just killed a farmer's prize sheep! He's holding me to ransom! I don't know if I'm going to make it out of here alive!" The project is an important example of what can happen when you take a trans-disciplinary approach to media with a provocative individual.

Shoot Everything: Capturing the Mood of the Zeitgeist

Mark Sanders *Dazed & Confused* was always about collaboration, so for *Safety in Numbers* Nick chose four cities, and it was really about the interconnection of youth in all of those different places. It was essentially about paradox, so it was about difference but also about similarity. The book was also a portrait of so many different backgrounds that showed it doesn't matter what nationality you are—you still share the same group counterculture mentality.

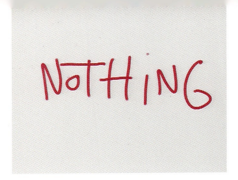

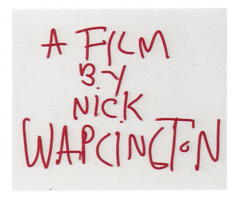

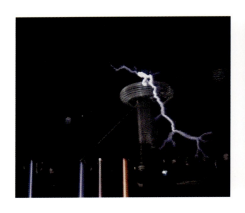
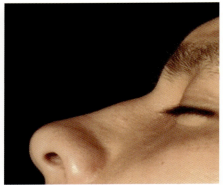

Nick Waplington There are a lot of pictures in *Safety in Numbers* that were taken on dance floors, where I would wait for the strobe to come on and quickly put the camera right in people's faces to try to capture the moment. At one stage in the project, I ended up living with two hookers in New York, and that was really interesting—they worked days and would come in with huge piles of cash we would spend in the evening; it was a hilarious time. Nothing was another strung-out adventure and my assistant went crazy on that trip—he thought I was tracking him for MI5. In the end, it got heavy, and I had to continue shooting the project alone. There is one bit in the film where ants are eating a live cockroach that is kind of great, but the rest of it is a fairly unruly mistake. It was a good way for Orbital to generate ideas for their next album, though—perhaps that is the best thing that came out of it.

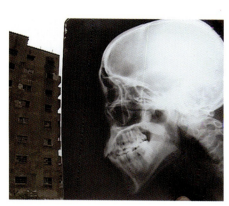

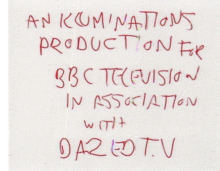

KM3D-1

In the KM3D-1 project I really wanted to push 3D technology as far as it was possible to go at the time. Baillie Walsh had been commissioned by Alexander McQueen to shoot Kate Moss for the famous hologram project and KM3D-1 was really a follow-up to that installation. Baillie had the idea of shooting it on a Phantom camera so that it would be the first slow-motion 3D film, and what was really important to me was that we would create the greatest feeling of three-dimensionality possible. In the end, there was something really transcendental about the experience of seeing it in a purpose built room on a triptych screen. Kate throws these diamonds at the camera and they float through the air, suspend, and then shatter into thousands of pieces of crystals, creating an explosion that has a depth of twenty metres. This means that when you stand in the installation watching the screen, you actually see crystals flying over the heads of the people in front of you. It was a very real attempt to disorientate and disturb reality. It got shown in London, Rome, Berlin, so, in some ways, it was as though Kate could appear in these cities without showing up — a mythical 21st century godess.

Three-dimensional Fashion: Being Everywhere at Once

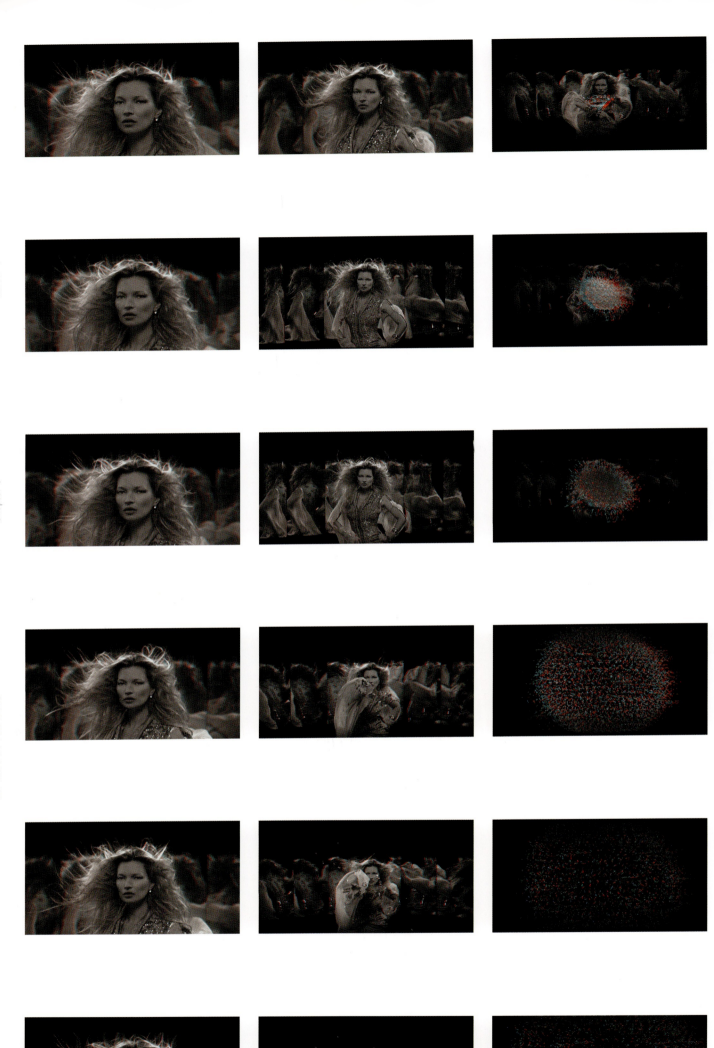

Jerry Stafford When Jefferson first approached me about this project, I was travelling in Bhutan and Northern India where I was becoming very interested in the ceremonial and ritual aspects of both those cultures. And so, when he started talking about this project with Kate [Moss], I was thinking of the idea that we would make Kate into a different incarnation of herself, from what we'd previously seen. The first reference point was the work of Kenneth Anger and the way that he had used shamanism, ceremony, and ritualism in his film work. Other influences came in, one of which was Ray Harryhausen, who was, for me, the original special effects man. It was a starting point that then evolved through the choice of director, Baillie Walsh. When you are working in 3D, it is about depth of field, not just about the foreground, which was our subject, Kate Moss. And what the mirror effect gave us was this ad infinitum, this void in which she could evolve as her character. The use of 3D, and the use of high-speed cameras, like the Phantom—had never actually been done. It was the first time that a camera rig had been invented with two Phantom cameras shooting at 1000 frames per second. This was very exciting because we were being as experimental as people like Kenneth Anger had been, because we were slightly working in the dark . . . it had never been done before.

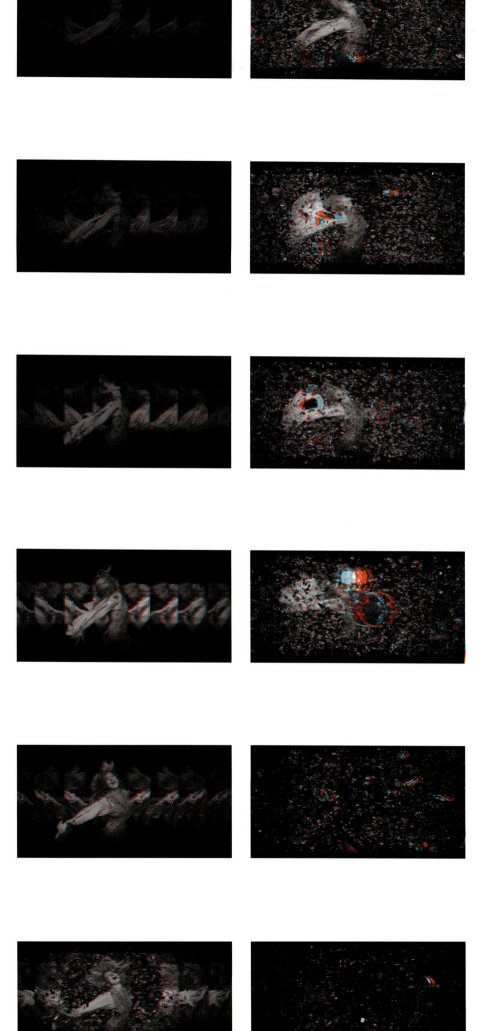

SX70

This was the idea of doing a collectable CD compilation that was a mix of the music I was playing at parties. I called it SX70, because the SX70 was my favourite Polaroid format camera. I took Polaroid pictures for the album artwork and I asked the incredibly talented design studio M+M to do something very analogue with them, so in terms of its tactility it kind of felt as retro as a Polaroid camera. It was about celebrating music, and the influence of music in all of my work. I think M+M did a really beautiful job; Mathias' illustrations really surprised me, he transformed it into a collectable and artistic collaboration — it's definitely more memorable for the cover than the mix of music on it!

Music as Conversation

SX70 by JEFFERSON HACK for colette

Guillame Salmon We invited Jefferson to make a compilation for us because music and fashion are intertwined; you can't have one without the other. For many years, Michel Gaubert curated all of our compilations and Jefferson was one of our first guest curators. He immediately had the idea to call the compilation *SX70* and to ask M+M Paris to make the cover. We knew it was going to be unique.

MAKING IT UP AS WE GO ALONG

The Dazed Exhibition at Somerset House was a celebration of twenty years of kicking against the pricks and all of those people who had helped us achieve it — the private view brought together two generations of contributors and collaborators and it was definitely a night to remember! I guess we had seen lots of other great titles rise and fall and we wanted to celebrate the fact that we were still here, and still going strong with an experiential, immersive exhibition that also launched the book *Making It Up As We Go Along: Twenty Years of Dazed & Confused*. I co-curated the exhibition with Emma Reeves and it is something I'm still very proud of. It featured some fantastic installations, such as the three-dimensional audio-visual representation of McQueen's classic Salò shoot, and it was a poignant visual journey through the era we had lived through, with amazing portraiture from Rankin and Juergen Teller that really defined the early days of the magazine aesthetically. It was, of course, impossible to represent everything that had been in the magazine over the course of twenty years and it was a tough process making decisions as to what did and didn't best represent us. Overall, it was essentially a celebration of the family we had created and the cultural provocation of which they had been the beating pulse—from Alexander McQueen to Björk, Jake & Dinos Chapman, Thom Yorke, Damien Hirst, Chlöe Sevigny, Jarvis Cocker, Kate Moss, Milla Jovovich, Katie Grand, Alister Mackie, Katy England, Phil Poynter . . . I mean, the list goes on, like the beat.

Celebrating   Twenty   Years   of   Cultural   Disruption

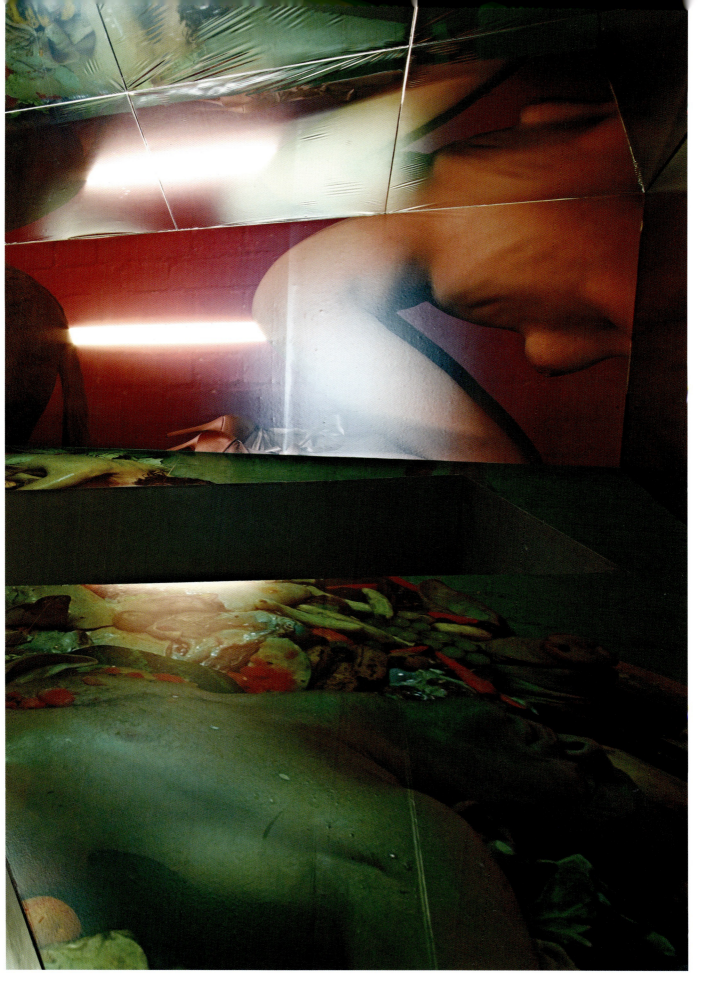

Emma Reeves In the early days we had the *Dazed* gallery, and that was always an "open door policy" — there were people constantly coming through. So there was always this sort of physical entity to the magazine, this social hub for a tribe and constant fluidity. When you're working on a magazine nothing is ever final, it's all just a work in progress, and that was the energy we wanted to take into the exhibition — the notion that you can't accept finality. So the exhibition was a physical representation of this constant stage of flux, an attempt to immerse the audience in the cultural phenomena that is a magazine, rather than just fetishising over the pages, or the past. If you just take the pages and put them in a frame you are doing it a disservice. You have to create an atmosphere, and inject it with that sensibility of collective action — we always wanted the exhibition to be something you have to engage in, like the magazine.

THE TRI OF OPTIM

"No one should compromise. Compromise makes people dull."

Alexander McQueen, *Another Magazine*, 2010.

DEFIANT

"If you live the way others want you to you just end up caring less anc less about life. You become more and more selfish and forget to fight back."

Malcolm McLaren, *Star Culture*, 2000

DEFINED.

PUNK POS

UMPH

"In art and dream may you proceed with abandon. In life may you proceed with balance and strength."

Patti Smith, *AnOther Magazine*, 2006

ISM.

"I need to respect the freedom I have and not use it vaingloriously to exercise my ego."

Jefferson Hack, *Purple Fashion Magazine*, 2010

NOT

"I certainly don't have the answers. I'm confused and full of contradictions: I don't believe in counter-culture, I don't believe in hype, I don't believe in Jesus Christ, the government, the revolution, an alternative culture, them and us, drugs, hedonism or peace. I rebel and conform at the same time; siphon like a sponge and squirt like a burst pipe. I don't fit in, but I don't want out. I like it easy, but I don't mind doing the hard work. I lie, I cheat, I steal, I experiment, I think I'm special, but I know I'm just the same as millions of other people. Maybe I'm the same, because I'm different. The one thing I do know, as I search for some elusive truths, is that I want to ask questions and set new ideas in motion."

Jefferson Hack, *Dazed & Confused*, 1997

ITIVISM.

THE CHANGE

"I surfed the revolution of the open spirit."

Jefferson Hack, *Purple Fashion Magazine,* 2010

"Is this live? Are we really live? This is really live, there's no faking it? Okay, so I can say fuck as much as I like and you can't edit it? Fuck, fuck, fuck, fuck, fuck, fuck, fuck, fuck, fuck, fuck, fuck, fuck, fuck, fuck . . ."

Jefferson Hack, *SHOWStudio.com,* 2014

ANTI-

ONLY

"Extreme acts of individuality propel the world forward but it takes individual people and passion to make things happen."

Tibor Kalman, *Dazed & Confused*, 1995

IS SOCIAL.

What's the most romantic action you've taken?
"Once, in a previous life, I scaled the tallest mountain and crossed the vastest desert to find her."

Waris Ahluwalia, *Anothermag.com*, 2013

NO STALGIA.

"The authentic isn't something that is easily assimilated by capital, so therefore what is authentic isn't necessarily what the culture wants on location because it's complicated, it's messy. It's difficult. Authenticity is dirty, it's horrible, it's disgusting. It has built into it this uncomfortable idea of chaos, where anything can happen."

Malcolm McLaren, *Star Culture*, 2000

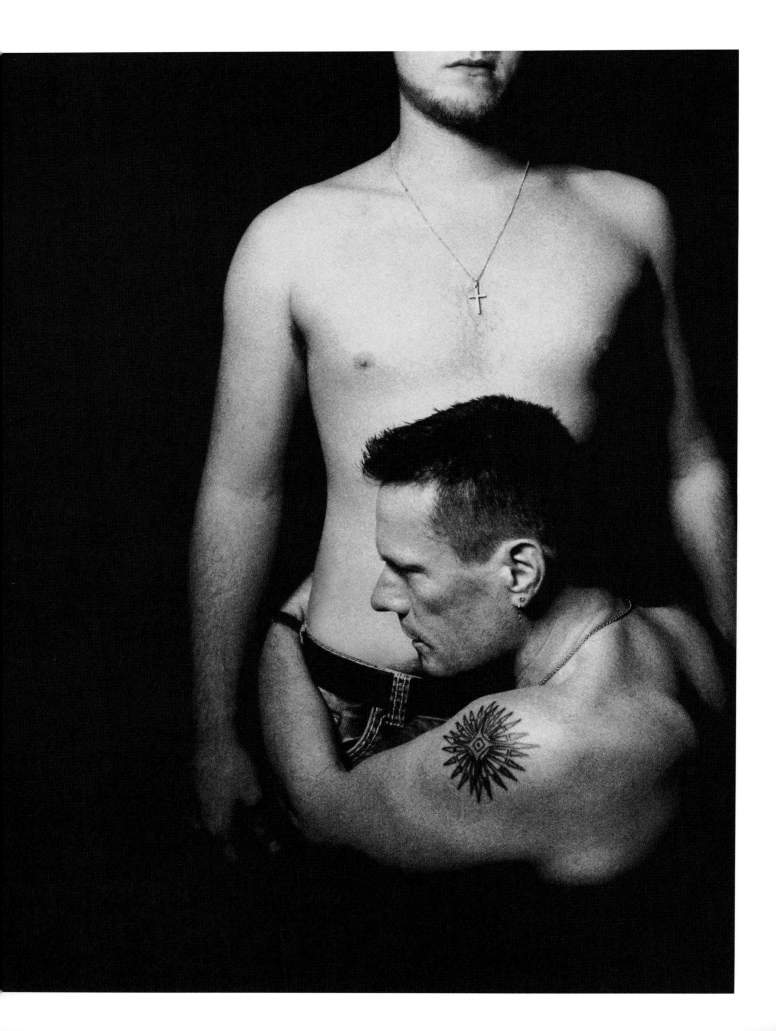

U2   SONGS   OF   INNOCENCE

U2 wanted to create a very personal cover image for Songs of Innocence, an image that represented a dialogue between the older self and the younger self. It was Bono's idea to stage it with Larry, the idea of the younger Larry holding onto his older self was evident but it also threw up other more ambiguous questions and connotations. Glen Luchford shot it on the back of a press shoot he did with the band with a Caravaggio-style lighting. It was a test, and the test stuck. At least 500+ alternative album cover designs were generated in between the test shoot and the final artwork going to press, but what won through was the ultra simplicity of this one test image with absolutely no type at all on the cover.

As the digital release of the album preceded the physical by two weeks the band needed an alternative cover. iTunes had the exclusivity so it meant that we had to create artwork that would stand out within this digital-only environment and then disappear. Gavin Friday inspired the idea of a white label "promo" sleeve, which is how the record industry used to promote vinyl releases prior to the invention of CDs. We mimicked the white label concept for iTunes and the fact that we got away with it still really surprises me, because it's actually a photograph of a vinyl white label record reproduced only for a digital release. It was an ironic subversion—doing a physical master for a digital only purpose.

Overall, the project became an exercise in stripping things down to very iconic, very graphic, very simple, very emotional, very direct, honest and upfront facets. We wanted to give the sense that what you were getting from the band was from the heart. There was a lot of thought that went into making something incredibly simple, and the crux of the idea was really to shine a light on the value of the physical and what lies beyond the surface—just because less people are buying physical, doesn't mean you care less, to me it's the opposite, it means the people who are buying the physical actually care more.

Retro-Minimalism   and   the   Eternal   Dialogue   of   Reflection

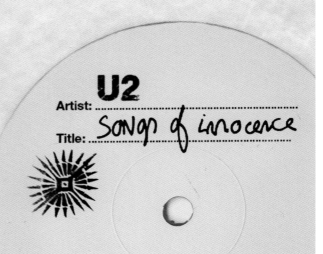

SKATEISTAN

Skateistan is a groundbreaking film about skater kids in Kabul by the director Orlando von Einsiedel. The pilot launched on *Dazed Digital* and then went on to become a long-form documentary that launched a movement. It really shows how a great idea and authentic story can pick up serious traction and how it can grow far beyond its initial parameters. The film took us behind the scenes of the world's first skateboarding school in Kabul, and provided a fly-on-the-wall view of the daily lives of kids facing serious hardship with immense positivity. In many senses, I almost feel that *Skateistan* held up a contemporary mirror to the ethos that had defined Nick Waplington's *Safety in Numbers* many years earlier [page 112]. It had exactly that same sensibility that somewhere, hidden under the surface of whatever is going on, even if that is conflict and violence on a massive scale, there is a youth culture committed to resistance; a youth culture expressing itself in ways that go completely against the grain of the cultural paradigm they are handed by the generation that precede them.

The Short Film That Became a Movement

Orlando von Einsiedel I got word that *Dazed* was looking for stories about youth subcultures and I had wanted to do something about the skate kids in Kabul for ages. *Dazed* is very open to making projects that might not get a look-in elsewhere and there is a real unique creative free-line in their approach. *Skateistan* premiered on *Dazed Digital* and was quickly staff-picked on Vimeo. It very swiftly got hundreds of thousands of views and a lot of press coverage, which brought it to the attention of Sundance—it was a whirlwind. The success of *Skateistan* through the support of *Dazed* has enormously inspired all of the film work I have done since. I now try to tell really positive stories from parts of the world you really don't hear those kinds of stories from, and, ultimately, the first point of that was *Skateistan*.

I really like skating and I won't stop.

STUDIO AFRICA

The ethical fashion brand Edun came together with Diesel to make a commitment to supporting organic cotton farming in Uganda, creating a collection from sustainable cotton farmed in Uganda that was sold in Diesel stores worldwide. We created Studio Africa as a response to that action and surveyed the youth spirit of different African countries—everything that was coming out in terms of photography, art, and music. Studio Africa had two purposes that ran in parallel—it was a creative space, but it was also a means for production. What we soon realised in the process of setting it in motion was that there was an amazing synergy between the new youth energy that was coming from Africa, those who were very proud of their African heritage, and the influences they were taking from the rest of the world - influences they were assimilating back into their own voices. Studio Africa became an umbrella for that globalised African mindset. It was emblematic of a movement that was already in full swing—what I wanted to do was identify that movement and give some fuel to it. The personalities featured are: Sy Alassane, Flaviana Matata, Uviwe Mangweni, Baloji, Yannick Illunga, I See A Different You, Tanya Mushayi, Adbellah Taia, Laurence Chauvin Buthaud.

Fuelling the Fire of Positive Change

Sara Hemming Studio Africa was a very unique project in that Jefferson did the matchmaking between Renzo [Rosso], Bono, and Ali [Hewson], all of whom share a passion for Africa and support trade on the continent. Knowing that all the involved parties were curious of the other, Jefferson orchestrated a trip to the Festival in the Desert in Timbuktu for everyone to get to know each other better. It was during this trip that the Diesel+Edun collaboration was born. The decision was made to make a denim line produced in Africa using African cotton, promoting trade not aid – this we knew, the rest was carte blanche. We decided that we needed to dedicate this platform to the amazing young generation of creative Africans, and communicate the positive aspects of what was happening on the continent to an international stage. We spent months working on the casting. The intention was honest and genuine and everyone could feel it. The first season was shot on location in a small town in Senegal called Saint-Louis, and to call the production epic would be an understatement. In total, we spent a year and a half working on Studio Africa and I have never felt such genuine passion from every single person involved in a project. It felt like one big adventure from start to finish.

Rankin I think that anything that creates awareness is a great thing. Jefferson and I both share the notion that anything that creates awareness about a problem is helping people debate and discuss that problem. One of the things we were both always very against was treating the readers like they were stupid. We put things in the magazine because we thought readers were clever, we thought they'd get it; they'd understand. A lot of what we were doing in those instances was provocative, and by doing that you are not necessarily giving a solution, because a solution is far more complicated than an article or a debate, but you are taking a social position. Lots of people thought we were doing things like Project RED or the South Africa issue of *Dazed & Confused* to get attention, but you're not, you're actually trying to provoke a reaction that comes from being inquisitive, and we always talked about the issues with a social conscience.

THE FIRST TO KNOW ✳ MUSIC ✳ FASHION

DAZED

The Freedom Issue: Know Your Rights

BUSY UNMAKING THE WORLD

They blind your eyes and drain your brain

BARBARA KRUGER / DAMIEN HIRST

I wanted to do an issue that celebrated the anniversary of the Declaration of Human Rights placing it into the context of pop culture—really explaining to our audience just how important this document is, in fact to show how it's even more important now than ever. We asked both Damien Hirst and Barbara Kruger because we thought one was going to say "no", but Barbara wanted to do it and Damien wanted to do it, so after that response, commissioning one cover wasn't an option anymore. How could you turn one of them down! Damien wanted a bullet hole in someone's chest on the cover complemented by text from the declaration because he thought it would be very provocative, confrontational, and stirring. Barbara's presented a powerful slogan on top of a found image in her classic layout style—"they blind your eyes and drain your brain".

Kicking   Against   the   Pricks

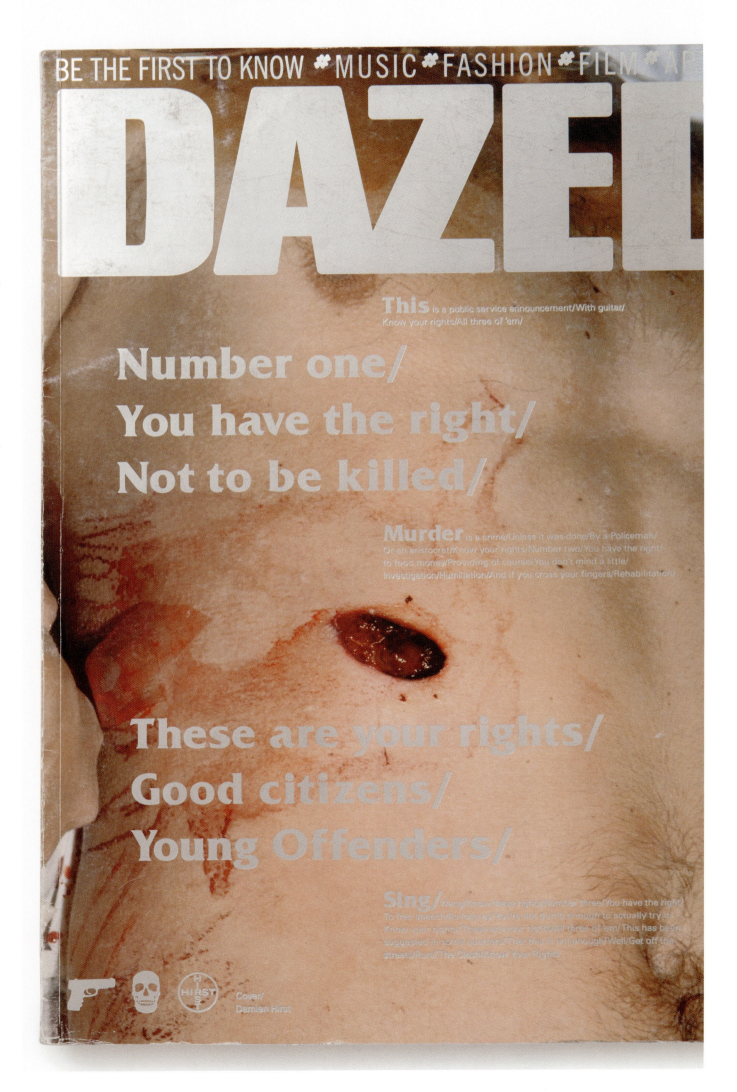

Mark Sanders During the first years of *Dazed* when money was tight, Jefferson and I would always talk about the magazine acting as a collective and collaborative platform that would allow us, our peer group, and readers to become proactive participants in the culture around us as opposed to passive consumers. The use of the magazine and its front cover to fight for human rights issues around the globe was therefore a key moment in *Dazed*'s history and one that has continued to evolve through *Dazed Digital*. Collective Action was the byword for *Dazed* in the 1990s and continues to be so today. Since its inception the magazine has always believed in collaboration and the free flow of ideas. Being proactive within culture means freedom and freedom of expression is what *Dazed* is all about.

I have never hurt a living thing, how fortunate one must be to be able to say that. We can't help but hurt one another, sometimes in our evolution we spin away from another we love or loved us. The wounds that are produced become precious. The wounded center of the heart erupts petal after petal to form the rose. The wounded center – the rose of Genet. Our walk is scattered with these roses, the haughty stems crushed beneath the cleated boot heels of passersby. The thorns strung above the porcelain necks of heroines who become saints and the breath of poetry. In my little space I begin again what I might have begun so long ago to commit a body of work there will be nothing but renewal

PATTI SMITH

The interview was conducted mostly in bed with Patti. I arrived at her house, and she came down in her dressing gown and said: "I've been up all night with a migraine. I think I need to do this interview in bed, I don't feel well." She was jet-lagged and fell asleep, and when she came to, we did the interview. It was amazing because she was in an ultra-relaxed state. What we wanted to achieve visually with the story was to shoot an invisible portrait of her, so we incorporated a lot of her notebooks and other elements into the pages, such as her Polaroids, which hadn't ever been published before. Patti is a vociferous notebook writer and writes almost every day in her notebook, so it was great to have all those layers. I was, and still am fascinated by how layered and deep a person she is. She told me to be bold and fearless in my work, compassionate and kind in my life and not let the cliché of rock'n'roll subvert that notion. It was the best advice anyone could have given me at that point in my life.

Cultural Provocation and Questions in Bed

Patti Smith
"A photograph is a secret about a secret, the more it tells you, the less you know." —Diane Arbus.

There is a hidden quality to Patti Smith that no amount of talking to her, no amount of uncovering her past or looking at her photographs or reading her texts will reveal. A visionary and a mystic, Patti has held on to that sacred quality most of us have erased to make it easier to get on with living. For the artist, the poet, it's the gift that makes them respond to the world in an original and extraordinary way. You feel it as powerfully in her silence as you do in her words, in her absence when she leaves the room, when she walks off the stage, as much as when she's there in front of you. It's a kind of noble truth; a vibrant stand-off between the divine and the destitute, the hardy and the heartbroken.

In Patti Smith's house, we come face-to-face with her material and ethereal mindset. The urban folklore of her inception as an artist is played out in her opened notebooks, her early memoirs. Volumes of Rimbaud, Genet, and Blake, in which she immersed herself during her youth are present, well-thumbed, still referenced today. A set of drums belonging to Fred "Sonic" Smith, her late husband and dearest love (who died in 1994), or the monogrammed slippers of Robert Mapplethorpe, her best friend and first love (who died in 1989), take on a talismanic quality, a power beyond the physical. Her home is not spooky in any way, it's just that all around her are the memories, the influences, the rites of her passage, and the codes that inform the person she is today.

The world-changing events of September 2001 and the subsequent invasion of Iraq have been key themes in Smith's recent output. In artwork she recently exhibited at the Andy Warhol Museum, we see the skeletons of the Twin Towers silk-screened with a meditative fastidiousness. On her last album *Trampin'* (2002), the incantations of "Radio Baghdad" call out to the souls of those who condone acts of war and perpetrate religious hatred. "Suffer not your neighbours affliction." She begs, but, "extend your hand, extend your hand." Smith is a political weapon, always has been. Since she released her first single "Piss Factory"/ "Hey Joe" in 1974, she has campaigned against social injustice and has stood up for greater human understanding.

Patti Smith's vantage point is that of the perpetual outsider. "Outside of society, they're waitin' for me, outside of society that's where I want to be," she sings on "Rock 'n' Roll Nigger," one of the tracks from her album *Easter*. It's a position she shared in the 1970s with friends and collaborators like William S. Burroughs and Gregory Corso, and artists like Mapplethorpe and Jackson Pollock, all long gone from the cultural front lines. Today, through events like the Meltdown Festival, she continues to "be a thorn in the side of the establishment" and has come to share this role with a new generation that includes Kevin Shields, Antony Hegarty, Cat Power, Fugazi, and filmmaker Jem Cohen, uniting them in new creative and political explorations. Surely, if such a thing as new countercultural movement could exist once more (and it might well do), then Patti Smith could be, as she was in the late 1970s, its revered figurehead.

In the foreword to *Early Work*, a collection of her writings and poetry from the 1970s, Smith states, "An Artist wears his work in the place of wounds. Here then is a glimpse of the scores of my generation. Often crude, irreverent—but done, I can assure you, with a fierce heart." It's an acknowledgement of the idealism and naivety perhaps with which she first presented her ideas—the incarnations of great songs, anthems, and lyrical mind bombs. This kind of bravery in putting new ideas on the line, to be inventive against what is so popular in your time, is something that is lost in rock 'n' roll today. It is not that brave artists don't exist, but that bands are fast tracked by the record industry into the super-annuated promotional machine—into an entertainment vortex where they all look and sound the same. Patti Smith reinvented the language of rock 'n' roll in the same way that Jimi Hendrix reinvented its sound, in the way that Pollock reinvented painting. This kind of development, the space for cultural experimentation and cross examination of the form, is almost lost now in a time when artistic freedom is short-circuited by the pre-packaged requirements of the entertainment machine.

In a glass cabinet, Smith keeps her Commandeur de l'Ordre by the French Republic to artists and writers who have contributed to furthering the arts. For someone who used to refer to herself as "The Field Marshall," she sees it as the ultimate medal in cultural war—in her spiritual crusade. It's not about brandishing guitars as weapons as she once felt she needed to, but about mining the depths of the personal and political. "The artist's calling is a sacred one," she reminds us, "and the artist's duty, a political one."

In her new volume of poetry and writing, *Auguries of Innocence*, Smith's duties pour into her words. It's a slim book, but one that is rich in its evocation of love, devotion, dedication, and the divine. It's a homepage to those close to her who she has lost along the way: Fred "Sonic" Smith, Robert Mapplethorpe, Richard Stohl, the pianist in the Patti Smith Group, and her brother and road manager Todd Smith, all of whom died long before their time. It's as if their ghosts are urging her, provoking her to challenge, question, and reveal more.

Patti Smith, however, managed to give death the cold shoulder. Her performances in the 1970s were unconventional, unrehearsed; she would bend and twist, and hurl herself around the stage. She would simulate masturbation, howl her babelogue, and pump her fists in the air, invoking, challenging the audience. In 1977 she fell off the stage in Tampa, Florida, and broke two vertebrae in her neck. It laid her up for a few months but didn't lay her out; she recorded *Easter* in 1978. It took something much more profound—emotional not physical—to end Smith's public life.

In the late 1970s, at the height of her fame, when the Patti Smith Group were playing to stadiums in Italy and had just released their biggest selling album *Wave*, Smith decided to retire with her husband so they could raise their children Jesse and Jackson (now aged nineteen and twenty-four) away from the limelight. It was graceful and unconventional and a totally unexpected exit from the game.

In many ways, Patti Smith is the ultimate rock 'n' roll visionary not just for what she did, but also for what she didn't do. She is an artist who has found a way to balance the sacred and the profane. She ignites the mythological potential of rock 'n' roll with the reality of living as an American artist under coercive regime. "People have the power." She tells us on *Gone Again* from 1996, and that's the point she will always make. The truth is that it may only take one artist like Patti Smith to change rock 'n' roll, but the people, you and her as one, can do much more than that; you can change the world.

AnOther Magazine: You're performing a lot at the moment. Are you enjoying it?
Patti Smith: Yes immensely. When I was younger I didn't know so much about performing, it was all intuitive. I didn't train to be a singer or a musician, I just did it. And I was pretty fearless.

AM: Were you surprised by how much of a physical performer you could be?
PS: Yeah, I was always shocked at how aggressive I was, because normally I'm pretty even tempered. But I have these feelings in me, because there is so much injustice in the world, that I can't help feeling a certain amount of rage. Performance has always been a way for me to channel that rage. It's been a very good vehicle.

AM: How did it feel to play the entire *Horses* album at the Meltdown festival last year?
PS: That was one of those nights where the people really ruled. They were really electric and I could feel their energy—it was a beautiful thing. We recorded the show, but I felt like somehow, if I could have captured the audience and recorded them, it would have made it great, not because they were cheering and clapping, but because there was an electricity in the air that was really fantastic. Our bass player mixed the recording for the anniversary CD and he brought "Gloria" round, and we sat in the car and listened. It made me cry. It had a real spirit. Sometimes you attempt things like that but you don't know if they're really going to come across well. But I was happy with it. I felt like the spirit of that night wasn't that different to the early days. For me "Gloria" was a declaration of the existence. What I'm trying to say is that we weren't just going through the motions. I felt like that authenticity came through.

AM: Do you feel as creatively powerful, as free in your expression as you did when you wrote *Horses*?
PS: Well, hopefully I feel more powerful. Even though I'm older I still feel that I haven't accomplished all of the things I want to, nor have I reached the place I want to get to, so I'm still struggling and working, just like I always did. In that way, I'm connected with all of my selves. I don't feel like somebody who produced a bunch of genius work at one point and now I'm in my declining years. I feel like I'm still trying to communicate something through a song that will touch people. I'm still working on things.

AM: Do you think that you have certain codes in your life and in your work?
PS: When I was younger, I didn't really think about how my actions or work would affect people—how it might redesign their thinking. Or if I hurt somebody, how that resonated in their life. So I am really trying to be more conscious of that and think that a lack of codes or having certain personal standards just leads to a murky chaos. Not an exciting anarchy or anything, just people hurting each other, people getting sick, I think it's important to have that. I learnt a lot when I lived in the Chelsea Hotel in the 1960s. I would see people spinning out of control all over the place. Some died, some committed suicide, some got so disconnected from reality that they could no longer work or form a sentence straight. I certainly didn't want to get like that.

AM: So you never had a long period when you used drugs—had a serious relationship with them?
PS: When I was young, I was only exposed to drugs in books. I'd read about the hashish eaters in Afghanistan, and the French poets who took opium, and it seemed really romantic and special. For me, drugs were like rituals. Like when American Indians go to the sweat lodge and take peyote and have a specific vision that informs the rest of their life. I thought it was important for jazz musicians so they could explore their music, allowing them to improvise. When I came to New York in the centre of drug culture in 1967, I saw all these people around me, all this drug use, without any spiritual or aesthetic meaning, or any kind of direction, just partying, using drugs, being slaves to them, and I didn't understand that. I found it very disrespectful. I didn't think people shouldn't take them, but I thought that they should be taken seriously. I don't believe drugs should be taken for recreation and so casually. I thought that then and I still believe it now.

AM: Did that have any bearing on your relationship with Burroughs, the most famous junkie in America?
PS: When I met William he was no longer doing drugs, because of his poor health. I've never seen William strung out. But, ironically, he was a good example for me, because he was really disciplined. Only sometimes he would be at the bar and have a little too much to drink, which he wasn't supposed to do. He had a medical cabinet, and he was very disciplined, he lived till he was eighty-three. I saw William as a man with lot of dignity. He was always well dressed, wore a shirt and a tie, overcoat—always a gentleman. I mean this is what I remember as my perspective for him. Of course I had a big crush on him, he was very kind to me. The example he set was of a person with self-discipline who really respected drugs. Sometimes, I would look around me and everybody seemed so messed up. What bothered me most was the inability of people to have a normal conversation. Everybody was like Dennis Hopper's character in *Apocalypse Now*. I didn't understand that kind of rap. Even though I was well read and intelligent, I was still a New Jersey girl. It was hard for me to comprehend the way people seemed insincere and surface with each other. However, within that world, I did meet a lot of really interesting people who I could communicate with. Like Gregory Corso who I would talk with for hours about poetry, performance, political issues and Sam Shepard, who had this cowboy aspect to him.

AM: So within the lifestyle you found what you wanted . . .
PS: It's about codes again, or a way of working . . . artists have a certain lifestyle. I believe that if it is your calling to be an artist, you have a real responsibility to that work and, one could say, to God. Also if you believe, being able to animate God within you, your work is a gift. And you know, everyone has the potential to animate God in some way or another; it might in the way they tend the plants in their garden, or in the way they raise their children.

AM: God being exactly what?
PS: I mean . . . look at someone like Jim Morrison . . . who I believe could have evolved into a great poet . . . people would have really profited by his work, and I think he wanted that. I don't think Jim Morrison wanted to die, but he abused himself so much with drugs and alcohol that he died at just twenty-seven.

AM: So you see that as a tragedy, as a waste?
PS: Yes, I see it as a waste. I suppose it's judgemental of me, but I didn't want to be like that. I would pay a certain price for art, I would be lonely, work really hard, sacrifice material things, I'd even sacrifice having fun, whatever one had to, but I was not willing to sacrifice myself. I think about these things even now, in terms of my own longevity. In another year and a half I'll be sixty, and I think that's a real milestone for a human being. I feel very connected with my whole self. I feel in touch, you know, with my eleven-year-old self, with all my selves, and the work that I want to do. I feel connected with all of the steps I've taken through the years. I'm glad that I've lived for so long and hopefully I have a few more decades so I can do better work, or more inspirational work for other people.

AM: When you spoke to the audience in Ghent [editors note: Patti was speaking at the Fusebox event curated by filmmaker Jem Cohen] about your political views you said, "we are the disenfranchised." What did you mean by that?
PS: I perceive this period of life on our planet as very dark. The people in power are very powerful, and I don't see them being toppled too quickly. Not only the government, but also the corporations, the pharmaceuticals, and oil companies—they're all sleeping with governments. The world seems more corrupt than ever. And I feel that our cultural voice is weak.

AM: The music, art, and media worlds are really putting up no resistance. There is no sense of a counterculture like there was in the 1960s. Now there is a series of highly developed micro-cultures that aren't unified.
PS: That's it. That is the idea of disenfranchisement—we have this umbrella, but we don't seem to have any sense of unity.

AM: In America, post 9/11, there is a kind of McCarthyism, which says if you're not with us, you're against us, and if you're against us you are anti-American. It puts people who are patriotic in a lose-lose situation.
PS: Especially after 9/11, because that, unfortunately, caused a resurgence of nationalistic sentiment. After the attacks people united, and that brought nationalism back to America, which I think is really unhealthy. Being nationalistic to me is being self-orientated. Patriotism is completely different. The Bush administration would like us to think that if we question the government we're not patriotic, but what Thomas Jefferson did in penning the Declaration of Independence was highlight the absolute need for Americans to constantly question the government. I mean Thomas Jefferson said rather overthrow your government than be sheep.

 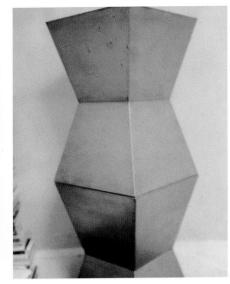 

These are the utensils of the beloved poet and adventurer Arthur Rimbaud. He brought them from Abyssinia to France before his death in 1891. They dwell in the Charleville Museum of Rimbaud with his scarf, cup and valise.

My good friend Michael Stipe gave me a set of stainless steel night tables as they resemble work of the great artist C. Brancusi. I located this homage to Brancusi in my hallway.

This piece of cloth has little material value save it was the handkerchief of William S. Burroughs whom I adored.

 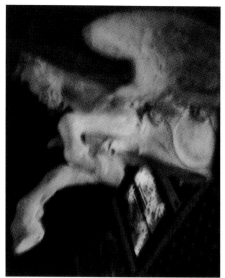 

I photographed the typewriter of Hermann Hesse in full sun. I wanted the keys to appear like beads, for the great Hesse wrote The Glass Bead Game on this humble, enduring instrument.

This is my earliest existing polaroid. The practice slippers of R. Nureyev in a length of mosquito netting in the cold Michigan light.

An ancient Islamic prayer shawl draping a discarded column is my homage to the citizens of Iraq. It represents the shrouded but proud women who stands the ruins triggered by the American invasion and occupation of her country.

AM: Another code...

PS: Yes absolutely, the true American code is against the Bush administration. You know, George Bush is a nothing but the new King George. He fears, or his administration fears, the organic way the laws evolved on which the United States was built, and has set up a smokescreen so that the people are very disconnected from their rights as citizens. And not only our rights, but our duties. It's our duty to question, it's certainly the media's duty to question and I think they have failed completely and betrayed us. They failed and betrayed us in their reporting of the Iraq occupation, and they're failing us now. And that's why I talk about being disenfranchised. I was heartbroken when the Bush administration said they were going to invade Iraq. I couldn't believe that the people would let them do that. I couldn't believe that the Democratic Party would support him in giving him the power to do that. We were betrayed down the line. So again, where are our examples today? The Democratic Party has, since I was a child, been the torchbearer for doing the right thing.

AM: Not supporting the war and wanting a change of government are two different things. That's the danger of having a two party system, they become so closely aligned. Kicking out the reds and getting in the blues doesn't necessarily work.

PS: That whole colours thing is bullshit—that polarisation of people. During the Vietnam war, the red and the blue didn't mean shit to the 50,000 parents who lost their sons. Suddenly nobody cared if they were Democrat or Republican, it didn't matter. People wanted the war to end because their children were dying. It was a huge emotional and physical drain in our country—the guilt and confusion, all the death. Fifty thousand Americans died, but hundreds of thousands were maimed or psychologically damaged, and so the nation had a strong, unified voice against it. When we protested against the Iraq war, 150,000 people gathered in Washington, and Jesse Jackson spoke, along with various other strong speakers, but it was never reported. The press gave us a small paragraph somewhere. I had five different interviews set up with CNN, but they cancelled every one of them. I realised that the only way you can influence political change in America is for huge numbers to come forth, and I don't see that happening right now. So what I feel is that we who believe, and are not heard, and have no real voice or real power, because of our media, have to find each other and unite. And I think that is really important. We can't become depressed or feel ineffectual, we have to start building a counterculture, a new underground, and just do our work.

AM: Like your heroes, Rimbaud and Blake?

PS: I always come back to William Blake because in his time, he saw so much injustice, saw women being beaten to a pulp in the street. Eleven-year-olds as prostitutes, toddlers as chimney sweeps, children in the mills working through the night with no food. He just walked the streets, and saw so much rampant human degradation, and was so moved by it, that he tried to make changes. He tried to join political movements, but they were so disorganised that he had to withdraw. He spoke out and was nearly hanged for dissent, and so finally he did the best thing he could: he worked. And he spoke about issues and offered new possibilities, or laid out the horrific situation children were put in. People didn't listen in his lifetime, but the future generations did. And now, William Blake's work and thoughts inform our culture. So I don't have an "if you can't beat them join them" philosophy, but I also don't have the "if you can't beat them, curl up in a ball" philosophy. If you can't beat them, just do your work. And as I like to put it, it becomes a thorn in their side—just keep pricking them and pricking them and pricking them until they bleed.

Interview originally published in AnOther Magazine, Issue 10, 2006

INSPI(RED)
David Sims

PROJECT RED

A Social Network for Change

We asked our contributor network to send images that contained some evocation of the colour red as a show of support for Project RED, which sought to bring awareness about HIV/AIDS in Africa and life saving drugs to those without access to them. We reached out to photographers, fashion designers, and artists, and it was an amazing response—a fabulous cross section of talent, from Peter Blake to Rankin. We published the images in the magazine, but then we also used them for the *Independent* newspaper, which produced a special edition on Worlds AIDS Day. The images appeared all the way through the newspaper, and again, it's a project that took on an unexpected life of it's own, evoking the power of multiple voices and perspectives to create a profound and inclusive way of looking at things and reaching a really wide audience beyond the magazine pages.

BA(RED)
Peter Blake

Jefferson Hack Red Alert was a twenty-four hour live web cast on World AIDS Day in 2006. People sent images of support and text messages in real-time response to the call to action. Behind the live layer, we had stories relating to HIV/AIDS activism in Africa and we invited the audience to take action. We created a microsite and a twenty-four hour digital event broadcast, and, just to put it in to context, this was before Facebook existed and probably around the time that MySpace was starting to make waves, so it was a big thing for a publisher at our level to achieve. We had multiple servers all over the world backing us up, because of the immense amount of data we were handling. These were dial-up days, pre-broadband, so it was an ambitious digital-first project of which I am very proud, and the contributors were all phenomenal.

SCO(RED)
Gillian Wearing

COVE(RED)
Jenny Van Sommers

IGNO(RED)
Ola Bergengren

NO.

"We seek nothing more in these pages than to break through a one-dimensional take on celebrity, entertainment culture and the world around us. When faced with a search for truth or meaning in film, fashion, art or music, it seems there are fewer and fewer credible voices, image-makers, or thinkers. Throughout AnOther Magazine we aim to reclaim a sense of purpose and the freedom to be different. Everyday we face that which destroys the very fabric, the beauty and the honesty of our differences."

Jefferson Hack, *AnOther Magazine*, 2003

THE

"What's on screen is a pure vision. The way things are structured is that people leave me alone. I have nothing to do with anyone. I have no idea about how other people make their movies. I don't make very much money. I don't concern myself with others.`I don't fraternise with the enemy. I just work, and I love and I fight and just do my own thing."

Harmony Korine, *Dazed & Confused*, 1999

BROKEN. RE-

Where do you feel most at home?
"In a plane, on a long-distance flight, with a big view."

Alain de Botton, *Anothermag.com*, 2013

CODE: RECODE.

5

"I hope wherever you are reading this—at home, on the road, or via some form of digital screen—that you can take a moment to ruminate on this quote from visionary inventor and philosopher R. Buckminster Fuller, who did more than anyone to re-think our relationship to the planet, each other, our environments and home: 'Our beds are empty two-thirds of the time. Our living rooms are empty seven eighths of the time. Our office buildings are empty one-half of the time. It's time we gave this some thought.'"

Jefferson Hack, *AnOther Magazine*, 2013

RULES ARE

"Another set of discoveries, another way of looking at things, another 30 minutes of your time, another kiss, another curious idea that just came to mind, another reason to get out of bed in the morning, another sense of déjà vu, another chance to do it all over again . . ."

Jefferson Hack, *AnOther Magazine*, 2001

WRITE THE RULES.

MEDIA OUT

ILLUSION

What's the most spiritual action you've taken?
"Following my heart all the time, even though I know it is destructive."

Alison Mosshart, *Anothermag.com*, 2010

THE
OF
PARA

LAWS.

"Being recognised for a style is as much a trap as a marker of your influence. You have to move on because culture will move on and your style will become co-opted, mainstream and sanitised. Our mission at *Dazed & Confused* and my personal mission has always been to inspire the self belief to challenge them. To keep fuelling the revolution. But we cannot just work against them, we have to work with as well to change things. Use them or be used. We find the cracks in the machine and work within those, find the crackpots who are in charge and work with them, find the simple idea and crack on with it, working mostly in the dark with the odd crack of light and then just making it up as we go along."

Jefferson Hack, *RCA Open Lecture Series*, 2004

OF FREEDOM. POWER

"The only reason I can see to do an interview is to voice political or philosophical ideas that are usually absent from the celebrity mania. I have a distaste for any subject perceived from an entirely subjective point of view—serving as it does the present day obsession with individualism."

Julie Christie, *AnOther Magazine*, 2004

DOX.

AI WEIWEI

Ai Weiwei is a cultural hero because he stands against oppression; he stands for the rights of ordinary people and he does it with grace and great humour. I went to Beijing to interview him in his compound. As soon as I arrived, there was a power cut and all the computers went down. His team lost all their unsaved data. I said to him, "Does this happen to you a lot?" and he said, "Yes, they are just reminding us who is in charge." He's the real deal — a leading voice of a cultural resistance movement. He is an exceptionally humble man, and an exceptional artist. He has chosen to stay in a situation where he is constantly under threat and constantly under harassment in order to keep fighting against the regime.

Defining the Age of Craziness

Ai Weiwei

China's foremost artist and provocateur invites us into his Beijing studio and explains how he maintains a sense of home in an inhospitable state.

Beijing is a tough city. A hard and colourless city where glass and steel skyscrapers stand anonymously alongside concrete flyovers. It's a city where beauty and treasures are hidden deep behind impenetrable walls, within ancient courtyards, and in winding hutongs. A city where memory is buried in the rubble of high-speed building projects and where economic prosperity for a few has torn a hole in the fabric of reality for many still living without a justice system and freedom of expression. I flew to Beijing to visit artist and provocateur Ai Weiwei in his studio home in Caochangdi, an area of the city whose identity he helped define by building a series of beautifully simple artists' studios and housing spaces there. Given the immense output of Weiwei and his studio, it's easy to forget that he is also a prolific architect, involved in over sixty architectural projects internationally, including a beautiful memorial to his father, the poet Aì Qīng, in the Jinhua Aiqing Cultural Park under the auspices of his studio FAKE. The most famous of his architectural projects is the Bird's Nest national stadium in Beijing, his collaboration with Herzog & de Meuron, which brought him to international prominence both as an artist and a political force: when he denounced the building and the Olympics it became a significant act of defiance against the state, and made him one of the few recognisable cultural voices of dissent in China.

In 2011, during the height of the Jasmine Revolution, Weiwei was arrested and I published a cover story in *Dazed & Confused* magazine bearing the famous image of his cut and shaved head, and the magazine joined a global movement led by Amnesty to call for his release.

Weiwei was held for eighty-one days without access to family or lawyers. Many imagined he would never be seen again. Protesters around the world took to the streets, the media, and the Internet. Weiwei became a symbol for freedom of speech and resistance, as well as simultaneously the most famous and the most fragile international artist, under constant surveillance and intimidation by the state. It was during this time that Penguin published the book *Ai Weiwei Speaks*, a series of interviews conducted by Hans-Ulrich Obrist that helped bring his creative thinking and message to a wider public.

Weiwei's critics suggest that his international fame has given him a form of protection, and some would say that his very existence shows China is opening up to dissenting voices. But Weiwei continues to put his work, his reputation, and his life at risk. Despite censorship of his blog and restriction of his movements (the government has seized his passport) there seem to be no boundaries for him in his commitment to changing the fabric of society through his melding of art and activism. Weiwei's powerful blog was shut down in 2009, but he still uses Twitter daily (although unavailable behind mainland China's firewall), keeping him connected to his many followers (191,203 at the time of publication).

A surveillance camera overlooks the deep blue door to his studio. Outside a policeman plays sentry. The doors open electronically to reveal a calm and inviting two-storey courtyard, with ivy crawling delicately over the blue-grey brick walls, and large metal letters spelling out F.U.C.K., a piece from the seminal *Fuck Off* exhibition, which he co-curated in Shanghai in 2000. It's a serene utopia in a traffic-bound city with one of the highest pollution levels and populations in the world. I walk inside the simply proportioned space, designed using locally sourced materials, and see Weiwei hunched over a computer in his studio, tweeting.

Despite his dissident status, he is incredibly warm and calm. We sit down to talk but as soon as we begin the power in the studio goes down. His staff shriek as unsaved files are immediately lost. Is it a form of government intervention, or just a blown fuse? "At the time of my arrest, before they would come to search this place, they would first have a power cut and then they would come and take all the computers and materials away." Is this the signal for a police visit, I ask? "I don't think so," laughs Weiwei reassuringly. "They're quite relaxed with me now, they're not as nervous as they were two years ago."

We begin by talking about architecture and his feelings about home as a philosophical space. We are soon joined by Hans-Ulrich Obrist, who Skypes us at three in the morning London time. Social media is another form of home for Weiwei, and his pastiche of Psy's "Gangnam Style" video is a prime example of how this deeply philosophical thinker uses humour as a political tool, satire as conceptual art, and digital means to escape the confines and contradictions of life in 21st century Beijing.

Jefferson Hack: I wanted to ask you about building this studio home. When you became an architect, was it really that simple—did you build a home and then you were an architect?
Ai Weiwei: It was as simple as that. I never thought about the work as architecture before or even after I built my first house. Later I had to think about what contexts I dealt with, what's the connector—occasionally it's about a book of Wittgenstein's, he built a house for his sister in Vienna.

JH: And had that image of a house always been with you—when you built this place, was it an early reference?
AW: It fascinates me, but I think everybody can build, everybody can have their own house in their own mind . . . a mute can still have a clear thought about the world, he just cannot talk about it.

JH: You call it "ordinary architecture"—what do you mean by that?
AW: Ordinary architecture occured rather directly from the usage; it's applied for the necessary purpose. And it doesn't require higher aesthetics, or for me what are high aesthetics.

JH: So talk to me a little bit about the layout of this particular complex.
AW: Most of the area was used for growing vegetables, but as this doesn't make much money, they had the intention to rent the land and service it. When I was in New York, I never had a real studio, so I took the chance to come back and build one, even though at that time I wasn't making art. I made a simple drawing: I would have one window, one door, like a child's drawing of a house, and a chimney and a road. And then we started to build it. I grew up in the countryside and people build houses like that, they don't need sophisticated plans. But every day, I came to the site, and I was very excited because building something from nothing is very exciting.

JH: How old is this studio complex?
AW: It's thirteen years old.

JH: And so the character's changed dramatically?
AW: At first, it was intended for myself, so I had one bedroom, one kitchen, one bathroom. Then, on the second floor, there is one bathroom without a wall because it's just a private house, we don't need a wall to separate the bathroom; it changes the whole feeling. But also there's no privacy needed because it's a private house.

JH: It's interesting to me, because there's so much multidimensionality to your work, yet I wanted to ask you if you have a routine in your life, with so much craziness and so many different multidisciplinary projects going on?
AW: If I can see a routine, I have to eat three times a day but besides that, at all other times, I am always expecting something new to happen and to surprise me—a new day rather than a repetition of the last.

JH: Do you live within this complex?
AW: I have always lived here, ever since I built it. I never think I should leave here, except when I travel.

JH: Could you give me a little walk-through and explain the different uses of the space and how you constructed some of it?
AW: This is a warehouse. I have a little, humble house for people who help us to cook and take care of the house, and they live here and grow vegetables. It's so appreciable, even if you have just one-quarter of this, you care for more than you can eat. It just takes sunshine and it comes up.

JH: Is this very common, to have a vegetable garden in a courtyard?
AW: No, nobody does that. It's a cliché to have grass, nobody wants to be farming in the garden.

JH: It's seen as a sign of poverty?
AW: It's not modern to have a vegetable patch. We already have so much, it's symbolic: we grow so much more than we need that we can give it to people, and it's very nice. We also have some chickens.

JH: Do people usually use the brick as a pathway? The incredible thing is how it's wearing, it has such personality.
AW: Most people think it's terrible, I think it's nice.

JH: And this is your living quarters?
AW: Yes.

JH: The volume is really unexpected when you walk inside. It's almost like a trick.
AW: Many people say so. It hasn't been touched since it was built.

JH: I wanted to ask you about the concept of home—what does the notion of home mean to you, and more than that, the sense of home when your homeland is in direct opposition to your beliefs?
AW: A sense of home is something you can ignore, it exists but at the same time, it is most convenient to be there. It's like magic, you can get whatever you want but you don't have to get it, you can ignore it, it doesn't bother you, you don't need it. That sense of home gives you extra power; of course, you don't have to use it.

JH: But you're unusual in the sense that your private life and your work life are one, your studio and your home are combined. Home is a place of constructing reality, it's not a place of escape from a work situation. It has all of those dualities.
AW: We're twenty, thirty people here, we normally do different things, research or archiving or communications. It's really become part of me.

JH: How do you conduct this orchestra of productivity?
AW: I think you have to be very relaxed. The costs here are lower than in the West, so you have to let everybody, every part of it, try to reach their best and to be themselves. Then when you need them, or you are working on the same task, they have to have a sense of contributing something you really want. I think that all sides are very important. In that sense, your surroundings are always an extension of the message of who you are. And the way you look at others is the way you want yourself to be, or what you want people to understand about you.

JH: But also, you've changed the kind of practises you're doing, they are evolving and changing—for instance, your architecture practise FAKE has stopped functioning and you've taken on producing social investigative films, so there's a kind of refocusing of purpose that is constantly going on.
AW: I think that the ideal of the house is to leave a space that is unpredictable, in mysterious conditions—you don't want to get too familiar with everything. You want to leave a space that is wild, that you can sometimes search and explore. I think you should always have that, because that gives your life a very special colour, and possibilities; you have a space that is not yet reached, and it is also important to include that into a master plan. I think that's important in anybody's life, because it's like a chessboard: this guy has only a few steps to move, and that's the end of it. It's better to create a game that grows itself and it doesn't matter how you do it, it's far from the end of it.

JH: But the government has banned you from communicating via Websites, banned you from foreign travel by taking your passport, banned you from showing your work in your own country—in a way, they've pinned you into a chessboard, into a corner, and pinned you into these walls. Do you have freedom to leave the building?
AW: Now I do.

JH: But conceptually, in a way you've made this house your playground. I think your "Gangnam Style" parody for instance is a way of saying "fuck you, you'll never take away my playfulness." And also you just invited several million people into this environment to party with you, so you kind of dissolved the chessboard.
AW: I think that's the game; that difficult moment is my most exciting moment.

JH: You've invited more people than can probably fit into Caochangdi.
AW: People start to believe in personal power, young people on the Internet, they think my existence provides a kind of truth, that freedom exists within ourselves, no one can take it away. It's just a question of how to recognise it and exercise it. That's the most important thing, even in the most difficult conditions. They put you in a cooking pot and when the time is up you start to think, oh this is the end of it, but actually it's the beginning. That's art. So when they put you in this cooking pot, I try to imagine when they open the cover they would see a very different dish than the one they expected.

JH: Do you feel most able to create under some form of extreme condition or resistance, rather than when you were in New York and didn't produce so much?
AW: When there's a required condition you have to deal with, because that condition is so special, the solution becomes new. So of course, Duchamp's famous line is that there is no solution because there's no problem and that really reflects his understanding of the time.

JH: Did New York feel like a home to you, or did it feel very transient? It was obviously a period of discovery and research and finding yourself, but did it feel like home?
AW: I used to see New York in the 1980s as the loneliest place for a young man. It had very little romance, I didn't have any real communication, I just went there to receive information, to experience the life, a very different life than the one I had during the Cultural Revolution. Like being on a long boat journey, it's new but your means of doing anything is limited because you're not part of the crew, you're just sitting there watching it. So I watched for a long time.

JH: You met lots of people in New York and had lots of experiences that informed your thinking and gave you a lot of insight and power to be able to do what you're doing now. But the idea of a crew, of belonging was really when you came here and you did the *Black Cover Book* and curated your first show.
AW: In the beginning, you think you can offer something, which is obviously lacking here. You have your experiences, or your way of understanding things, but you have to have a solid material through which to explain or introduce that to people—it could be a book, a magazine or a space.

JH: At the time, when you created those books, and those shows, were you doing it to have an impact on society, or more for your group?
AW: At that time, the kind of society I cared about was the art community; I didn't care about farmers' or workers' conditions. I only saw that much.

JH: Your view was only that far at that time.
AW: Conceptually, the thing most capable of changing things effectively was a book. Later, after I built this studio in my home, people started realising that it was something they could relate to. There were so many people coming to ask me about the definition of home; people started to realise it themselves by identifying what belonged to them.

JH: Home is about the curation and creation of your own space. But you've said that Beijing's greatest problem is that it never belonged to its people, it creates a facade of a city. So do you think that's another reason why you creating your own home in this city was so powerful and symbolic, and really captured the imagination of the people?
AW: I think when I created something here, people could see that this guy did something so private, extended his message to the maximum. Even that is ridiculous because we rent the space, it's never safe.

JH: It's temporary because you have a lease.
AW: I maybe have another seven years, but at any moment they can destroy it. So I'm not only creating a space, I'm also challenging the idea of so-called property. I think property is something you use; it's not just something that belongs to you. It's like money—your only fortune is what you spend, not what's in the bank. That's just numbers.

JH: But this is fundamental to people's psychological fragility, that there is no land right or ownership.
AW: In China, in a communist society, the property belongs to the nation and not to the private individual. That's why the old houses deteriorate so fast, because this is a nation in which there is no ownership. If you don't have individuals who own their own place, you don't have ownership of the country. The consequence is that the whole nation has no memory, no responsibility, nothing to care about, nothing to pass on to others, no generosity, no sense of relation to another person's pain or joy, because they have no place to share it. It really very deeply affects this nation's mindset and very few people talk about it.

JH: It's critical; it's critical not just here but globally, too.
AW: Even the poorest beggar has something he treasures; it could be a piece of rock or cotton, and he might pass it to the one he loves—that's important, that's humanity, culture, warmth. But in this nation, they try to destroy, as so-called communists, anything that has that kind of sentiment.

JH: In the interview we published in *Dazed & Confused*, you talked about a nightmare you had where you were in a secret society and you saw horrible things: you saw people crying, you were followed constantly, you weren't allowed to take anything with you. And then you said the most shocking thing was that there were so many tourists in that society who saw all of these things, but they didn't care, they just pretended everything was alright. Do you remember that nightmare?
AW: I remember it so vividly, I had such a grand vision. At the time, I was under so much pressure, I really turned to the pages our brain doesn't normally flip to. In our minds, we have a sense of the worst conditions, and I think the most danger comes when you wonder if you and the society are on the same page, we're reading different things, the consciousness is not on the same level. That's the nightmare of the past, in Soviet or Cold War times.

JH: So you think the visitors to the city need to open their eyes more, be more engaged, be more informed, or do you think they are complicit somehow in the system?
AW: I think the visitors are a metaphor for tourists.

JH: Which could be Chinese tourists . . .
AW: It could be any tourist, it could be me, going to a place for no real reason, where it's impossible to approach the visitors or tourists.

JH: To be a tourist in one's own reality is to have a passive consciousness; it's a metaphor for a state of being.
AW: Sure, I think Kafka used to say we have two conditions, two kinds of mental conditions: one careless, and another impatient. Because of our carelessness, we were kicked out of Eden, but because we have no patience, we will never go back. But tourists have both!

JH: But that's humanity, humanity's flawed.
AW: That's true, but it's most extreme in the case of tourists.

JH: "Twitter is a city" is a phrase you've used, so you must feel very at home on the Internet, you spend a lot of time online, and I want to ask you if you feel ultimately the geography of the Internet and the Twitter city you inhabit provides a more natural and real sense of home for you?
AW: It fits my definition of home: you have your own corner, it's very private, very comforting, but you are always facing a person, it is confrontational as well as comforting—that means you always have areas that are familiar but that you never really know.

[*Hans-Ulrich Obrist enters the conversation via Skype*]

Hans-Ulrich Obrist: I wondered if you could tell us a little bit more about your extraordinary video, your version of the "Gangnam Style" video by Psy. I was in Gwangju recently and everyone there was speaking about your video, picking up on this mass phenomenon on the Internet.
AW: It looks from our video like something we planned but in reality, we jumped into it quickly, we danced with maybe half of the office staff for about ten minutes. That's why I look so very energetic, like I'm on drugs, because if it had been a little bit longer, I would have had to call the hospital! We edited it in about fifteen hours, and we put the video on the Internet at midnight, because at that time, nearly eighty per cent of the Internet police in China are sleeping. It survived the whole night in China until the next morning when it was discovered. But by then a great many people had already watched it. Within half a day of our posting, we noted several hundred articles internationally in major newspapers like the *New York Times*, the *Wall Street Journal*, the *Washington Post*, the *Los Angeles Times*, the *Guardian*, all those major papers. It became such a phenomenon, but that really shows the character of today's media, it's always so eager to see something new and something unpredictable, something instantly happening, and people are happy to receive it before they understand it.

HUO: It's fascinating because more people will see this than will ever see an exhibition in a museum, it reaches out to a completely different group of people. But also I was interested to hear more about this piece, which you called *Grass Mud Horse Style*—there is this detail with the handcuffs in it, I was wondering if you could tell me a little about that?
AW: I think when we call something new, it means it has to destroy part of the old. That means we have to offer a condition that we are not used to, so that means our vocabulary has to be new. You always have to introduce something new. Even with the most popular video clip, somebody has already used it—it's like using the Coca-Cola logo, you have to write something really surprising. So it is at the same time recognising the reality but offering a new vocabulary.

HUO: When I was in the studio where Jefferson is now, about four months ago, I saw the preparations for the exhibition *According to What?* at the Hirshhorn Museum in Washington D.C., which opened to huge public and critical acclaim. You were preparing these wonderful works, these very realistic crabs made out of porcelain and you told me you were going to make thousands of them. It would be great to hear a little bit more about this exhibition.
AW: It's my first ever show in the United States in a public institution but I cannot attend it. The crabs are really more like a joke, because when the Shanghai government, due to my political stance, decided to destroy my studio without an explanation, I said before it's destroyed, let's have a party and eat river crab, which is very famous in Shanghai.

JH: But the title is also significant.
AW: *He Xie* means river crab but also sounds like "harmonious society"; it's exactly the same pronunciation. But of course the announcement of this party triggered the nervousness of the police, because there were thousands of people wanting to attend and people flowing in from all over China, from some twenty provinces—it was a record.

JH: This was the moment you were put under house arrest.
AW: Yes, the first time, and they said, "Can you announce to them that the party is over?" And I said, "How?" The security just said, "Tell them you have been arrested." I said, "I cannot tell people when I am not arrested that I have been arrested—that's unacceptable." Then they said, "Now we have to arrest you."

JH: When you were under house arrest, did they give you a time period for that?
AW: I asked them, how long, what's the definition of the arrest? They had to think about it . . . Well, you cannot leave the house to go to Shanghai, they said. I said, how long for and they said, until the party. So it was that kind of back-and-forth argument, but it was quite enjoyable actually.

JH: It's enjoyable because you get to highlight the hypocrisy through the exchange? So it's a form of interview?
AW: It is a form of interview; it's about communication. It's about trying to deeply force somebody to speak what's in their mind, or what's not in their mind, or what they are not prepared for.

JH: But the other thing is, you were not prepared for the actual demolition, because from what I've heard they didn't give you a date for when the bulldozers came in. You had someone from your own team on-site who called you—can you explain just a little bit about that famous image of you standing there with the hard hat, how did that happen?
AW: We had an agreement. The government said, OK, Weiwei, we're very sorry, we invited you to make this studio, but we have to destroy it, we cannot give you a reason why, but we can at least pay you back everything. Which they did, they paid back more than what we paid and in cash, without a receipt. Then, you get really scared—you say, gosh, who are they? Are they the government, or are they just a mafia? We told them, we have to record it, before you tear it down, take some photos. They said, yes, we will not do it before Chinese New Year's day, but if we do it, we'll give you time. But since we cannot completely trust them, based on our previous experiences, we told the local farmers, the neighbours, if you hear anything being destroyed in this building, just give us a call. So one morning at five am, we received a call saying that they had started to destroy it. I had to book the ticket, and fly over there and it was already halfway done—we could not record the destruction from the beginning. Which is very sad because of course we built this building, we love it, and we need to record how it's being taken down, which is not a luxurious demand, but even that they don't like. The most interesting thing is that after they destroyed it, we said maybe we could get some of the destroyed material, all the rubble. But they put it in a warehouse—not a wasteland, a warehouse.

HUO: So like a Weiwei piece, all the rubble is preserved in a warehouse, like some kind of gigantic installation.
AW: We tried to talk to the people to get into the warehouse but they said, by very high order we cannot let you have a single piece of rubble. They destroyed it in twenty-four hours. It was so fast and they took every single brick and immediately turned the land into farmland.

JH: So the memory is completely erased.
AW: The need to erase the memory, even though it's been recorded—still the need is so strong. It's stronger than in any other animal or species. So to this day, all the rubble is still sitting in a warehouse.

JH: Do you know the location of the warehouse?
AW: Yes, we're still negotiating, but they say it's impossible, they have an order from on high not to give even a piece away—you ask why and they think this guy, this artist, must want to use this for some kind of artwork, which is half true. So I start to think even an event like that, a very deep, personal experience, very real—how to use it as an artwork? You need some kind of symbolic gesture, so I naturally made those crabs with porcelain and they are very well-crafted. It's very hard to fire things like that, because they have eight legs stretching out and are all hand-painted.

HUO: Obviously, another context in which rubble plays a role is in your work dealing with the collapsed buildings during the Szechuan earthquake.
AW: This work started in 2008 as a way of answering a simple question: during the earthquake, how many students died and who were they? As an artist I said, let's make a phone call. I always want to make a direct confrontation, to actually confront the party that holds the answer. The result was so amazing—they said, you must be a spy, this is a top national secret. We realised that we had to do the research ourselves, and so I just very quickly announced that we'd do a citizens' investigation. Then the response was, Weiwei, how far do you want to go? And I said, as long as there is a name we cannot find, as long as I'm still alive. That answer really cost us a lot. It almost cost me my life. I had so many problems as you know for it, but which I never regret, I still think it's the strongest effort I've made in any circumstance. We did so much, we put all the names online so people could read them, and every day we reported our discoveries. We did it very precisely, we made sure every name was correct, we interviewed all the parents, we made documentary films to tell them what happened that day, why their children did not come back from school, what was the last thing their children said to them.

JH: There was also this interactive piece that was very powerful, where you invited members of the public to read the names out loud, and it created an audio memory.
AW: The memory needed something to carry it: language. So we asked people on the Internet, what can we do? An overwhelming 10,000 people read those 5,000 names. We put together an audio piece and it sounds very simple but it's not so simple, it's really from the Internet and the pieces were recorded in very different conditions, in the mountains, in the farming areas, with phones, and these were sent to us and we edited them. But of course those cannot be experienced, so I had to do something with the rebar salvaged after the earthquake. We collected about 200 tonnes of iron, and we straightened about 150 tonnes of these twisted pieces, one by one, so it looks as if it just came out of the factory, as if it never bore the weight of a structure or landed on a human body. Every one takes over 200 punches to make really straight as a pencil, and then we displayed the finished piece so it looks minimal. I always like to play with art history: you always have to cook something people can eat. It's easier on their habits but I think misinterpretation is a way to acceptance . . .

HUO: You create so much energy—where does your energy come from and how could one define energy? Joseph Beuys talks a lot about energy principles and I'm curious if you could talk about this mysterious energy.
AW: I think energy is something you need and you can really stretch—because we cannot stretch time, and we cannot stretch our luck, but we can stretch our energy. I will never wake you up at three in the morning again!

JH: No, we will, it will become an annual event. A ritual!
AW: To rest, to rest, Hans.

[Hans-Ulrich Obrist exits the conversation]

JH: So to continue to make the link to Hans-Ulrich, in an interview with him you said that taking photographs was like breathing, it becomes a part of you. You started taking photographs right at the beginning in New York, taking pictures of some of the protests going on in the streets, and then obviously photography has been important to your diary. But I wondered how photography has evolved over time for you?
AW: I think one misunderstanding about the artist is that he consciously knows what he's doing. Photography is one example. Very often, a photograph only takes a very short moment to take but really photography is already cut off from reality, a photo is never reality for me. I realise we take so many images, we have no time to really look at them; you don't get to take your breath or clear your throat, you don't get to look at the reality twice. That's a real luxury and despite all this technology, maybe only God can look at reality twice.

JH: Does that make you more conscious of how you're taking photographs now? You are being simultaneously photographed and spied on by the state...
AW: My assistants are artists and they see this guy in the park with a camera every day when I'm doing my exercises. I once ran after him, grabbed him and said, show me the pictures—if I have made a mistake, then just prove I'm mistaken. And he wouldn't give them to me. I said please call the police, and still he wouldn't talk to me. I grabbed his camera during the struggle and I took the memory card and gave the camera back to him. But he didn't know I had taken the memory card. Then I came back and sat down in front of my computer and I was so surprised—this guy was not only taking photos of my assistants from far away, but also my baby boy's carriage—I don't know why he took that. And the restaurant I used to go to, they had taken photos from every side of the restaurant, the corridor, the rooms, the tables. I was so shocked!

JH: Incredible detail.
AW: It is a different society here, nobody understands what they're doing. And the photos from during the Jasmine Revolution—they were taking them far away from the students but I was still quite shocked at how close and personal it was.

JH: What does political progress mean for you?
AW: I think political progress means re-shuffle. It's when we have problems with a kind of condition we think we cannot solve, one in which we have to adjust the whole situation to the new possibilities.

JH: Should China be defining a new form of democracy or should it bring democracy in wholesale from the West?
AW: I think each Western nation has a very different form of democracy. So much relates to the culture, memory, and the past. It's like China always has this argument, should we have Western or traditional Chinese medicine? It's a completely different kind of thinking and logic. But it seems that both have gradually worked because both are dealing with our belief in how to cure illness and how to maintain a good quality of life. So that argument is always on, that argument will always be on, it goes much deeper than the political: the situation is much more about aesthetics or philosophy.

JH: What are the political solutions?
AW: I think the political solutions only come when individuals' rights have been fully protected and promoted. I think any political demand has to benefit individuals' well-being in a society, in a collective situation. You have to trust that human beings are not only equal in terms of rights, but are equally smart and equally good-willed to others. Only by giving them full rights can they bear this responsibility fully. That's very critical, so anything that ignores those rights ignores the dignity of life, because life cannot be borne foremost without liberty.

JH: When you get your passport, what do you think you'll do?
AW: First option is to destroy it—always tempting. It's mine, I can do whatever I want with it.

JH: The social documentaries you're making—how long have you been making them, three or four years?
AW: I have been making them for about four years, and putting them on the Internet. We still have three DVDs yet to release, but we are trying to find the right moment, because there could be a lot of danger when we do. One is an investigation into a village that was crushed by a truck, and one is about a small incident, a physical fight. The documentary is a very nice format, because first you can make the story very comprehensive and dense with information, but at the same time, it also leaves a record; otherwise after a while, people have no way to know what really took place.

JH: Are they sincere acts?
AW: They are sincere, because in a life and death situation, you use certain material and as a consequence you can be hurt, you can be hated. You know, we had a documentary about one young boy who killed six policemen. The police hated that one the most. The only time they lost their temper with me was when they saw my film; they interpreted it like I hate the police. I told them I don't hate any police, the police is not like one person. It's just their position, but to have a structure that makes the police the victims is questionable, too. They are also victimised by this structure.

JH: Is your dream to have a show in China, or are you ambivalent about your artworks being shown here?
AW: I never really dreamed of having a show in China, because to have a show you need an audience, you need a platform, you need criticism, freedom of communication. If you don't have those, having a show doesn't make any sense.

JH: It becomes a facade.
AW: Yes, and there's already such an effort to make me not exist—in this sense, they are giving me a chance to have a show every day in China, because all the young people are seeing me and asking, why is this guy always having to be censored, this guy who is here without a passport but at the same time is not here? That's magic.

JH: But also, as Hans-Ulrich said, your "Gangnam Style" parody reached many more people than any museum show could. In a way, you're still able to be creative within the confines that you're given. These are completely extreme conditions, but you're finding ways to navigate them.
AW: When you can do something, you always have to be critical, you have to find a different position, which is not a surprise for other people, but you surprise yourself.

JH: It's interesting because in the documentary your staff refer to you as "teacher Ai." It's not something that's ever been attached to your name—you've had artist, architect, activist, diarist, photographer, all these labels, but never teacher.
AW: I think in China, most young people think I am a teacher, through my daily chats with them, answering their simple questions, joking with them... many people say I have been a teacher for years, and I really appreciate that.

Interview originally published in AnOther Magazine, Issue 24, 2013

BARBARA KRUGER

"Barbara Kruger is an amazing artist, who started to feel disillusionment with the language of how things are sold, designed, and packaged as a magazine designer in the 1970s. This project is about her de-codifying the codes of magazines and wider culture and communication. And the beauty of it is that she is de-codifying it inside a magazine that is also trying to de-codify itself—so, you have this weird schizophrenic thing going on, which is what makes it really interesting." —Mark Sanders

Decoding the Magazine

DAZED VS. WARHOL

How Upstarts Took the Mantle

The BALTIC approached us to do a show called *Dazed & Confused Vs. Andy Warhol*, because they said they considered the *Dazed & Confused* generation to be the children of Andy Warhol—a contemporary version of the Factory. I think it was the first time we were truly recognised by an institution for being more than a magazine, and essentially being a network, a community, a movement. We gave an open brief to friends and family, such as Rankin, Gareth Pugh, The Kills, the design duo M+M, Robert Montgomery and Matthew Stone: all contemporary artists we felt were directly influenced by Warhol or reacting to Warholian ideas. I absolutely loved the exhibition because it really pushed that idea of reframing and rewiring history, and it took us far beyond the confines of the pages.

Gareth Pugh BALTIC is kind of the North East's answer to the Tate Modern, and to have a big, cultural institution land on the River Tyne was quite a moment for Newcastle. The fact that *Dazed* was asked to be part of that is a testament to what it stands for and how it can cross-over boundaries between art, fashion, design, and culture and be part of all of those conversations at once. I made huge silver balloons for the exhibition, and, while that was a nod to Warhol, it represented temporality – the disparity between the optimism that they represent and the finite amount of time something exists within. It's an ephemeral object by virtue of the fabric that it's made of – you know, you go to a funfair as a kid and get a huge balloon and then you take it home and the next morning it's a shrivelled lump of rubber; so it's very much an object that signifies all of those things in its very nature. It was a really well-curated show and a great thing to be part of. I have always felt flattered to have the opportunity to be part of the conversations that drive *Dazed & Confused*.

MOVEMENT

I have always loved the interplay of dance and fashion and the ways in which they have inspired one another. I think the conversation between the two genres has been really important in pushing culture forward, in creating a heightened aesthetic experience. But every time it's been done, one has always been in the service of the other—choreographers have invited fashion designers to design for their stage, and designers have invited choreographers to perform on their catwalk. What we wanted to do with MOVEment was to take these two disciplines into a neutral place and for them to work together collaboratively, to create movement designed for the screen—the idea of putting them together allowed the designer and the choreographer to push each other equally hard, without one being in the service of the other. The choreography was not made for the proscenium stage; it was made purely for the camera, and the aim was for that third party view, or eye, if you like, to provide a window into which dance and fashion could be explored with new relevance for the 21st century.

It was really important for me to partner with Alistair Spalding and the team at Sadler's Wells for their expert counsel on making these pairings. Some were blind dates and some were existing relationships, but all were paired to bring something new and original to the table.

Where Fashion, Dance and Film Unite

p188 and right: Designer: Prada; Choreographers: Dancers of Tanztheater Wuppertal; Director: Kevin Frilet | p190 top to bottom, left to right: Designer: Iris Van Herpen; Choreographer: Russell Maliphant; Directors: Warren Du Preez & Nick Thornton Jones | Designer: Calvin Klein Collection; Choreographer: Jonah Bokaer; Dancer: Julie Kent; Director: Daniel Arsham | Designer: Gareth Pugh; Choreographer: Marie-Agnes Gillot; Director: Daniel Askill | Designer: Chalayan; Choreographers: Aya Sato and Ryan Heffington; Director: Jacob Sutton | Designer: Stephen Jones Millinery; Choreographer: Alexander McQueen; Director: Ruth Hogben | Designer: Wayne McGregor; Choreographer: Jasmin Vardimon; Director: Matthew Donaldson

Alistair Spalding Dance has always been open to collaboration; it can rarely exist on its own. With fashion, it shares a strong relationship with the body, its movement, and one's sense of identity. While rooted in history, both art forms are equally at the forefront of what's new and constantly move forward. The fruits of creative partnerships between dance artists and fashion designers are usually seen in performances that are, by nature, ephemeral, so we were really excited by Jefferson's idea to crystallise these collaborations through the eyes of highly talented filmmakers.

DRESS ART

"Dress Art was about exploring the notion of clothing as art, and it's a great example of how a radically open dialogue creates the space for absolute freedom. The genesis of the project was a picture of the Dadaist poet Hugo Ball taken in 1916, where he is dressed in a cardboard outfit he used to perform his poems in. It's infused with a truly provocative and pure spirit. Dress Art was a wild celebration of that spirit—introducing artists and designers and then just letting them do whatever they wished; we didn't seek to control the process at all. That's key to the approach we took to everything, particularly in fashion—we were always taking fashion outside of its box. I always smile when I think of Bernhard Willhelm's piece; all of those pieces of linoleum wrapped around the body with a couple of holes cut for the eyes! It was just so pure in terms of presenting clothing as art. The piece with Riccardo Tisci and Paolo Canevari was also truly wonderful—Paolo's work is made exclusively from inner tubes and tyres, and to see that aesthetic transformed into an enormous rubber cloak was really something. It's hard to see where the fashion ends and the art begins in Dress Art, and it's that kind of process that pushes culture forwards." —Mark Sanders

Fashion   Collides   with   Art: Transdisciplinary   Style

p192, Bernhard Willhelm; Olaf Breuning | p193 top to bottom, left to right: Dolce & Gabbana, Ann Duong | Christopher Bailey for Burberry; Annie Morris | Stella McCartney; Jeff Koons | Sophia Kokosalaki; John Isaacs | Maison Martin Margiela; Gotscho | Francisco Costa for Calvin Klein; Ghada Amer | Jean-Charles de Castelbajac; Meredyth Sparks | Ann-Sofie Back; Annika Von Hausswolff | Rifat Ozbek for Pollini; Manfredi Beninati | Agnes B, Ryan McGuiness | Giles Deacon; Simon Periton | Rick Owens; Ian Kaer | Issey Miyake by Naomi Takizawa; Yoshitomo Nara p195 top to bottom: Riccardo Tisci; Paolo Canevari

FILMS OF INNOCENCE

The idea for this project was to create a visual accompaniment to U2's album *Songs of Innocence* and the band asked me to take the murals of Northern Ireland as a jump-off point because the "Troubles" had been such a reference for them in the recording of this album. I started researching contemporary muralists, and artists that were using public space to express themselves in ways that had moved on from graffiti or tagging into some extraordinary new expressions. Once we had chosen the artists we asked them to be inspired by a song and do whatever they liked in response — it was a carte blanche proposition, so the films were very much a reaction to the music; these were not music videos, they were a new form of video storytelling. All twelve of the films were released simultaneously online as a group exhibition. Oliver Jeffers, Robin Rhode, D*Face, Mode 2, Chloe Early, Ganzeer, Vhils, Maser, ROA, DALeast, and Todd James were given complete creative freedom to showcase their personal responses to U2's music. They really celebrated the unique democratic power of urban art and what was most satisfying was that none of the artists apart from Jeffers had worked in moving image before. It really helped them push their work to new unimagined places.

Anti   Retro   Futurism

p.196, Raised by Wolves, Artwork by Vhils | p.198 and p.199, top to bottom, left to right: Sleep Like A Baby Tonight, Artwork by ROA | California (There Is No End To Love), Artwork by D*Face | Iris (Hold Me Close), Artwork by Chloe Early | The Troubles, Artwork by Todd James | The Miracle (Of Joey Ramone), Artwork by Oliver Jeffers | Cedarwood Road, Artwork by Maser | This Is Where You Can Reach Me Now, Artwork by DALeast | Every Breaking Wave, Artwork by Robin Rhode | Volcano, Artwork by Ganzeer | Song For Someone, Artwork by Mode 2

PRINT EMPOWER

"Pleasure is as important as work, and you get your identification from both."

Hugh Hefner, *Another Man*, 2007

"Who are you? What do you do? How did you get to be reading this?"

Jefferson Hack, *Dazed & Confused*, 1995

INDE WAY.

"We are fighting a cultural war against the 'Non-ness'. If everything looks the same, reads the same, feels the same we are doomed. If new ideas are not given a chance we are doomed. If there is no funding for alternative ways of thinking we are doomed. We are constantly attacked by those who hold the balance of power; those who control the mode of distribution or manufacture, because they want things to remain the same. They don't want change, because it will destabilise their control so they undermine and criticise all new things. They will sneer at your bravery, challenge your self-belief and dismiss your achievements."

Jefferson Hack, *RCA Open Lecture Series*, 2004

"I can only do it the way I do it. That's why they chose me, and if they can't accept that, they'll have to get someone else. They are going to have no choice at the end of the day because I work to my own laws and requirements."

Alexander McQueen, *Dazed & Confused*, 1996

6

MENT.

"What I still think the power of a magazine is capable of, is to give people a sense of freedom, to make them feel like they're not alone, that they can be empowered, and through that empowerment they can create a better, more interesting, and vibrant society."

Jefferson Hack, *Purple Fashion Magazine*, 2010

THE PENDENT

"Even the poorest beggar has something to be treasured; it could be a piece of rock or cotton, and he might pass it on to the one he loves—that important; that's humanity, culture, warmth."

Ai Weiwei, *AnOther Magazine*, 2013

VALUING

"What I believe in a lot is intuition, intuition in everything. Our intuition is our real person getting out and being free."

Nicole Kidman, *AnOther Magazine*, 2003

INTAN

TRUST
IN

What's the best advice you've been given?
"No advice."

Yoko Ono, *Anothermag.com*, 2011

OF

"There is something incredibly attractive and powerful about people who are in tune with their intuition. In a world with so little to hold onto that feels real or credible, a world with so much disinformation, hypocrisy and confusion, not just to go with the flow and follow everyone else, but be able to stop and listen to your own feelings, is key."

Jefferson Hack, *AnOther Magazine*, 2003

THE GIBLE.

"I perceive this period of life on our planet as very dark. The people in power are very powerful, and I don't see them being toppled too quickly. Not only the government, but also the corporations, the pharmaceutical and oil companies—they're all sleeping with governments. The world seems more corrupt than ever. And I feel that our cultural voice is weak."

Patti Smith, *AnOther Magazine*, 2006

THE YOU IT.

"There is a form of repression in the world; everyone wants to keep you serious and reasonable. There is never space for dreams or the realisation of big ideas. If many people push it in different ways this could be the moment that starts a new period. I'm really hoping for that."

Miuccia Prada, *AnOther Magazine*, 2005

ANOTHER MAGAZINE

AnOther Magazine was really born of two things—wanting to hand on the running of *Dazed & Confused* to the next generation of provocateurs ten years in, and wanting to create a high-impact magazine for the global stage; to create something that felt it had more permanence and that was more like a book. It's kind of testament to *AnOther* that after just one decade it was actually turned into a series of books by Steidl that stripped away all the context. The *AnOther Art Book*, *AnOther Fashion Book*, and *AnOther Portrait Book* are beautiful timeless, classic photo books wonderfully designed by David James Associates that have emerged from these temporal magazines. I don't think we knew what to expect when we began. I mean, *AnOther* wasn't the first, biannual but it was definitely blazing that trail, and it was definitely the first fashion bi-annual to be proudly non-gender specific, to be for women and men. We wanted to do things differently and I suppose, in a sense, it was a product of a change in our perspective—we were all older and we had been through the sound and the fury of *Dazed & Confused* in the 1990s, so we were more confident of our ability, or more assured, and we wanted to use that confidence to push the outside culture into the lens of the mainstream even more. I think we have pulled off some amazing interventions in art and fashion in *AnOther*, and the team still continue to do so.

Going Global: the Emergence of Another Point of View

Foreword

Alex Wiederin Working on AnOther Magazine was an incredibly exciting experience. Jefferson and I were both strongly invested in the goal of creating a very different magazine with a unique vision. We wanted to create a cultural publication that would not only document fashion but also truly inspire men and women alike. Jefferson was based in London and my offices are in New York, so there was some real culture-clash between differing sensibilities in fashion and design—in a really good way! In fact, I think we probably created the very first bi-coastal magazine ever. We put all of our effort into every single page—each custom font, for example, was created by myself—specifically for the magazine. In the end, we were both immensely happy that our work had created this strong, unique voice. AnOther Magazine was, and still is, a very powerful tool for new collaboration and, ultimately, what we created was a platform for talent all around the world.

AnOther Magazine: another point of intervention, another set of discoveries, another way of looking at things, another thirty minutes of your time, another kiss, another curious idea that just came to mind, another reason to get out of bed in the morning, another sense of déjà vu, another chance to do it all over again next season. Another damn fine day.

We wish our lives to be less complicated and more spiritually rewarding yet we are creatures of extremes. Taken to habit and spurred by random acts of chaos. We laugh when we should cry and make others cry when we should make them happy. We are silly and smart, selfish and caring, the modern metaphysical children of Adam and Eve. This is our Original Sin. Our humanity, our right to fuck up and pick up the pieces. To learn as we go along and make the same mistakes again. To lose ourselves in the moment and put things off for another day.

AnOther Magazine explores these themes through the writing, fashion, photography, and vision of its contributors. The cover of this issue by Nick Knight shows two young lovers in a personal embrace. To show real love, in a real situation with real people is something few contemporary magazines would attempt or even think to do. That's our cover statement for this season: to keep a sense of romance alive in a world where ideals are often replaced by deals, and desire easily subverted by greed. It's about an attitude that carries through the fashion and literature to influence and effect contemporary thinking. There is little time in our culture to allow surprises, radical ideas, and thoughts to emerge. We are moving, consuming, and communicating so fast that it takes real control to slow down rather than just go with the flow. Recessions, wars, global and personal disasters continue, and often lives remain uninterrupted. As our culture accelerates and people jump on the latest money-go-round, we see a uniformity of opinions and ideas, a homogenisation of theories, images, and fashion. It's as if the faster things become the smaller the sphere of reference revealed.

AnOther Magazine is not going to change the world we live in. It exists to expand that sphere of reference, to show that there is more to our lifestyles than the obvious. That there is a need to slow down and assess, as much as there is a desire for constant entertainment. *AnOther Magazine* juxtaposes these extremes in a magazine "for men and women," a magazine "for people".

Art directed in New York and produced in London, *AnOther Magazine* traverses a continental style divide. Its writers and photographers come from all over the world. Some of them are visionaries whose names you may recognise others are emergent protagonists in the media landscape. These are our protagonists; producing images you will want to rip out and stick on your wall, articles you will want to highlight and keep to reread. They have come together to fire inspiration and action, style and reflection into the ether; to kick through our daily realities and fuel the fantasies of a generation caught in the slipstream of the extreme.

Jefferson Hack
Editor-in-Chief

ANOTHER PERFUME 13

The idea that you could tell stories through scent was really revolutionary to me—I really wanted to transfer the fashion-focused story-telling that we were doing in the magazine beyond perceived boundaries.

The Sweet Scent of Print Addiction

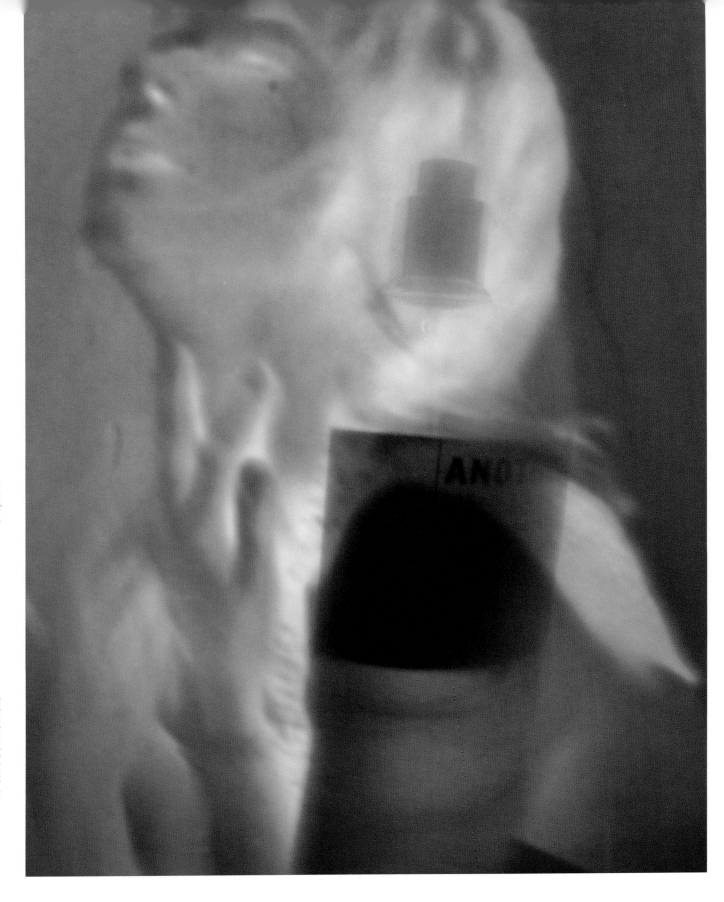

On 2009/06/23, at 17:51, Eddie Roschi wrote:

It's me again

I have arranged to send 4 samples of 2 versions of what Fabrice and I think is the definite AMBROX 13 for the AnOther work we are doing together.

Pls tell Jefferson to wear this for a while as this theme is truly outstanding. I will not go into the difference between the 2 versions you will receive as I want you to smell them on your skin, wear them, and let your nose decide. We can go into the technical details later. We have a clear favorite and we think we should go with that one but we'll divulge that once we get your feedback.

This theme is truly what we think is "another" perfume. Completely unconventional yet totally wearable and addictive. It's grows on you. It's intellectual but very sensorial too. It's a blend of out of this world muscs which are very, very pricey with the main one being AMBROX (hence the name). Other muscs are also present in the ingredient list and other notes too to round off the very raw result and create an addiction that sticks with you and clothing.

Pls spray your clothing with it and be generous in your sprays, you will smell the Ambrox 13 for a long while. It's a skin scent: it doesn't diffuse a lot but has a staying power and wake that is truly exceptional. Your t-shirt will smell of it even after it's washed. AMBROX 13 gets better with time and over the hours that you wear it. Judge for yourself, we are proud of doing this under Le Labo and co-branding it with AnOther as it totally nourishes the purpose of this partnership.

I have been wearing this for months now and have had a very difficult time wearing something else.

Final word—it's polarising, people will love, others won't even smell it. Trust your nose and trust us ;)

Speak soon,
Fabrice and Eddie

BLOW UP

"Blow Up" was really important in the history of *Dazed & Confused*. Without it I'm not sure we would have survived past issue one. We literally couldn't afford to get a second issue of the magazine done. Issue one was out, and we were sitting around trying to get a sponsor to come in to help finance issue two and it was taking forever. I said to Rankin, let's not wait for someone to give us permission to print a magazine, let's just make something happen; let's make a live magazine experience. So I contacted a series of London's underground clubs and asked if we could put a black backdrop up inside and I ran around grabbing people and asking them to stand in front of Rankin's lens. Rankin took brilliant photographs that really captured the early days of house and ecstasy culture and the characters that were inhabiting London's nocturnal scene. It was important for us both, because it taught us that if you want to make something happen, then you have to do it yourself, and that doesn't necessary mean hustle the money, but just create the energy and the rest will follow.

A Live Magazine Exhibition and the Art of Not Giving Up

Rankin In the early days of *Dazed & Confused* we weren't able to access people that were famous, so we were like, okay, so let's just make people famous—let's give people the opportunity. That's where the nightclubs came in, and there were two elements, really: one was meeting people, and the other was making money putting on club-nights, which was really important because obviously a magazine needs funding. We really liked the idea of being in all of the "scenes," so we would go to all the different clubs. The intention behind "Blow Up" was to meet people and document what was going on across the whole spectrum, because, at that point all the subcultures were merging—the Manchester thing was really the last subculture, so all these clubs were incredibly different. I think "Blow Up" is the perfect example of what we were about—we were documenting the experience. It was about you. I think that's where we changed things quite dramatically.

DAZED &CONFUSED

Special Guest Editor Paul

NO OTHER MAGAZINE LIKE IT

16

Björk

+ ONE TO ONE INTERVIEWS WITH:
LL Cool J, Rei Kawakubo,
Douglas Coupland, Kathryn Big

CLOSE-UP AND INTIMATE WITH:
Kylie, Louise Wener, Isabel Monteir
& Marijne van der Vlugt

GUEST ART EDITORS JAKE & DINOS CHAPMAN

ISSN 0961-9704
DON'T THINK ABOUT IT, BUY IT!
£2.50

THE FIRST COVER STAR

Björk was our first personality cover star, the previous ones had all been very conceptual covers. I was hugely impressed by Rankin who was so creatively focused on the cover and image direction of Dazed & Confused in those days. He did incredibly playful and raw images of Björk, and was absolutely adamant that he only wanted to see her eye on the cover of the magazine. I also remember the interview so clearly, I was talking to her a lot about dreams, about magic, and I was kind of letting her dictate where she wanted to go in terms of all the mystical and arcane things that were informing her musically and spiritually. I love that spiritual dimension to her and there was just a natural synergy. The basis of much of the editorial ethos of Dazed & Confused at that time was the multiculturalism of 1990s London, the DIY club culture, the positivity of ecstasy culture; that whole sense of a new identity being formed. It was a very experimental landscape and Björk was the archetype of that moment in culture. Her career has grown in parallel with ours — she's constantly opened up new doors and new possibilities for us and is, in many ways, the patron saint of the magazine.

The Patron Saint of Dazed & Confused

Nanu Nanu: Björk Calling Jefferson

When lunar astronaut Björk crashed back down to earth during the US leg of her recent world tour, those closest to her wondered if she was going to be able to withstand the shock of impact. Her reentry through Earth's atmosphere was caused by physical exhaustion; its by-product was she began to lose her voice. There was panic in camp Björk. After a back-to-back schedule of interviews, gigs, and promotional chores she crashed for three days. A specialist was brought on tour. She had to cut her live set a little short, leaving out the encores at some of the less important shows. She stopped talking unless absolutely necessary, communicating by means of a notepad and pen. Björk was saving every last vocal chord for the remaining dates of the tour, determined to fulfill the commitments she'd already made.

In 1987 the Sugarcubes released "Birthday," bringing Björk's voice to the attention of the British music press and a few thousand indie kids for the first time. It was alien, other worldly, an escape into the imaginary situations and characters that shaped her hopes and desires. Four Sugarcubes albums and her own three million worldwide selling *Debut*, which captured the zeitgeist with a soundtrack to the summer of 1993, have seamlessly imbued Björk's voice into mainstream public consciousness. You either love it or you hate it, but you damn well know it's her when you hear it and that's what matters. What was once considered too weird for commercial success is now accepted, as Björk flouts convention at every opportunity, bringing experimentation and new musical ideas to the charts.

This year, *Post* shone new light onto planet Björk, after the clouds began to settle on the peaks of the mighty but now overfamiliar *Debut*. *Post* spans a similar emotional radius, but the musical production breaks with any sense of the fluidity of its predecessor. While *Debut* appears carved by water and ice, *Post* seems shaped by fire and volcanic action; the lows are much more precarious, the highs more jagged and steeper to climb. Individually co-produced with Nellee Hooper, Graham Massey, Howie B, and Tricky, the songs reflect the personalities of Björk's male counterparts. These are her collaborators in the sexually charged, creative act of making beautiful music. Björk takes liberties with melodies, and form is avoided in favour of impression. You can imagine Björk still gasping at her own reflection in water, still seduced by the sound of the echo of her own voice.

Björk is now back on form, after a strict diet, rationed talking, and plenty of rest. Last night she broke with convention and went on a binge, ending up back at her house with some friends, drinking and talking until five in the morning. Tonight she's in a hotel room in Liverpool, with a four-poster bed and a four-poster bathtub "dead princess-like." She describes the telephone she's talking to me on as being gold with roses painted on it, "Jeff Koons would love it." It sounds like they knew Björk was coming.

Dazed & Confused: How did you feel when you were losing your voice?
Björk: I was basically faced with, "If I can't sing, it's not only me and my life, but a lot of people rely on that," you know? It was kind of strange to be confronted with it.

D&C: But I heard that you had nodules (whatever they might be) on your throat.
B: I got nodules, but basically it is physical exhaustion. It's so clever the way the body functions; it makes you crash and makes you rethink everything.

D&C: How long did you crash for?
B: I crashed for a few days, but then I did the whole tour very carefully. I called it my "monk tip". So my last few months of touring has been Björk on the monk tip. If you're sort of really bored, Jefferson, and you want a new angle on life: don't do drugs, stop talking. It's amazing. The amount of energy that goes into communicating is just outrageous. And you end up just writing what is dead important. Everything becomes so precious. And it's very interesting. You start very quickly listening to completely different music as well, and reading completely different books and you get this urge for completely different films as well.

D&C: Are you at the end of your monk tip now? Are you talking more regularly to people?
B: I can still go completely bonkers. That's kind of how I was brought up, my drinking manners with my mates, was "go for it", and do it for twelve hours and then don't do any of it for a month and I really like it like that. But it had become that I was going out all the time and it's not as precious. I went out last night and got drunk and it's like I've cleared up a lot of crap, and I wake up like this rucksack full of rocks has been lifted off my shoulder.

D&C: For me it's definitely the other way round. If I've been out drinking I feel like I've got a rucksack full of stones lying on my head.
B: Yeah, that's what it's like when you do it often. When you do it rarely and go all the way, it's better than any fucking psychotherapy. Because your body just screams for these needs and just goes and jumps on a table if your body needs to.

D&C: You've become very good at analysing your own psychology, working out what makes you tick. Have you ever been to see a psychiatrist?
B: No. I want to be quite self-sufficient like that. I think people should only do that in the case of emergency, but at the end of the day you've got to learn to live with yourself and if you need constant assistance just to do that . . . also I think you are supposed to be able to solve those things through friends and your relationship, not in an analysed, calculated manner, but in a free-flowing, natural way, so you don't end up stuck with the same problems for ten years.

D&C: When was the last time you cried?
B: Listen, I cry all the time. I cried this morning. I'm over emotional.

D&C: What was that all about?
B: Well, after my binge last night, we ended back at my house and I ended up in a one-to-one talk with one of my oldest friends and we were just crying, not because of sadness, but because (*laughs*), it sounds so wack now, we were being fragile, we weren't on drugs (*laughing*) just fragile, and when you feel too much in a happy way.

D&C: Close your eyes for a minute and tell me what you hear inside your head.
B: (*long pause*). It's some sort of movement similar to cream I think. You know when they squeeze the cream out of the gas thing. Like really pretty when it's got a spike at the top, and it's got a circle. Sort of slow circle movement in the same way whipped cream would move. Very still and very satisfied.

D&C: So you're happy at the moment.
B: You know this touring thing is definitely one of the most difficult things I've done, like an Indiana Jones thing, and me dealing with my body, like "time's out, Björk".

D&C: What were the overriding emotions you felt during this tour?
B: Goldie was with us, and all of Goldie's crew and our crew got on and it was the best vibe on tour.

D&C: So how come you didn't ask Goldie to co-produce any of the songs on *Post*?
B: I don't know really. It wasn't like I was trying to get the whole world on the album.

D&C: Yes it was . . .
B: (*laughs*) Yeah, I know, it looks a bit like that. I'm very much a person who has intimate musical relationships with people and they are almost like love affairs, you see. But I'm very loyal. So me and Nellee got through half the album and then we just stopped turning each other on. We remained friends, but we would just kind of know each other's taste too much for it to be a surprise. And at that point I met Tricky, so we did those tunes, half of which have come out on my album, the other half is coming out on Durban Poison.

D&C: And Graham Massey and Howie B, how did your personal relationship with them affect the music?
B: The tunes I wrote with Graham, I actually wrote before *Debut*, and I saved them for this. I met him in 1990; that was when we were really sparking big time off each other, and for a few years we sent each other tapes, and then when I started doing *Debut* with Nellee it just became very obvious that it would end up as a very musical affair between me and Nellee. So I talked to Graham and decided to keep the other songs because they were just too different. So I saved "Army of Me" and "Modern Things" for this album, and then Howie has been one of my closest friends in England for over three years and that just kind of happened one afternoon. That song we wrote in an hour.

D&C: It's a very spontaneous-sounding song.
B: It's not even produced, I just decided to keep it raw, like it is. (*Pause*) I'm just going bonkers now, I had a three hour conversation with Nellee yesterday. I fucking wake up in the morning with a far too big heart, I don't know what to do with it really. I love so many people so deeply I could happily die now. It's scary. It's so scary it's outrageous. If it wasn't for my kid I would . . . emotionally-wise, I think I've achieved as much I think I can achieve

D&C: I don't think you have.
B: But do you know what I mean?

D&C: No. But you've probably achieved more than what you think is possible . . .
B: That's true . . .

D&C: But I don't believe that you've given as much as you're ever going to give.
B: (*sighs*) And the band as well; when I went through my monk tip, they developed this amazing way to tell me jokes without making a noise, they worked their way around it.

D&C: It's funny because, when you're more serious, your accent is more British, and when you're speaking more emotionally it's more Icelandic.
B: It's definitely that. For me Icelandic is my instinct and English is me being clever. Icelandic is unconscious and English is conscious. And when I speak English, especially when I do interviews and stuff, I can very easily see myself from the outside and describe myself. But then again I would have to be pretty stupid not to have developed that thing, because I've done interviews now for 900 years. But it's impossible for me to do interviews in Icelandic. I just listen to myself and I sound so fake and so terribly pretentious and so Little Miss Know-it-all, I just want to strangle myself. The Icelandic media is going bonkers because I do one interview there every five years.

D&C: Do you feel like you have multiple personalities you can switch into at any time to suit the mood or occasion? Like when you do interviews, or when you're with friends or when you're performing. Or do you feel a lot more sorted than that?
B: I think I'm learning to combine them. And that's kind of what *Debut* and *Post* are all about. Like, I would love to do one experimental electronic song with Graham and the next day I would love to be a diva walking down the staircase being a drama queen. The day after, I would love to do a punk song, and that's very much how I've done my music so far, but I can feel very much that I'm starting to become more everything at once. Like I have one friend who I'm very humorous with and another friend whom I'm very sexy with; and another friend that protects me and another friend that I protect; but now I can see it, I'm not planning it or anything, I can just see myself being able to be everything with each person and just being more spontaneous about it, and just let it flow. But I think everyone is a bit like that and that is kind of the target; combine all those things without leaving any of them out. Because it's very tempting, as we grow up, to leave one of them out.

D&C: Are you in love at the moment?
B: (*pause*) I am, actually. I haven't eaten or slept for two weeks.

D&C: And there's me thinking that's because you've been working really hard, not shagging.
B: But it doesn't really bother me. I just look at a plate of food and I just think it's rubbish. It looks like wood to me or coins. It's just impossible to put it inside my system — it's got nothing to do with me.

D&C: But you seem to fall in love very easily.
B: I think my reputation has gone a bit funny, because I've got a lot of friends, but I get very precious when it comes to love things, you know?

D&C: What do you think your reputation is?
B: I dunno, I guess everyone thinks I fall in love every five minutes, and I have nine boyfriends.

D&C: Yeah, they probably do.
B: It's not true.

D&C: So you've just got one on the go?
B: This is definitely the strongest, though, for many, many years. I'm on natural E; I don't even want to drink, because that will make the feeling go away. I just have to drink one glass and push me a little bit up, and I'm ecstatic.

D&C: What's he like? Does he work in the same industry as you?
B: Don't ask me please, (*pause*) Let's put it this way, I don't meet a lot of people other than the people I work with. You know, it's not like I hang out with shoe salesmen. Or gymnasts.

D&C: Or psychotherapists.
B: Not in my line of work.

D&C: With you and Tricky. Why was it so short-lived?
B: With me and Tricky I don't think we ever knew if we were going out together or not. I mean, we were going out together and then we weren't. Because, basically, the way our relationship functioned was that we were a support mechanism for each other, and we still have this kind of, like, permission to call each other in the middle of the night, when I'm in fucking Munich and he's in fucking Tokyo. It's a very strange job we've got, and we don't have to explain it: we know. And we know the pressure. So that's more what our relationship is like and still is. And I think it didn't last a long time before we realised that is why we'd met and sucked like a magnet to each other.

D&C: So are you writing at the moment?
B: Yeah. Pathetic Michael Jackson songs, (sings "Don't Stop 'Til You Get Enough") My next record is going to be happy Smurfs or something, I dunno. It's very happy, which makes a change.

D&C: Tell me about one song. Have you got one in your head at the moment? Apart from cream?
B: It's very happy, very simple and very poppy. I usually have two at the same time. And they are usually opposite to each other. It's like that mood and that mood, black and white. I've got about five songs that I could go and record tomorrow. Basically, what happens to me is I write the melody first and then, if I work with someone, then the other person adds the other half.

D&C: So who's next on your hit list?
B: I think I have to start being a bit self-sufficient.

D&C: Especially if you have to jump into the studio with some geezer every time you want to record a song.
B: I just love doing music with people; it's the biggest kick ever. But what I need is patience to make the song finish in my head because now in my head I've got a lyric, a string arrangement, a bass line, the sounds, what instruments I want to use, I've got the rhythm, but if I would have met a person that I would have musically fallen in love with, say, in June, that probably meant that I would have only written the melody and the bass line by then, so he would have written the rest. But if I wait, I end up finishing the song myself.

D&C: What kind of person do you fall musically in love with?
B: I want people to be strong characters and personalities; I thrive on that, I'm motivated by very strong characters, I don't get any kick out of bossing people around, you see.

Interview originally published in Dazed & Confused, *Volume I, Issue 16, 1996*

DECADE IN STYLE

For the tenth anniversary of AnOther Magazine, we came up with the theme "Decade in Style" — the idea was to take an outfit from the last ten years from a designer's career and have a brilliant woman wear it. Forty muses for forty designers representing a decade of looks in fashion. Negotiating between the designers' wish lists, the photographers' ideas and our casting was unbelievably difficult. Shot over eighteen months, it was conceived as an attempt to push AnOther out of being just a cool London magazine to a global proposition. The casting process was insane but I kept pushing it because I wanted it to do something with celebrity and fashion at an epic scale. I have to say a huge thank you to Greg Krelenstein for all his patience and casting support. I felt it was important to use really glamorous and seductive techniques to broaden our voice and show the reader and the industry that we had come of age. To do that on such a grand scale really created an event moment for us as an international title. Here are a selection of the pairings all shot by Craig McDean.

Growing Up: Ten Years of AnOther Magazine

p.222: Kate Moss in John Galliano | p.224 and p.225, left to right: Charlotte Gainsbourg in Balenciaga by Nicolas Ghesquière | Milla Jovovich in Prada | p.226 and p.227, left to right, top to bottom: Sophia Coppola in Chloé | Courtney Love in Givenchy Haute Couture by Riccardo Tisci | Winona Ryder in Marc Jacobs | p.228 and p.229, left to right: Christina Ricci in Gucci | Michelle Williams in Louis Vuitton

Susannah Frankel I worked on the *AnOther Magazine* prelaunch, and at its heart it was—and still is, in fact—simply about presenting another point of view. The magazine is a pioneer and often takes an anti-establishment stance, but it also has a foot in the mainstream—a lot of its content embraces the very well known, just portrayed in a different and hopefully surprising way. Maybe that drives the magazine—the wish to amplify something different, something that celebrates diversity, always pricking away at the status quo from the inside. Cathy Edwards was the fashion director and was always the person I liked talking to about fashion the most because she had incredible knowledge and an amazing eye—quite twisted and perverse at times. She loved messing about with reality. She was the dream fashion director because she could think in the way a researcher or writer would and was an amazing analyst of not only what was going on on the catwalk but also outside of that. The result is a brilliant and very quietly subversive aesthetic.

DROP DEAD LETTER CLUB

The Drop Dead Letter Club was formed in 2005 in Paris at the Ritz Hemmingway Bar. It was a place that Hemingway went during the liberation in Paris and it was festooned with literary history and memorabilia. There was an old typewriter there, and I loved collecting old typewriters, so I asked Colin Field, the head barman, if we could set up a club where I could leave letters for friends who would also frequent the bar. He loved the idea because he loved the sound of the typewriter and how it played into the atmosphere of the place. The protocol for our club was that once you dropped a letter, it remained dropped. The name came from the "dead drop" in spy culture, which is a prearranged place where one leaves a message or object that is going to be transferred between two spies. I received some of the most honest and beautiful, heartfelt and also hilarious letters through the club. It has a magical quality. There was one night where Jack White, Alison Mosshart, Garance Doré, Philip Andelman, Sarah Andelman, Mike D, Paul Yauch, Dean Fertita and Jack Lawrence were all typing, drinking, and dropping dead letters around.

Inspiring the Art of Letter Writing

CHANEL

Karl Lagerfeld told me that magazines are too disposable and you have to make a book if you want to make your magazine last one hundred years. That conversation was really the genesis of the *AnOther* book series we created with his imprint at Steidl, art directed by David James. Through that, my relationship with Karl developed and he invited me to creative direct the Chanel in-house magazine called *31 Rue Cambon* and obviously, I said yes. I mean, when Karl Lagerfeld asks you to create a magazine for him, you say yes! The first thing that came into my mind was the image of mirrors. Every time I think of Chanel, I think of mirrors because of the famous mirrored staircase that goes up to Coco Chanel's bedroom, so we used actual mirror board for the cover and it became this incredible gateway from Chanel past to Chanel present. It was very expensive to produce, but if you are going to do a magazine for Chanel, it has to feel like the most extravagant thing ever.

No Expense Spared: Reflecting on History

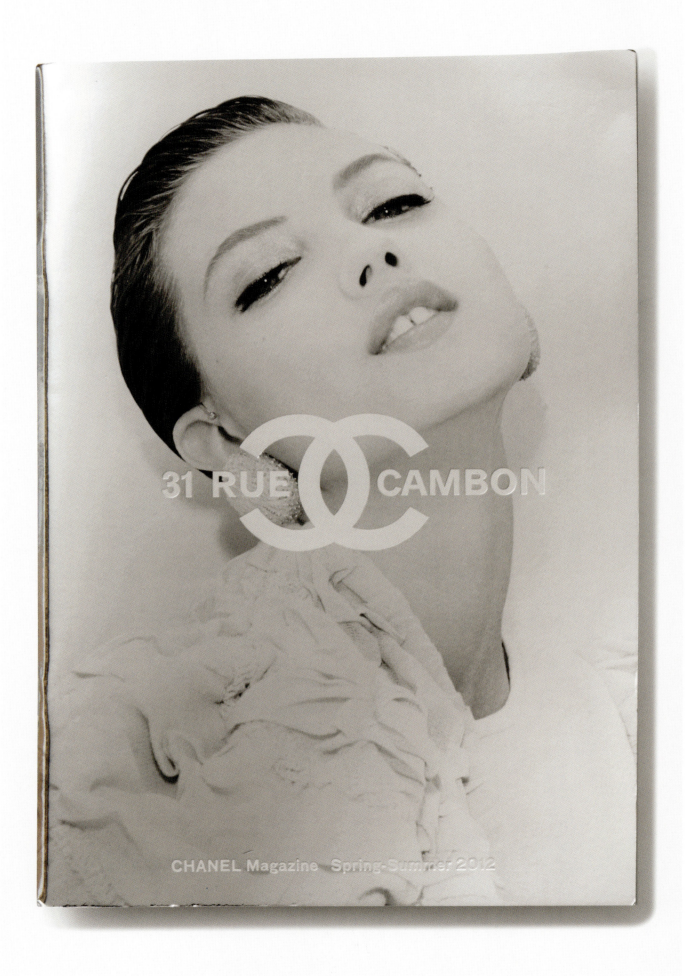

RAG & BONE

Creating this campaign for Rag & Bone was a great process because we wanted to approach it as an editorial shoot and then apply that approach to advertising, but with an onus on each individual insertion in a magazine being unique. I asked Michael Pitt to be in the campaign and I wanted him to run around New York and be shot by Glen in a very reportage way. It was an homage to the amazing pictures Glen took of Kate Moss in the early 1990s which are shown alongside the campaign images. This idea of the English in exile in New York appealed to me as it was also a part of the brand's own story as David Neville and Marcus Wainwright of Rag & Bone found their fame in New York and their ethos echoed that same spirit.

Keeping it Real: Documentary as Fashion Advertising

Glen Luchford This campaign was born from a mutual desire from both Rag & Bone and Jefferson to move away from the advertising that was dominant at the time, which was essentially imagery created in Photoshop rather than in camera. The desire to return to the negative was overwhelming and needed to be honest, so it was refreshing for me to be "unleashed," so to speak. Michael Pitt is totally unique. He comes to you fired up and full of ideas, and he's rather beautiful in my opinion, in that brooding movie star kind of way, so as a photographer you just load the camera and let him go — the rest is easy.

MUL

"I never wanted to be a product of one identity. Besides, I wasn't a citizen of any country. I had a non-identity."

Jefferson Hack, *Purple Fashion Magazine*, 2010

"When everyone is a star, who are the outsiders? When everyone can have an opinion, whose opinion matters? When the cult of celebrity robs celebrity of glamour and permanence how will our cultural icons (or countercultural commentators) be remembered? Any sense of the mystery found in the legend of Studio 54 or the archived covers of magazines like Rolling Stone or Interview is vanishing fast in today's cultural climate."

Jefferson Hack, *AnOther Magazine*, 2003

PERSPEC

SEX

&

"Living life is always more interesting than films. I find life is more exciting because it's limitless. Films can only imitate life."

Harmony Korine, *Dazed & Confused*, 1998

TIPLE SELVES. 7

"You know, if I go to St Peter's gate, I would most comfortably describe myself as an artist's model, certainly more than actor or performer. It feels most accurate . . ."

Tilda Swinton, *AnOther Magazine*, 2009

SHIFTING TIVES.

"In 1989, 1990, I wanted to be in Andy Warhol's Factory. That to me was a spiritual home—a group of people from different backgrounds and with different ideas creating a new way of living."

Jefferson Hack, *Purple Fashion Magazine*, 2010

IDENTITY.

WHO
DO YOU
YOU

What do you most dislike about contemporary culture?
"The acceleration of constant distraction and the loss of distance: both hinder the imagination."

Christopher Bollen, *Anothermag.com*, 2015

CONVER

"Imagination is a weapon against negativity."

Viktor & Rolf, *AnOther Magazine*, 2011

CREA

"Fashion—it should be a hallucination. It should be about a commentary on culture not just a commentary on clothes. It should be about the ultimate expression of your fears and your desires."

Jefferson Hack, *RCA Open Lecture Series*, 2004

THINK

ARE?

"I can't differentiate between notions of underground. Underground film, underground music, alternative culture—to me it doesn't exist. To me the future is either good or bad, and it's about kind of making sense of both those things."

Harmony Korine, *Dazed & Confused*, 1998

SATION
IS
TION.

"Do you think this can be a form of ballet, this new transdisciplinary dance in print? That maybe through all the energy and networking and conversation that's going on it could actually have a real-life component. Could that work?"

Jefferson Hack, *AnOther Art Book*, 2010

MCQUEEN / BOWIE

The Synergy of Radical Creativity

David Bowie is just so culturally tuned in to the cutting-edge of art, music, and fashion, and he really loved Lee [Alexander McQueen]. I asked Bowie to interview him for *Dazed & Confused* and the first question that Bowie asked Lee was: "Are you gay, and do you take drugs?" It was such a great conversation because neither of them could really bullshit the other. Personally, I just found it such an extraordinary achievement to get two people together who were both so private at that time. Bowie's anti-establishment thinking and his creative, imaginative mind was as expansive as Lee's, and vice versa, and their background was incredibly similar. They both came from nothing; working-class boys made good. It's a trajectory that's always inspiring to me because it's about sticking to your guns and not caring what people think.

Fashion: Turn to the Left. Fashion: Turn to the Right

British designer of the year Alexander McQueen in conversation with David Bowie.

This conversation took place on the phone, as is always the case with my conversations with Alex. We have worked together for over a year on various projects and never once met. It's a beautiful Sunday afternoon and he is in the verdant garden hills of Gloucestershire visiting at the house of his friend, Isabella Blow. Ring ring. Ring ring. Ring ring.

David Bowie: Are you gay and do you take drugs? (*laughter*)
Alexander McQueen: Yes, to both of them. (*more laughter*)

DB: So what are your drugs of choice?
AM: A man called Charlie!

DB: Do you find that it affects the way you approach your designing?
AM: Yeah, it makes it more erratic. That's why you get my head blown up shot. (*In reference to a Nick Knight photograph at the Florence Biennale.*)

DB: Well, I once asked you to make me a specific jacket in a certain colour and you sent me something entirely different in a tapestry fabric, quite beautiful I might add, but how would you cope in the more corporate world?
AM: I wouldn't be in a corporate world.

DB: Even if you're going to be working for a rather large fashion house like Givenchy?
AM: Yeah.

DB: So how are you going to work in these circumstances? Do you feel as though you're going to have rules and parameters placed on you, or what?
AM: Well, yeah, but you know I can only do it the way I do it. That's why they chose me and if they can't accept that, they'll have to get someone else. They're going to have no choice at the end of the day because I work to my own laws and requirements, not anyone else's. I sound a bit like yourself!

DB: Unlike most designers, your sense of wear seems to derive from forms other than fashion history. You take or steal quite arbitrarily from, say, the neo-Catholic macabre photographs of Joel-Peter Witkin, to rave culture. Do you think fashion is art?
AM: No, I don't. But, I like to break down barriers. It's not a specific way of thinking, it's just what's in my mind at the time. It could be anything—it could be a man walking down the street or a nuclear bomb going off—it could be anything that triggers some sort of emotion in my mind. I mean, I see everything in a world of art in one way or another. How people do things. The way people kiss.

DB: Who or what are your present influences?
AM: Let me think. I don't know. I think that's a really hard question because in one way, one side of me is kind of really somber and the other side of my brain is very erratic and it's always this fight against the other and I choose so many different things. This is why my shows always throw people completely: one minute I see a lovely chiffon dress and the next minute I see a girl in this cage that makes her walk like a puppet and, you know, they can't understand where it's coming from because there are so many sides of me in conflict. But influences are really from my own imaginations, and not many come from direct sources. They usually come from a lone force of, say, the way I want to perform sex or the way I want people to perform sex or the way I want to see people act, or what would happen if a person was like that. You know what I mean? It's not from direct sources. It's just sort of from a big subconscious or the perverse. I don't think like the average person on the street. I think quite perversely sometimes in my own mind.

DB: Yeah, I would say, from just looking at the way you work, that sexuality plays a very important part in the way that you design.
AM: Well, because I think it's the worst mental attitude. Sexuality in a person confines you to such a small space and, anyway, it's such a scary process trying to define one's sexuality. Finding which way you sway or what shocks you in other people and who accepts you at the end of the day when you're looking for love. You have to go through these corridors and it can be kind of mind-blowing sometimes.

DB: There's something a lot more pagan about your work compared, say, to Gaultier. Your things work at a more organic level.
AM: Possibly. I gather some influence from the Marquis de Sade because I actually think of him as a great philosopher and a man of his time, where people found him just a pervert. (*laughs*) I find him sort of influential in the way he provokes people's thoughts. It kind of scares me. That's the way I think but that's the way my entity has grown and, all in all, in my life, it's the way I am.

DB: Do you think of clothes themselves as being a way of torturing society?
AM: I don't put such an importance on clothes, anyway. I mean, they are, after all, just clothes and I can't cure the world of illness with clothes. I just try to make the person that's wearing them feel more confident in themselves because I am so unconfident. I'm really insecure in a lot of ways and I suppose my confidence comes out in the clothes I design. I'm very insecure as a person.

DB: Aren't we all? Could you design a car?
AM: Could I? It would be as flat as an envelope if I designed a car.

DB: Could you design a house?
AM: Yes, very easily, very easily.

DB: Do you paint or sculpt?
AM: No, I buy sculptures. I don't do it, I buy it. I buy lots of sculptures.

DB: Do you ever work in the visual arts?
AM: No, but I just did a show the other day. I don't know if you heard, but we did this show, it was on water and we did this kind of cocoon for this girl made of steel rods and it was in the form of a three-dimensional star and it was covered in this glass fabric so you could see through it and this girl inside it, but we had all these butterflies flying around her inside it. So she was picking them out of the air and they were landing on her hand. It was just about the girl's own environment. So I was thinking about the new millennium in the the future thinking you would carry around with you your home like a snail world. She was walking along the water with a massive star covered in glass and the butterflies and death-faced moths were flying around her and landing on her hand and she was looking at them. It was really beautiful. It threw a lot of people completely sideways.

DB: It's interesting how what you're talking about is somewhere between theatre and installation.
AM: Well, I hate the theatre, I hate it. I used to work in the theatre. I used to make costumes for them and films, and it's one thing I've always detested—the theatre. I hate going to the theatre, it bores me shitless.

DB: Well, I'm not talking about a play.
AM: I know, but I just wanted to tell you that anyway! (*laughs*)

DB: All right, change the word to ritual.
AM: Yeah, that's better. I like ritual . . . (*laughs*)

DB: Armani says, 'Fashion is dead'.
AM: Oh, so is he . . . I mean, God . . .

DB: Now you sound like Versace . . .
AM: He's close to dead. I mean, no one wants to wear a floppy suit in a nice wool—the man was a bloody window dresser. What does he know?

DB: Do you think that what he's really saying is that maybe . . .
AM: He's lost it . . .

DB: He might still be making an observation in as much as the boundaries are coming down . . .
AM: Yeah.

DB: The way fashion is presented these days is a quantum leap from how it was presented, say, five or ten years ago. It's become almost a new form, hasn't it?
AM: Yeah, but you know you can't depend on fashion designers to predict the the future of society, you know, they're only clothes and that never strays from my mind for one minute.

DB: Is the British renaissance a reality or a hype, do you think? The world is being told that it's so. Through all strata of British life and from fashion to visual arts, music, obviously, architecture, I mean there's not one aspect of culture where Brits haven't got some pretty fair leaders, English designers in French houses, you know what I mean? It's like we're invading the whole zeitgeist at the moment.
AM: Being British yourself, I think you understand that Britain always led the way in every field possible in the world from art to pop music. Even from the days of Henry VIII. It's a nation where people come and gloat at what we have as a valuable heritage, be it some good, some bad, but there's no place like it on earth.

DB: But why is it we can't follow through once we've initially created something? We're far better innovators than we are manufacturers.
AM: Yeah, exactly. But I think that's a good thing. I don't think that's a bad thing. It makes you holy, it makes you quite respectable about what you do and the actual moneymaking part of it is for the greedy.

DB: So you're not greedy, Alex?
AM: I'm afraid I'm not. Money's never been a big object. Well, I mean I like to live comfortably, but I've been asked by this French fashion house how would I put on a show and I said, well, the sort of money these people buy these clothes for in this day and age, you don't want to flaunt your wealth in front of the average Joe Public because it's bad taste and with all the troubles in the world today, it's not a good thing to do anyway. I'm sure these people that have this sort of money don't feel like showing their face on camera, so I said it would be more of a personal show and people with this sort of money who do appreciate good art and good quality clothes and have these one-off pieces made just respect the ideal, not the actual chucking money around. They can do that anywhere.

DB: When you are affluent, which I'm afraid is probably on the cards for you, how are you doing to deal with that?
AM: I'd like to buy Le Corbusier's house in France . . . (sniggers)

DB: Here's a nice thing. What was the first thing you designed ever? Like when you were little or a kid or something?
AM: Oh. I can't think that far back, but for my own professional career, it was the bumsters. The ones that Gail, your bass player, wears.

DB: Was there a point when you were sort of playing around with stuff, and when you used to dress up and go to clubs when you were a kid, and all that, where you would do original things?
AM: Actually, yeah. I would wear my sister's clothes and people wouldn't recognise it because I'd wear them in a male way. I did go round my street once in my sister's bra when I was about twelve years old and the neighbours thought I was a freaky kid, got dirty looks and all that . . . and you're talking about Stepney here.

DB: My father used to work in Stepney.
AM: Yeah?

DB: What age were you when you left home?
AM: Nineteen.

DB: Did it give you an incredible feeling of freedom? Or did you suddenly feel even more vulnerable?
AM: I felt really vulnerable actually. Because I was the youngest and I was always mollycoddled by my mother, so that's why I turned out to be a fag, probably. (laughter)

DB: (laughing) Was it a clear choice?
AM: I fancied boys when I went to Pontins at three years old!

DB: Did you ever go on holiday to Butlins or Bognor Regis or Great Yarmouth?
AM: No, I went to Pontins in Camber Sands.

DB: Camber Sands?! I used to go there too!
AM: Oh my God!

DB: They had a trailer park with caravans . . .
AM: Exactly.

DB: . . . and next door to us we had a, at the time, very well-known comedian, Arthur Haynes, who was sort of like a bit of a wide boy; that was his bit onstage, you know, and I used to go over and get his autograph. I went three mornings running and he told me to fuck off every day. (laughing) That was my first time I met a celebrity and I was so let down. I felt if that's what it's all about— they're just real people.
AM: Two memories of Pontins—one, was coming round the corner and seeing my two sisters getting off with two men. (laughter) I thought they were getting raped and I went screaming back to my mum and I wound up getting beat up by my two sisters! The other one was turning up in Pontins when we first got there and looking out the cab window 'cos my family was, like, full of cabbies; it was like a gypsy caravan-load to go to these places, and I looked out the window when I got there and there were these two men with these scary masked faces on and I shit myself there and then in the cab! I literally just shit my pants! (laughter)

DB: Which comes to . . . who is the shittiest designer?
AM: Oh my God . . .

DB: Who is the worst designer?
AM: In my eyes?

DB: Yeah, in your eyes.
AM: Oh God, I'm open for libel here now, David . . .

DB: Do you think there's more than one?
AM: I think you've got to blame the public that buy the clothes of these people, not the designers themselves because it turns out they haven't got much idea about, you know, design itself. It's the people that buy the stuff. My favourite designer, though, is Rei Kawakubo. She's the only one I buy, the only clothes I buy ever for myself as a designer are Comme des Garçons. I spent about a thousands pounds last year—I shouldn't say that—on Comme des Garçons menswear.

DB: I've never paid, Alex! (laughs) Until . . .
AM: Until you met me! (more laughter)

DB: Until I met you! Yes, but I knew that you needed it!
AM: I did at the time! But I tell you what I did do when you paid me, I paid the people that actually made the coat!

DB: No, listen, you were so kind about the couple of things that I didn't need that you actually gave me. I thought that was very sweet of you. You work very well in a collaborative way as well.

I thought the stuff . . .
AM: I still haven't bloody met you yet! (laughs)

DB: I know, I think it's quite extraordinary that we've done so well with the stage things that we put together. Do you enjoy collaboration?
AM: I do, but the one thing you have to do when you collaborate is actually respect the people that you work with: and people have phoned me up and asked me to collaborate with them before and I've usually turned them down.

DB: Do your clients really know what they want and what is right for them, or do you usually have to dress them from the floor up?
AM: It can work either way and I don't resent either because, at the end of the day, I'm the clothes designer and they are the public. If you want a house built you're not expected to build it yourself.

DB: Here's a fan question. Who would you like to dress more than anyone else in the world and why?
AM: There's no one I'd like to dress more than anyone else in the world, I'm afraid. I can't think of anyone who deserves such a privilege! (laughs)

DB: The sub-headline there! (laughs)
AM: Oh my God no, 'cos I'm an atheist and an anti-royalist, so why would I put anyone on a pedestal?

DB: Well, it does draw one's attention back to your clothes and what you do is actually more important than anything else.
AM: Well, I think it would limit your lifestyle somewhat if you said your music is just for that person down the road.

DB: You just sort of hope there's someone out there that might like what you do.
AM: And there's always someone, I mean the world is such a big place.

DB: Yeah. Prodigy or Oasis?
AM: Prodigy, I think they're brilliant.

DB: Well, you haven't answered this one. I have to drag you out on this one. Armani or Versace? (laughs)
AM: Marks and Spencer. I'm sorry. I don't see the relevance of the two of them put together. Actually, they should have amalgamated and sort of formed one company out of both. If you can imagine the rhinestones on one of them deconstructed suits . . .

DB: What do you eat?
AM: What do I eat?

DB: Yeah.
AM: Well, I've just had a guinea fowl today . . . it was quite an occasion to come here . . . It's such a lovely place and I love to come here. Bryan Ferry comes here a lot. It's an amazing place and it was built in the arts and crafts movement by Isabella's husband's grandfather. It's on a hill in Gloucestershire and it overlooks Wales and everything. And my bedroom is decorated with Burne-Jones' Primavera tapestry—I always come here to get away.

DB: So this is your sanctuary, is it?
AM: Yes, it is. Very much so.

DB: Did you ever have an affair with anyone famous?
AM: Not famous, but from a very rich family. Very rich Parisian family.

DB: Did you find it an easy relationship, or was it filled with conflicts?
AM: No, he was the most wonderful person I have ever met and I was completely honest with him. Never hushed my background or where I came from, and this was when I was only nineteen or twenty, I went out with him and I said to him whatever we do, we do it Dutch and he didn't understand what I said. He thought it was a form of sexual technique! Going Dutch!! (laughs) I said it means paying for each of us separately.

He thought that was great, but he gave the best blow job ever! (laughter)

DB: How royal! Was it old money or was it industrial wealth?
AM: Long-time industrial aristocratic wealth.

DB: Do you go abroad very much? I mean just for yourself, not for work?
AM: No, not really.

DB: So you really are happy in your home-grown environment?
AM: I like London, but I love Scotland! I'd never been to Aberdeen before and I went to see Murray's friends in Aberdeen for the first time and it was unreal because I stepped off the plane and I just felt like I belonged there. It's very rare that I do that because I have been to most places in the world, like most capital cities in Japan and America, and you feel very hostile when you step off the plane in these places. I stepped off the plane in Aberdeen and I felt like I've lived there all my life. And it's a really weird sensation. I like more of the Highlands. My family originated from Skye.

DB: Are you a good friend, a stand-up guy, or a flake?
AM: I'm afraid I have very few friends and I think that all of the friends I have, I can depend on and they can depend on me. I'm very aggressive to people that, if I read through 'em in a second, they've usually found the wrong person to deal with. So if you have got me as a friend, you've got me for life. And I'd do anything for them, but I don't really have associates that use me or abuse me, unless I ask them to! (laughs)

DB: Are you excited about taking over Givenchy?
AM: I am and I'm not. To me, I'm sort of saving a sinking ship and not because of John Galliano, but because of the house. It doesn't really seem to know where it's going at the moment and, at the end of the day, they've got to depend on great clothes, not the great name.

DB: Have you already formulated a kind of direction you want to take them?
AM: Yeah, I have.

DB: Is it exciting?
AM: Yeah, it is, because the philosophy is mainly based on someone I really respected in fashion. There's a certain way fashion should go for a house of that stature, not McQueen bumsters, I'm afraid.

DB: My last question. Will you have time to be making my clothes for next year's tour? (laughs)
AM: Yeah, I will. We should get together. I mean, I want to see you this time. (laughs)

DB: We could put this on the record right now . . . are you going to make it over here for the VH-1 Fashion Awards? I can't remember.
AM: When is it?

DB: October 24th or something . . .
AM: My fashion show is on the 22nd.

DB: So you're probably not going to make it. 'Cos you know I am wearing the Union jacket on that. Because millions of people deserve to see it.
AM: You've got to say, "This is by McQueen!" (laughs)

DB: Gail will be wearing all her clobber as well.
AM: Oh, she's fab!

DB: Oh, she wears it so well.
AM: I'd love to do your tour clothes for you again.

DB: Oh, well, that's great. I can't wait to be properly fitted up this time!
AM: Yeah, definitely. But I've got to see you. I don't want waist measurements over the phone, 'cos I'm sure you lie about your waist measurements as well! (laughs)

DB: No, not at all . . .
AM: 'Cos you know some people lie about their length! (*laughs*)

DB: I just said I'd never lie about the inside leg measurement.
AM: What side do you dress David, left or right? (*laughs*)

DB: Both!
AM: Yeah, right.

DB: No. Yes. Well, maybe.

Interview originally appeared in Dazed & Confused, *Issue 26, 1996*

RENEGADE TV

Renegade TV Gets Dazed was a Channel 4 commission and it was the very first magazine takeover of British television. The key thing for Rankin and I was a sense that we were bringing the pages of the magazine to the screen and doing it in a way where the aesthetic wasn't television but more proto-Internet—a sort of precursor to digital/web storytelling in the mix of hyper short form content including short film, fashion film, and moving portraits. It was meant to be provocative and there were a lot of firsts in it. It was the first time Lynne Ramsay's work was on TV—we screened her short film *Kill the Day*—and it was the first time Joe Wright and Jake and Dinos Chapman were featured on TV. Howie B created all the incidental music, which was just brilliant—minimal, emotional, circumspect. I think people were genuinely shocked by it, and we loved that. I love the whole hijack notion of TV culture because at the time it felt like a genuine intervention into the mainstream.

Bringing the Magazine Into the Living Room

EPISODE 1   EPISODE 2   EPISODE 3

  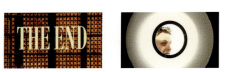

Rankin We really went to another place with *Renegade TV* and I'm always sad that we didn't go further with it because it would have pre-dated the Internet by a couple of years. It was one of the most exciting things we had done because it was a really amazing opportunity to experiment with a medium we were both fascinated by. Jefferson was very interested in open access TV. He loved the New York cable channels and was really interested in how we could hijack a TV station, so we approached it that way because we were both media outsiders, and we were both totally inexperienced as well. In a sense, we kind of missed the opportunity to take it further—I mean, we had talked about wanting to create a video magazine back in the very beginning. One of the things Jefferson always said was that we never wanted to just be a magazine—we wanted to be an exhibition, a performance, a night club, a live event, an experience.

EPISODE 4

EPISODE 5

THE END

BERNHARD WILLHELM worn by Leanne. Materials: cotton.

MASQUERADE

Masks have obvious connotations when it comes to how we define our identities on a deep level, and I wanted to create a project that would play with gender, identity, disguise, ceremony, the folkloric, and the futuristic. We wanted a multiplicity of voices, and that meant there were some interesting counterpoints in what was produced – the designers tackled it in so many different ways, from the romantic to the gothic, and the conceptual to the more graphic, all of them using masks as a tool for subversion in a cultural, historical, sexual or political context. There were no restrictions at all, you didn't even have to be wearable; it just had to explore the very notion of the mask. Alexander McQueen made one with dripping wax over an impression of his own face and that idea of impermanence was very interesting to me. I love that idea of the obsolescence of fashion. The masks were exhibited in Paris at Rond-Point at a really fabulous party with Michael Clark, so again, we were extending the realm of the magazine into physical space, as curators and exhibitors.

Scary   Monsters   /   Super   Creeps

ALEXANDER MCQUEEN Materials: paper and wax.

GWYNETH PALTROW

I think this was the first multiple perspective interview we ever published. I wanted to try out an idea that involved lots of people who had worked with a public figure asking them hyper-personal questions only they would be able to ask. Gwyneth Paltrow was perfect for this as she has such an enigmatic quality, so I reached out to people, including her family, to ask questions that I would deliver in an interview setting. What was important to me about the experiment was that she would answer a question that she knew her mother had proposed, or her brother, or Tom Ford, or Stella McCartney, in a very different way than if it was coming from an interviewer, because she would have the image of that person in her mind. In print it felt like a conversation that was happening with her peer group, friends, and family, and, as such, it had an amazing sense of intimacy and sense of scale. I remember Ingrid Sischy from *Interview* saying to me, "Wow, I wish we'd thought of that format for *Interview*—I'm going to steal it!" That's the biggest compliment I could have ever gotten!

Imagining — New — Interview — Formats

Gwyneth Paltrow

If you could ask her one question what would it be? Since winning an Oscar at twenty-six she has been a Hollywood icon. In celebration of her career so far and in anticipation of her latest film, *Sylvia*, AnOther Magazine brings Gwyneth Paltrow together with an all-star line up featuring her friends, fellow actors, producers, directors, and even her family. How much closer can you get?

Wes Anderson: How much of you is Welsh, if any? And, what else goes into the mixture of your bloodlines?
Gwyneth Paltrow: Zero of me is Welsh. My mother simply liked the name. She went to school with a girl called Gwyneth when she was very little. It stuck with her. I am glad it did. I like my name. My bloodlines are quite well mixed—I am a real mutt. On my mother's side I am German and English/Scottish with some Dutch thrown in for good measure. On my father's side I am Polish Jewish. Makes for an interesting inner dialogue.

Christina Applegate: What is the one thing that gets you up in the morning, keeps you going and working, giving everything all your grace even when you just don't feel like it anymore?
GP: I guess lately it's been sheer discipline. Because of the year I've had, I've taken work very seriously. I used to feel so inspired all the time and that's what kept me going. But since my dad died, I feel like I've been forcing myself a little. It's weird that Christina used the word "grace" because I feel like that's what I've lost—ease and grace.

AnOther Magazine: Things happened for you quite easily after *Shakespeare in Love*. Did you have that feeling of going with the flow, just enjoying it?
GP: Yes, exactly. There was an insouciance about the way I approached my work, my life. I reached the top when I was twenty-six. I won the Oscar and in a way I felt really liberated by that, because I thought, "Oh well, I can do whatever I want now." But with that came a lack of focus, a lack of seriousness that I've definitely got now, maybe for the first time in my life.

Tom Ford: I have always admired the fact that you are incredibly real as a person. I have watched other celebrity friends wall themselves in and become detached from the real world. Is this a constant struggle for you?
GP: I wouldn't say it's a struggle as much as just having to be conscious of it. I find that when you're famous and you're young, people are constantly removing obstacles for you. People you don't even see hear that you're coming to the airport and get the tickets ready, and all of a sudden you're not going through life like everyone else does. I think that what can happen, quite gradually, is that you come to expect things. Not in a horrible petulant way, it's just a natural thing that happens. I constantly have to remind myself, "Wait a minute this is not normal, you are being treated specially." It makes me feel sick, but I get a kind of guilty pleasure from it as well. I have celebrity friends who do wall themselves in. I'm lucky because I have people in my life who are always saying to me, "Wait a minute, hang on, this isn't normal, you're not seeing things how they really are."

Neil LaBute: Having had such success in your career so far, do you find it harder or easier to make decisions about film roles? What criteria do you use when deciding? Do you weigh your audience into it at all, or do you believe that people will follow you wherever you go?
GP: That's an interesting question. Before, I went on instinct and I would take a role just because it was something I hadn't tried. I'd just take it and wind up in something mediocre, but not really care. I do feel like I'm at a turning point in my life now and my criteria are getting narrower, definitely. But I will never factor my audience's opinion into it, because I can't. If I did, I would feel like a complete sell-out.

Sadie Frost: The character you play in *World of Tomorrow*, Polly Perkins, reminds me of Veronica Lake. If the movie had been made in the 1940s, which classic actress do you think would have been best suited to the role?
GP: It would have to be someone with a sharp tongue, like Katharine Hepburn. The character is very feisty and articulate.

AnOther Magazine: Does she wear the trousers in her relationship with the Jude Law character?
GP: Metaphorically, yes she does, but she's in a little tweed Stella McCartney skirt!

AnOther Magazine: Tell me a bit about Polly Perkins.
GP: Well, it's Polly Perkins and Sky Captain, who Jude Law plays. He's this RAF pilot, Polly's a reporter and they're on the trail of this mystery together. They've had a relationship in the past and there's a lot of sexual tension, mistrust, and banter, so there's a great dynamic between the two of them. The whole background is computer generated, all blue screen.

AnOther Magazine: How did you find that?
GP: I'd shot on blue screen before, but never anything substantial. It was tough and could get monotonous but Jude used to make me laugh. We were supposed to be in a cockpit of an aircraft and he would say, "I feel like we're six years old and you're over at my house." It was so fake! We'd laugh about it.

Wes Anderson: Who's your favourite hero or heroine from books and movies?
GP: My favourite heroine in fiction is Franny Glass or Jane Eyre. I don't have a favourite hero/ine in the movies because I don't really like them.

Neil LaBute: Now that you've made your London theatrical debut, do you have plans to return to the stage? And after so many film roles, how did it feel facing a live audience again?
GP: I had such an amazing time, it really awakened something and got me re-connected with why I started doing this in the first place. I would love to do a play once a year if I could. It was scary, but you know, I always realise these things about myself after the fact. Looking back now I think, "My God, wasn't I terrified to go in front of a live audience after all these films, especially in London?" I have this built-in bravery though, so it petrifies me now, but at the time I thought, "Yeah, let's just go forward."

AnOther Magazine: What would you call that? Blind optimism?
GP: I think so. My parents instilled great self-confidence in me. My dad always said the whole time I was growing up, "You are the greatest, you can do anything." It was very bolstering. I think that gets in there when you're a child, it really does. Of course I have the insecurities of any actress, of any woman, but deep down I have this understanding of what I'm capable of. I was fearless when I did *Emma* at twenty-two years old. I came over to England and I'd never done an English accent. And it wasn't until the movie came out and the press were asking "weren't you at all intimidated going over there?" that I realised what I had done.

Mario Testino: How do you manage to cry throughout a play like *Proof*, express such suffering, but still make the audience desire your performance; sit through it, and actually enjoy watching that suffering?
GP: If you're real, the audience will be engaged. If you fake it, half-ass it, you lose people. But if you're as exposed as you can be, they are really fascinated by watching true emotion. If you see a play and someone's standing a few feet in front of you hysterically laughing or crying—whatever it is—if it's real and happening in front of your face, then you have the thrill of live theatre.

Neil LaBute: What other job in your industry do you find yourself most attracted to? If you could do something other than act, would you write, direct, do make-up, produce..?
GP: I think I would be a producer because I think I'm quite good at arranging people and seeing holes in scripts or seeing great things in scripts. I don't think I could be a writer.

AnOther Magazine: What would your motivation be for producing?
GP: Getting things made that are worthwhile, because I'm really having a crisis about the kinds of films that are getting made and the kinds of films that are successful. I've realised that I just will not be in Whatever-It-Is Part 2 or Part 3, I won't be in these lowest-common-denominator romantic comedies. It takes too much out of my life. I'd rather make less money and take more risks, try to at least put something into the world that's worthwhile, that has something to say.

AnOther Magazine: It sounds like you're on a bit of a mission...
GP: It's true! I am on a mission! I would also like to be the crowd service person. They don't have them so much in England, but in America, on a movie set, there's a snack table where people make cappuccinos and smoothies. I'd make really healthy smoothies.

AnOther Magazine: What attracts you to that?
GP: I don't know, I'm a bit of a homemaker. I like to cook.

Harvey Weinstein: Who is the best-looking producer in New York? I'll give you a clue, his initials are HW.
GP: That would have to be Hal Wallis, producer of such great old films as *42nd Street*, *Jezebel* and *The Maltese Falcon*.

Amira Casar: Hola Sexy! I have this question we couldn't talk about on the set of *Sylvia*. My fear playing Assia was that fiction wouldn't do justice to a life already so mysterious and washed out of history. Her short, misunderstood, troubled life, and her suicide with Hughes' child saddened me. Did you feel this guilt or any guilt at all portraying Sylvia Plath?
GP: That's a good question. I was having this very interesting conversation with Nora Ephron yesterday. She's a writer and director; she wrote *When Harry Met Sally* and directed *You've Got Mail*. She's a brilliant New York intellectual. She was asking me about *Sylvia* and I was saying how difficult it is to know what goes on in biographies. In fiction everything is possible. For example if you read *Madame Bovary*, you understand the relationships, you know exactly why things went down the way they did. In biography, you can never really know. My worry came from how I would ever be able to portray all the facets of this woman—she's so complicated. My guilt was that she has children who are still alive and was I hurting them by participating in the film? It was a struggle because obviously I'm a person who really believes in privacy and in family.

Amira Casar: There were certain similarities between Assia and Sylvia. Naively, I like to think that without Hughes, these two fascinating women could have been a comfort to one another. What do you think? Did Hughes damage them?
GP: The very basic principle with which I approached the whole thing was that it takes two people to create a dynamic and I never in my mind vilified Ted Hughes or blamed him for her death. There was obviously something innately attractive to Ted Hughes about complicated women. I find the fact that Assia killed herself in the exact same way that Sylvia did was very manipulative and stagey, like "I'm going to show the world what you've done." I don't think that Sylvia had that kind of venom.

Christine Jeffs: Is there any other character you'd like to play based on a real person?
GP: I would like to play Catherine the Great or Marie Antoinette, some incredibly power-mad, complicated woman. I think it is my favourite thing to uncover the reasons behind why someone is reviled, unloved. I especially find it fascinating when historical women get assigned titles like "monster".

Alexander McQueen: Do you think the term "film star" is relevant to the 21st century?
GP: I think that we're moving into an age where everyone is a celebrity, everyone's a star. I think film stars are relevant because they're famous for actually putting something into the world, something that takes thought and creativity, as opposed to letting a camera watch them twenty-four hours a day.

AnOther Magazine: In the past, we didn't know as much about the lives of stars. Now, with celebrity culture the way it is, with magazines the way they are, the "ordinariness" of actors is exposed more and the mystery and glamour have gone.
GP: The romance and mystery of old Hollywood have gone. We're redefining what it means to be a film star in this day and age. Photographers take the worst pictures of stars walking down the street in sweatpants and people go through their garbage. The public are the ones shaping how they want to see things and it's their appetite for seeing Elizabeth Hurley with shopping bags in a market that's changing the way that the media is handling everything.

AnOther Magazine: Do you care about it?
GP: Do I? I think it's a shame that the sheen has rubbed off. The whole idea of a film star and films is that they're escapism. Films are two hours of your life when you can go in and feel something that you wouldn't feel if you had stayed home. It's like entering another world and it is a shame when the bubble bursts.

Blythe Danner: Does your natural gift for music, your ability to sing just about anything and play the piano by ear, inform your talents as an actress? The accents, your ability to inhabit such a broad stroke of characters.
GP: Awww. Well, I use music all the time when I work. I always have my iPod and I listen to music to get myself to the right emotional level.

AnOther Magazine: Did you have specific music you listened to for *Sylvia*?
GP: Absolutely. During *Sylvia*, I listened to the last Sigur Ros record. I listened to Jeff Buckley, the "Corpus Christi" song. There was a Sarah McLachlan remix which my friend Kevin Aucoin gave me right before he died and there's a song on that I listen to a lot. But to answer the question, I think if you have a musical ear you can hear things and harmonise and imitate stuff—it really helps with accents—it's the same part of the brain. But I get all that from my mom, she's incredibly musical. She always had instruments around the house.

Blythe Danner: Do you love me?
GP: Awwww. Is that what she asked? I love her with all my heart. What edgy, cool questions from my mom.

Stella McCartney: Do you think love and loss are similar emotions?
GP: I do. I don't know if it's what's happened to me with my dad, but sometimes I feel now that I love someone so much that the next emotional layer is fear of losing that person. I realise that the size of your love for someone is proportional to the size of your pain when they're out of your life.

Sadie Frost: One of the things I admire about you is your strength. What do you attribute it to? Where do you get it from?
GP: I don't know quite where it comes from, I suppose it's from my family again. No matter what happens I have them, so I've never felt alone in the world. I think the reason that Sadie perceives me as strong is because a lot has happened in my life. I have been emotionally decimated a few times. I lost a cousin at seventeen, a good friend in an accident a year later, my best friend's mother at twenty-one, my grandfather when I was twenty-six—which was a real blow because we were very close—and then my father who was the centre of my world. Within that time frame I had a broken engagement and a drawn-out, tortured relationship with a complete knucklehead. I have made and lost friends and seen people change. I have gotten the wrong idea about life and then righted myself. I have had a big life in the last decade. Sometimes it has made me feel heavy and weary and like the shine has worn off me, especially since my dad died. But life has a

funny way of equalising things, and in another respect I am happier than I have ever been.

Valentino: Gwyneth, would you leave forever your career to follow your boyfriend or husband to a little island in the middle of nowhere?
GP: (*Laughing*) I think I would if it was something that we were doing together. If I didn't feel like I was compromising everything I was and everything I have in order to do his thing. If it was "let's do this together" I would.

Steven Spielberg: (*This is what we received from Steven Spielberg's office*) This interview is certainly an interesting and unique approach. Mr Spielberg is leaving for the summer this week and is tying up loose ends, so he regrets that he won't be able to participate. Good luck!

AnOther Magazine: Let's turn that around then, what question would you like to put to Steven Spielberg?
GP: The thing that amazes me most about him is that he has this infinite capacity to imagine things. I would want an insight into how that works. He was saying the other day that his mother was a pianist and he used to lie under the piano and watch her feet and would never let her open the top of the piano because he was afraid of what was inside. He's always playing video games, he's so in touch with that thirteen-year-old boy, hyper-imaginative mind. I'd want to know how he maintains that.

Anthony Minghella: Gwyneth Paltrow is intelligent, intuitive, and unerringly true as an actor; capable of being, by turns, fragile, funny and forceful. She can be as good, as enduring, as startling, as she wants to be. It's in her hands. And that's a curse as well as a blessing.

AnOther Magazine: How would you respond to this statement?
GP: I see it definitely as a blessing. I feel frustrated by the fact that sometimes I hold back—or I have in the past. If I feel like the material can't support what I'm doing, I really withhold and then I think I'm just wasting my time.

AnOther Magazine: Do you ever think you can't support the material? Do you ever feel that if you want to do it as well as you would like to, you have to give parts of yourself that you might not want to?
GP: I've definitely felt that in the past, not knowing how I'm going to get there. But I think it just takes work and a relentless determination not to give up. I think you always know that it's in you. You have to in order to be an actor, you have to think you're capable of it all. I don't ever think of it as a curse that I have to go somewhere I don't want to go to. That's my job: to force myself into uncomfortable areas in my own heart and soul.

Interview originally published in AnOther Magazine, Issue 5. 2003

FASHION-ABLE

The Inimitable Beauty of Otherness

This project pretty much rewrote the rule-book in terms of placing a fashion focus on those outside of pop culture and was an act of cultural resistance against a mainstream that blatantly seeks to divide different groups in society from each other. In terms of fashion, this tends to mean the wholesale creation of a clear-cut hierarchical structure around notions of beauty, designed very simply to disenfranchise those not considered worthy to have a lens shone upon them. Katy England and Lee McQueen both shared a passionate social conscience and didn't give a fuck when it came to mainstream notions of beauty, or fashion for that matter — for both of them fashion was a tool for positive and radical subversion. Bringing those two indefatigable talents together with Nick Knight to shoot a fashion story featuring people with physical disability created an image-making triumvirate to be reckoned with — it was one of those moments when it was kind of obvious to me that the outcome would be timeless and iconic. The pictures of Aimee Mullins on the cover and also in McQueen were picked up by the national press and were a defining moment for *Dazed & Confused* in mainstream media consciousness — it was one of those moments when you realise a point of difference and willingness to do what has never been done before has genuine power and potential.

Fashion is a big bubble and sometimes I feel like popping it'
—Alexander McQueen, 2008

It is the summer of '98. Madonna's "Ray of Light" is fighting it out in the charts with Massive Attack's "Mezzanine"; France lifts the World Cup and the iPod is merely a twinkle in Steve Jobs' eye. Alexander McQueen has just shown his latest collection for Givenchy haute couture in Paris—a tribal collection inspired by royalty and the Amazon—and he is about to create the scene-stealing moment of September's London Fashion Week, when robot arms will spray-paint a white dress worn by stoic, revolving model, Shalom Harlow. Opening the show, No.13 (Spring/Summer 1999), Paralympic athlete and amputee Aimee Mullins strides out on a pair of prosthetic legs, intricately hand-carved in wood.

Aimee Mullins was also the cover star for the September 1998 issue of *Dazed & Confused*, guest-edited by Alexander McQueen. Stylist Katy England, McQueen's creative right-hand and visionary fashion editor at *Dazed & Confused*, had spent months preparing the cover story that cemented the relationship between the designer and the athlete. Lee (as we called him) had seen a picture of Aimee, reached out to her and fell in love. As was the case with everything he did, he wanted to push the boundaries of beauty, and so he began casting more people with disabilities, inviting his contemporaries such as Hussein Chalayan, Roland Mouret, and Philip Treacy to design and customise pieces for them to wear. Photographed by the legendary Nick Knight using his now antiquated 10x8 camera, "Fashion-Able", as the story was titled, was, Katy has since told me, "the hardest thing I have ever done". Katy, Nick and Lee believed sincerely in the beauty of the individuals they case alongside Aimee (Jo-Paul, Mat Fraser, Helen Mcintosh, Catherine Long, Alison Lapper, David Toole, and Sue Bramley) and they worked painstakingly with charity organisations and peer networks to navigate the hurdles that existed in mixing fashion photography with disability. "We were entering into a different world," explained Katy, "and of course we had to tread very carefully, with extreme sensitivity."

It was *Dazed*'s "Never Mind the Bollocks"; it took us from being indie-outsiders to being one of the most talked about magazines on the planet that year. Inside, beyond the "Fashion-Able" story, you really feel like you're walking into the mind of McQueen at that time. Photographers Inez van Lamsweerde and Vinnodh Matadin shot his Givenchy collection and Juergen Teller Grace Jones; Jack Webb documented underground sex clubs and the photographer and film director Robert Frank was profiled. Lee himself interviewed Helen Mirren. I think the only person who Lee wanted in the issue that we couldn't get to shoot was Joel-Peter Witkin.

Soon afterwards, Lee became our fashion editor-at-large, forging a loyal and amazingly rich relationship with *Dazed*, resulting in a series of special photographic projects. What was incredible about working with him was that he never intellectualised his ideas or actions. When I asked him why he wanted to profile Helen Mirren, he just said, "cause I like her". He was a natural storyteller with an exceptional, childlike wonder for the world, coupled with a polemic anti-establishment ethos. Lee was truly fearless and never really gave a damn about what anyone else would think, or how they might perceive what he did. His concept of challenging conventions of beauty was never political, always punk. That's why this issue is as powerful and provocative today as it was then. It was Lee who taught me not to say, "Why?" but more importantly, "Why not?"

Originally published in Alexander McQueen, *V&A Publishing, 2015*

Susannah Frankel "Fashion-Able" was a very brave and potentially risky project. It was an emotional and extraordinary process that wasn't without upset. Lee [Alexander McQueen] in particular always had an ability to push for the seemingly impossible. It was challenging and it was about all of the people we shot expressing themselves, about their power and beauty as physical beings, and also the power and beauty of fashion in an unconventional way—really, everyone worked so hard and was so giving of their time and energy, particularly the models. Katy England cast the shoot through relevant organisations, including the RNIB [The Royal National Institute of Blind People]. I felt that it was done with great sensitivity and it took months. All the people cast had to really want to do it and to feel comfortable in their own skin. Then Lee approached Rei Kawakubo, Hussein Chalayan, Roland Mouret... I talked to all of the people cast about being shot and, honestly, I felt out of my depth. I remember going to the house of the wonderful girl who had only recently lost her sight [Sue Bramley], and I probably made mistakes when I was talking to her because why would I, as a fashion editor, know quite how to approach that? That's kind of what was important though—the integrity and willingness to push everyone outside their comfort zone that went into "Fashion-Able" is so rare.

Aimee Mullins

When I arrived in London and was taken to the set, I was struck by how lovely everyone was. Nick [Knight] is an incredible gentleman and a bit reserved. He's like family now. He just seemed incredibly chic, very elegant. Then there was Lee [Alexander McQueen], who was a little bit giggly, very shy, and very protective of me, in a way. We began shooting a kind of mesh tank top and a jacket that went over the whole look. Nick came up to me very discreetly at one point, and said, "the jacket is really difficult," and he asked me if I could take it off and I went, "oh, yeah sure, but there are still a couple of layers underneath." Then Nick, slightly blushing said, "Do you mind taking it all off?" My heart just started stuttering, and I started thinking about my parents, but then I thought, "Well, no one I know will ever see this." Of course, it is the single image of me that has gone all around the world more than any other. I think Nick still gets asked about that image every week.

Lee had a real draughtsman quality, like an architect or painter. He asked me there and then: "I want you to open my show." I remember feeling elated. I mean, I had spoken about this idea in a magazine profile just weeks before, which he had seen—to seek people outside the medical community and go after artists, sculptors, NASA engineers; anybody who could create wearable sculptures for me, and there I was, not even six weeks later, in a situation that was making these ideas real. When Lee presented his idea it was as if everything else disappeared. He unrolled this crimson paper and it was a to-scale drawing of what became the carved wooden legs we used in his show.

I remember being very, very proud of the cover and it was seminal because it was about embracing otherness—not as a freak show, but as genuinely beautiful in its power to be other, its power to be provocative. There is still tons of imagery that is very limiting when it comes to the perception of beauty around women, but it's changing. I am now the face of L'Oreal worldwide. That's huge. It was seventeen years ago that I did my first fashion cover with *Dazed*, and now to be the face for the largest beauty brand in the world? That's progress. That time gap is closing more and more though, real acceptance is happening. The question that "Fashion-Able" posed is still valid—it should be consistently asked again and again of society.

BJÖRK: Obsessed w this…

http://www.theguardian.com/science/2015/jun/05/newly-discovered-vessels-beneath-skull-could-link-brain-and-immune-system

Newly discovered vessels beneath skull could link brain and immune system

•

JEFFERSON HACK: It's an unbelievable discovery. The doctor even admits "based on what we know they should not be there". What else will be revealed…. how little do we know, how much is waiting under the skin of our bodies to still be made sense of???? Biology, physiology and psychology are so linked in your work….Just listening to Stonemilker.

It's almost like the opening string section should be the soundtrack to this piece of news… What music did you hear? It made me also think of other things…. Vulnicura - Cure For Wounds in Latin - what if your wounds are not curable?

Mental Health….. is so far so little understood….. My favourite writer Robert Walser said, "My disease is one of the mind and difficult to define" - Auto immune diseases - the body attacks healthy cells by mistake…. it's so fucked up…. they say it's genetic… i imagine it as looking at the world through the eyes of Francis Bacon. Pain distorts the senses, sound, shapes, colours, darkness…

(I'm supposed to be interviewing (?) you so I'm conscious of not typing too much… but we need to start so I thought I would start with a splurge…)

Walt Disney has his brain Cryogenically suspended so he can be defrosted and return - apparently in the body of a professional basketball player…

•

Dearest Jefferson,
Sorry for late reply but Sardinia had less Wifi than I had hoped – I went into these incredible caves there, Neptune's grotto…

I noticed this article too and sent it to like all my friends ABOUT TIME they connect the gut with the brain: and it is a breakthrough for them that they connected it to the lymphatic system!!! did you see that medical drawing of those branches growing in the skull lol ? we all have those ha ha ha ha . the meninges gets an upgrade:

"meninges is often regarded as the brain's shrink-wrap packaging, rather than a piece of anatomy in its own right."

i have a personal connection to this discovery as this area swells up in me when i eat bread . and ive tried to explain this to several doctors and they just shook their heads . fair enough , me describing a swimming cap appearing on my brain and closing down my connections ha ha ha ha the odd icelander strikes again . but it is always sooo satisfying when science backs up your instinct like that . have you read a book called "proust was a neuroscientist" ? it is several lectures by jonah lehrer where he proves that creative impulses foresaw science often about 2 centuries . he describes how proust getting lost in how that french cookie sets off memory and 50 pages spent on describing how it travels from his fingers to his mouth is basically the promise of neuroscience much later . my favorite tale though is the insane french chef who discovered boullion by burning broth for days most people thinking he lost it . meanwhile he was isolating an enzyme which is now perhaps thought of as the 7th taste up there with sweet , sour and bitter . it is the same enzyme that gets stimulated by sex and it appears in odd collisions for example burnt cheese on pizza yeast . at the same time a japanese chef was frantically inventing miso not knowing of the french one ….

who is robert walser ? sounds super interesting

in the cornwall palm trees !! they always told me it had rain forest here and i didnt believe them !!!!!

enthusiasm,
björk

•

I'm sure it was a relief for you to be off-grid for a few days. A digital detox? I think this idea of individual pursuit of new ideas is a thread that is really interesting. The doctors who shook their heads are a reflection of society's failures and limitations in dealing with the complexity of the human condition. And how often individuals who are considered nutty or off-key who are obsessed with studying or doing the same thing over and over again to find a different outcome are often onto something fundamentally important, that is linked to the essence of life… It was Kerouac who tapped into that veneration of the genius/outcast dichotomy in On The Road in his speech about 'The Mad Ones…" which Steve Jobs later appropriated for his Think Different campaign for Apple which resulted in billboard sized images of Einstein and Muhammad Ali pasted over the high density traffic intersections of the industrialised Western World. I'm thinking of your Jonah Lehrer reference as its this intersection of science and creativity that is such a strong thread. How technology influences art: the clash or reappraisal of ancient and modern, hidden and visible, the known and unknown, in your work. It makes me jump to Jung , who you so generously introduced me to when you became obsessed with The Red Book around the very beginning of the writing of Biophilia, is there a connection to jung for you in relation to this?

(just a quick note on Walser... he writes observational short stories they are simple, almost minimal (reactive) tales. He influenced Kafka and Hesse and is credited with really birthing Modernist style of literature. He was penniless, had one suit and lived to write. His life became reduced to the bare essentials and in his writing you feel the link of spirituality and anti materiality especially in his view on man and nature. To cut a long story short as he descended into madness his writing became incredibly small until eventually he invented a microscript style of writing which was coded and so tiny you would need a microscope to even see it. It took decades for the code to be eventually cracked! - He has an unami way of writing!)

.

I had never heard of him , i can relate to this slowly disappearing writing ha ha ha ha ... i probably drive around reykjavík like this , gregarious some days and then humbly hide on backstreets on other ...

just googled your robert walser . interesting , was just recently introduced to this https://www.youtube.com/watch?v=b6Fvp8XyJys and rollo may :
a friend recommended his book love and will to me and i found this tone of friendly male matriarchs nourishing , them waving the flag of emotions and pioneering eastern philosophies in the mainstream early/mid 20th century ... not sure why im attracted to that right now, perhaps counterbalancing feminism somehow , a relief because of the latest gender awareness surge ? to find the root of sympathetic males ? or just feeling that at last we can erase the differences . patriarch industrial 20th century was always a bad idea , we all kinda knew it , lol

but so so so so so hungry for spoken word now , can someone explain that to me ? it is like the vitamin i never took !! and listening in that gap between wake and sleep and then just when you wake up ? it is not a coincidence that the worlds religions invented prayers for this moment , im feeding all sorts of youtubes in there and it sets up an explosive cocktail in my mind , we are so so receptive , arent we ?

which brings us back to the brain : obsessed w this https://www.youtube.com/watch?t=13&v=nEOpUypJgyw sooooo curious about how brain is the place in us that adapts and changes quickest , like all our lives we can develop different sections up there , i remember reading a book about all the hormones and the body offers us new ones every few years and even after 80 they are still introducing us to new ones we have never tried before , id like to think the spiritual wise ones .... (i wish)

.

Wow that's beautiful. We are constantly able to be enriched and excited by life and our bodies if we are open to the inner not the exterior development. That's a life lesson right there! Neuroplasticity is incredible. I first read about it in Wired. The idea of the constant re-wiring of our brain, the story was about the brain's malleability and how it's constantly re-configuring according to stimulation. There is a direct link between VR, gaming and Neural healing/ development... I found this on Wired... (not quite as academic as your link) http://www.wired.co.uk/magazine/archive/2014/05/features/game-your-brain)

Also quick side note but it reminded me of a story that I 'd heard about Albert Enstein's brain being removed - it was removed (with or without his permission no-one truly knows) after his death - the autopsy and studies reveal that he was missing part of the Sylvian fissure and also he had a high proportion of Glial cells. Lets see in the future if we can use VR to make us all into Einsteins?

Sometimes i feel like we are already in VR - just without the headsets.

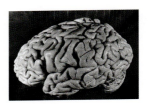

.

Sadness oliver sacks passing away ....but then again , strangely not ? didn't he REALLY live a full life ? did you see this ? he kinda wrote his own eulogy here:

http://www.nytimes.com/2015/07/26/opinion/my-periodic-table.html?smid=pl-share

i went to his house in june and was lucky enough to have tea with him and touch these rocks he was collecting , everytime he had a birthday he got the element which position in the element table corresponded to his age .... and he would surround himself with mercury on mercury year (when he was 80) and tin and osmium and we confessed we had the same favorite : bismuth . how graceful of him to leave on that year !!! (it is number 83 and he was on his 83rd year)

watched "awakenings" tonight again just appreciating how much he cared for people its kinda crazy . that he broke through to folks who hadnt talked for decades , were vegetables in institutions and the

amount of times he did it with the only thing that would reach : music !!!!! is reassuring , beyond faith and hope and all that pizzazzass ..... im not sure i would ever make that effort for a stranger , shy and selfish w my time . and somehow his life seems to be all about adding compassion to science ?

been doin a lot of research on those moments between sleep and awake and just before you fall asleep again and you look yourself into the eye , t h e   s u s p e n s i o n and that canyon that appears and it has made me curious how people build their own personal scaffolding for it. it can be words , music , mantras , whateva . and somehow i ended up listening to tibetan book of the dead in one long whack on spoken word. i recommend it , it is only 4 hours . i put 2 coats on and was lying on the beach by this icelandic lake and adoring the clouds choreographing these ancient words . its kinda crazy it was written in the year 600 , right ? like before or during viking shit . all my friends were reading it when i was a teenager and i decided they were too nihilist, like william boroughs or bukowski kinda cowardish antilife stuff . Meanwhile I was focusing on euphoric surrealistic ladies . but maybe i wasnt ready for it . not even about death that much , more about

```
were traditionally used for funerary purposes, much of it
was originally intended for advanced Tantric initiates who
used it to re-live the death process as a means of realiz-
      ing the mind of clear light while still alive.
```

•

I am really swept away in that image of you lying there listening to the Day of the Dead. That's a performance in itself. Could be staged at the next Venice Biennale! The word suspension really struck a chord for me, also this idea of the 'realising the mind of clear light'. Is that a possible state in which to compose and write music? Have you ever achieved a closeness to experiencing death? In yogic and Buddhist text it's Nirvana or enlightenment which is both death and birth or re-birth. Its interesting how the clear light is linked to both or the circle of life is completed through that 'transience' that Oliver Sacks talks about. What other suspensions are there? Drugs were always seen as a fast track to experiencing that spiritual connection, but in my experience that's a fake enlightenment. Even with so called natural drugs which i loved doing like Ayahuasca. There's always a dialogue still with self or a projection of self thats carried or a nihilism as you so rightly call it. Bringing physics and science into it is really powerful, especially through Neurology

That's so incredible that you got to spend time with Oliver Sacks. Reading his obituary makes me just want to never waste a second of any day, his enthusiasm for the future in it is so infectious and his understanding that there is so much to learn, so much to discover that will change our perception of the universe and the mind so positive......

•

Harvest time here, picking berries , getting lost up there for hours , question how much of it goes in your mouth and how much in the bucket .... also picking berries w headphones good , listened to a passionate playlist and crawled around a gooseberry bush in my garden meticulously removing every single berry off , like 6 buckets !!! amazing how many of them hid behind on the lowest furthest away branches i had previous years missed or not been too bothered about before thought of doing it w music !!!!! my hands got all delicately scratched though from the thorns but i didnt realize until in the local swimming pool using a citrus hair conditioner and a strong glowing sensation came out of the back of my hands . like dozens of thread of light glowing into the shower ha ha ha ha ha . confused at first not making the connections but then a silent giggle impressed with the gooseberry thorn / citrus hair conditioner ha ha ha . this post of ours is about inspirations , right ?

also incredibly inspired by viviennes (Westwood) tank .... might have to borrow it for our minister here . weve been for months preparing a national park in the centre of the island as the government has decided to undo the only nature preservation law .... to be continued

p.s. http://www.scientificamerican.com/article/scientists-discover-children-cells-living-in-mothers-brain/

•

Every activist should have their own white tank! Declare Independence - Raise Your Flag! Vivienne's protest was brilliant. Tell me more about yours?

•

just hearded sheep on horses for 6 hours

so magnificent

total merge of nature / animal / human / human rituals / weather

synchronized 50 folks on horsebacks and 200 sheep

in massive rain and wind

just like a musical

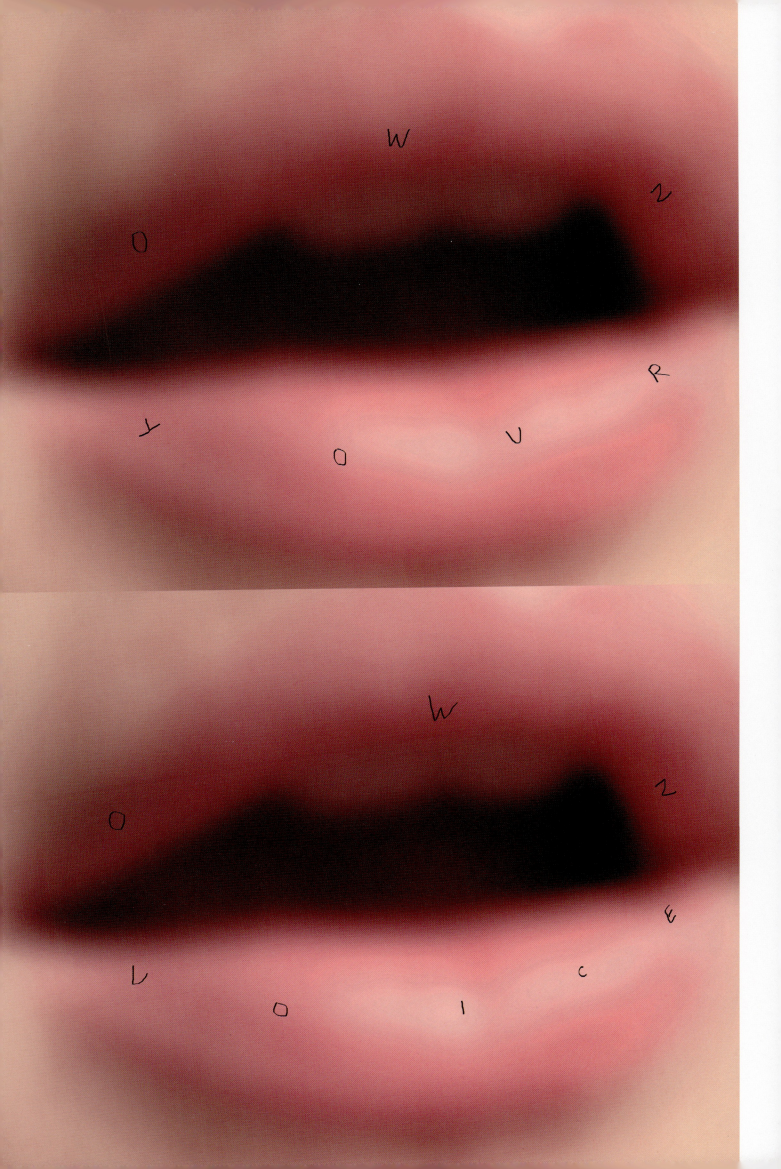

ask
unanswered
questions

Drop

Dead

Letter

Club

IF YOU STAND FALL FOR ER NOTHING ANYTHING

an independent state of mind

True   The Opposite Is Also True

The Opposite Is Also True

Another

 point

 of

 intervention

DEATH OF THE COVER STAR

BEEN THERE

SEEN IT

DONE IT

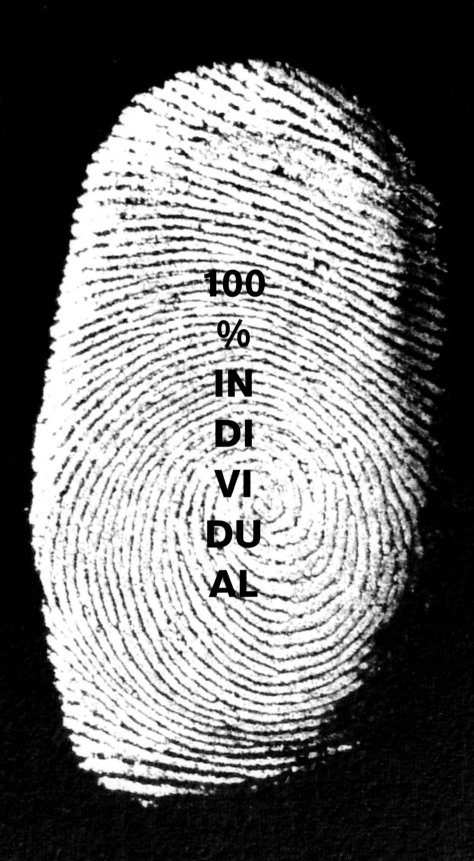

what remains of the future

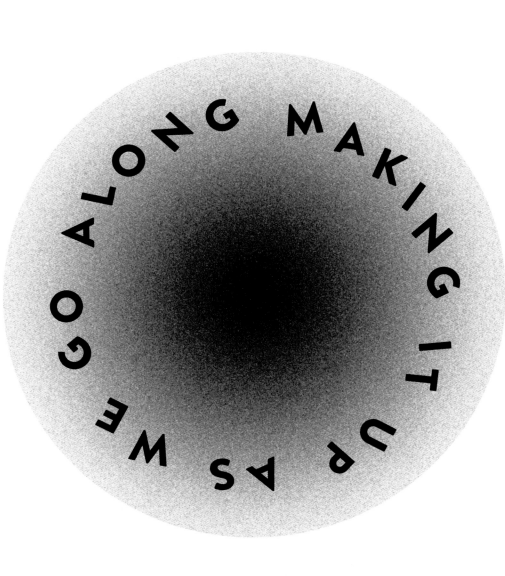

Acknowledgements

I would like to thank the following people for their dedication to this book, without whom it would not have been possible:

Art Directed and Designed by: Ferdinando Verderi
Edited by: Ferdinando Verderi and John-Paul Pryor
Produced by: Felicity Shaw

Design Team, Project Management: Piera Wolf and Stephanie Spech
Assistant Designers: Aline Stieger and Bia Kim
And: Enrico Pirondi, Elena Miska and Emily Okuda-Overhoff

And to: Charles Miers, Anthony Petrillose, and Gisela Aguilar at Rizzoli International Publications

Thanks to the following people for their fantastic contributions to this book:

Philip Andelman, John Baldessari, Ola Bergengren, Björk, Jeremy Blake, Peter Blake, Andy Brewer, British Film Institute, Linda Brownlee, Richard Burbridge, Richard Bush, Jasper Clarke, Ben Cobb, Peter Coffin, Douglas Coupland, Meg Cranston, D*Face, DALeast, Paul Davis, Corinne Day, Brian Degraw, Andy Delaney, Anne Deniau, Horst Diekgerdes, Matthew Donaldson, Tara Donovan, Chloe Early, Lena Emery, Saam Farahmand, Hans-Peter Feldman, Robert Francis Muller, Susannah Frankel, Tom Friedman, Albrecht Fuchs, Ganzeer, Johan Grimonprez, George Harvey, Jamie Hawkesworth, Sara Hemming, Damien Hirst, A.M. Homes, Martina Hoogland Ivanow, Todd James, Oliver Jeffers, Chris Johanson, Scarlett Johansson, Quentin Jones, KAWS, Brad Kahlhamer, Nadav Kander, Kacper Kasprzyk, T. Kelly Mason, Nick Knight, Alberto Korda, Barbara Kruger, Le Labo, Hart & Lëshkina, Wayne Liu, Richard Louderback, Glen Luchford, Maser, Melodie McDaniel, Craig McDean, Barry McGee, Jason Meadows, Albert Moya, Mode 2, Carrie Moyer, Aimee Mullins, Ben Murphy, Hans-Ulrich Obrist, Gwyneth Paltrow, M+M Paris, José Parlá, Laurence Passera, Paul Plowman, Gareth Pugh, Katja Rahlwes, Rankin, Emma Reeves, Jason Rhoades, Robin Rhode, Terry Richardson, Dario Robleto, Sam Rock, Guillaume Salmon, Lernert & Sander, Mark Sanders, Bill Saylor, Lina Scheynius, Nina Schultz, William Selden, Jim Shaw, David Benjamin Sherry, David Sims, Patti Smith, Mario Sorrenti, Alistair Spalding, Jerry Stafford, Matthew Stone, Jacob Sutton, Tilda Swinton, Christopher Taggart, Juergen Teller, Ed Templeton, U2, Christian van der Kooy, Inez van Lamsweerde & Vinoodh Matadin, Jenny van Sommers, Rory van Millingan, Vhils, Banks Violette, Hanna von Goeler, Orlando von Einsiedel, Baillie Walsh, Nick Waplington, Gillian Wearing, Ai Weiwei, Monty Whitebloom, Alex Wiederin, Timo Wirsching, WIZ, Yelena Yemchuk, Thom Yorke.

Very special thanks to the following unique individuals for their unwavering support: Rankin and Susanne Waddell, Kate Moss and Lila Moss-Hack, Douglas and Theresa Hack, Philip, Mandie, Scarlett and Harper Hack.

To the original *Dazed & Confused* crew:
Nicki Bidder, Sophia de Romarate, Cathy Edwards, Katy England, Nicola Formichetti, Katie Grand, Claude Grunitzky, Wendy Ide, Damian Lazarus, Alister Mackie, Callum McGeogh, Rob Montgomery, Lotte Ould, Phil Poynter, Emma Reeves, Matt Roach, Mark Sanders, Ian C. Taylor.

Special thanks to:
Imran Ahmed, Daniel Arsham, Christopher Bailey, Alex Betts, Olivier Bialobos, Derek Birkett, Tim Blanks, Bono & Ali Hewson, Laura Bradley, Stanley Buchthal, Sarah Burton, Ronojoy Dam, Hugh Devlin, Mandie & Karen Erickson, Marianne Faithfull, Mike Figgis, Ed Filipowski, Jack Flanagan, Tom Ford, Matthew Freud, Jean-Yves le Fur, Nicolas Ghesquière, Holly Hay, Iris van Herpen, David Joseph, Jan Kennedy, Greg Krelenstein, Karl Lagerfeld, Susie Lau, Evgeny Lebedev, Caroline Lever, Caroline Lynch, Stella McCartney, Gillian McVey, Suzy Menkes, Beth Mingay, Jimmy Moffat, Benn Northover, Karla Otto, Eric Pfrunder, Mark Phillips, Miuccia Prada, François Ravard, Scott Rodger, Jane Rosenthal, Renzo Rosso, Ingrid Sischy, Raf Simons, Jerry Stafford, Richard Thackray, Riccardo Tisci, Vivienne Westwood, Kerry Youmans, Olivier Zahm.

Nick Abrahams, Andreas Ackerup, Daniel Adeyemi, Sean Agass, Masuda Akihisa, Margherita Alaimo, William Alderwick, Benjamin Alexander Huseby, Cameron Alexander, Elizabeth Alker, Alistair Allan, Jan Aman, Ravi Amaratunga, Kevin Amato, Rachael Ames, James Anderson, Finn Andrés, Jamie Andrew Reid, Peter Andrew Bosch, Dan Annett, Faye Anthony, Mark Anthony, David Armstrong, Gary Armstrong, Matt Armstrong, Finn Atkins, KT Auleta, Michael Avedon, Samantha Avendano, Iphgenia Baal, Catherine Baba, Susie Babchick, Coline Bach, Pierre Bailly, James Baker, J.G. Ballard, Nick Ballon, Tim Barber, Anastasia Barbieri, Jeff Bark, Sandra Barron, Steve Barron, Erin Barry, Luella Bartley, Johanna Basford, Alexander Basile, Jessica Bateman, Zac Bayly, Ned Beauman, Jonnie Begood, Agata Belcen, Martin Bell, Riccardo Bellini, Helena Benjafield, Abby Bennett, Danielle Bennison-Brown, Jon Bergman, Giasco Bertoli, Phil Bicker, Camille Bidault-Waddington, Cass Bird, Marc Bird, Chris Birkenshaw, Dan Blackledge, Tamalyn Blackman, Devin Blair, Judy Blame, Joe Blanchard, Derek Blasberg, Emma Blau, Mel Bles, Anuschka Blommers, Alixe Boardman, Kasia Bobula, Victor Bockris, Christopher Bollen, Beat Bolliger, Polly Borland, Mark Borthwick, Joel Bough, Anne Bourgeois-Vignon, Joan Braun, Tal Brener, June Brigman, Mike Brodie, Chris Brooks, Sarah Broom, Alex Brown, Thomas Brown, Linda Brownlee, Laurenz Brunner, Cedric Buchet, Phil Buckingham, Richard Buckley, Brian Butler, Kira Bunse, Isabella Burley, Sara Burn, Abi Burnton, Tim Burrows, Jeff Burton, Philippa Burton, Jeff Busby, Jennifer Byrne, Jodie Byrne, Jeffrey Byrnes, David Calhoun, Victoria Camblin, Jenny Campbell-Colquhoun, Charlie Campbell, Chris Campion, Jessie Cape, Hayley Caradoc-Hodgkins, Elizabeth Cardwell, Asger Carlsen, Claire Carnegie, Sean Carpenter, Ed Cartwright, Darren Carty, Zoe Cassavetes, Alex Cassel, Raphael Castelmezzano, Hector Castro, Ali Catterall, Charlotte Chandler, Cody Chandler, Thomas Changeur, Michelle Chardin, Thea Charlesworth, Adam Chen, Jake Chessum, Leon Chew, Luciano Chianese, Andrew Chidgey, Esther Choi, Natalia Christina, Paola Cimmino, Harry Clark, Cath Clarke, Indigo Clarke, Aimee Cliff, Grace Cobb, Sarah Cobb, Jarvis Cocker, Sally Coe, Todd Cole, Aimee Coles, John Colver, Alisa Connan, Gracey Connelly, Jonathan Connelly, Pia Constenius, Fiona Cook, Celestine Cooney, Leonie Cooper, Tim Cooper, Anton Corbijn, Poppy Corby-Tuech, Bibi Cornejo Borthwick, Nicki Cotter, Mark Cousins, Daniel Coutinho, Kate Cox, Louise Cox, Michael Cragg, Elissa Cray, Phil Crean, Melanie Crété, Jennifer Croli, Alisha Crompton, Erica Crompton, Thomas Crossman, Dan Crowe, Farrell Crowley, Gavin Cumine, Chris Cunningham, Gro Curtis, Lizy Curtis, Joanna Curwood, Claude D'Avoine, Alessandro Dal Buoni, David Dalton, Paul Dalton, Tara Darby, Nick Dastoor, Daniel David Freeman, William Davidson, Susanna Davies-Crook, Lucia Davies, Rhys Davies, Arthur Davison-Sharp, David Dawkins, David Dawson, Neil Dawson, Amanda de Cadenet, Autumn de Wilde, Priya de Souza, Trevor de Cotta, Pierre Debusschere, Stevie Decanay, Roger Deckker, Godfrey Deeny, Joseph Delaney, Mae Delaney, Sophie Delaporte, Betty Demonte, Alex Denney, Chris Dent, Matt Dent, Justin Devon Moore, Lydia Dewdney-PalaLeon Diaper, Ronald Dick, Abi Dillon, Alex Doak, Pamela Doherty, Sian Dolding, Claudia Donaldson, Faye Dowling, Thomas Dozol, Yves Drillet, Jon Duckett, Lauren Dukoff, Johanna Dunn, Nathan Dunne, Jane Duru, Matt Dyson, Modesta Dziautaite, Emma E. Forrest, Kat Easthope, Jessie Economakis, Nancy Edmondson, Anders Edström, Alan Edwards, Scott Edwards, Courtney Eldridge,

Nicole Elias, Rebecca Eling, Sam Elliot Connor, Andrew Elliott, Emma Ellwood-Russell, Tracey Emin, Barrett Emke, Xavier Encinas, Brian Eno, Glen Erler, Reuben Esser, Roe Etheridge, Michael Evanet, Gareth Evans, Karla Evans, Oliver Evans, Helen Evenden, Michel Faber, Justine Fairgreave, Richard Fairhead, Sarah Fakray, Sam Falls, Naomi Falusi, Shelley Fannell, Max Farago, Sylvia Farago, Tony Farfalla, Leandro Farina, Dominique Fenn, Beth Fenton, Andrew Fenwick, Piper Ferguson, Gavin Fernandez, Lara Ferros, Hannah Fincham, Ana Finel Honigman, Agathe Finney, Ernst Fischer, Nicki Fisher, Steve Fisher, Adrian Fleet, Tim Fleming, Chris Floyd, Simon Fly, Paul Flynn, Ryan Foerster, Lauren Ford, Louise Ford, Luke Ford, Michael Fordham, Stephen Fortune, Richard Foster, Nina Fourie, Tom Fowlks, Katy Fox, Neal Fox, Neil Francis Dawson, Jermaine Francis, Elizabeth Fraser-Bell, Hannah Freeman, Tim Freeman, Francesca Fregosi, Sandra Freij, Arran Frood, Erwan Frotin, Stephen Fry, Matthew Fry, Warren Fu, Ricardo Fumanal, Nagasaka Fumi, Jo-Ann Furniss, Maksymillian Fus Mickiewicz, Adam Fuss, Lewis G.Parker, Ashlee Gagui, Pauline Gaiger, Stefano Galuzzi, Emma Gammon, Katia Ganfield, Michael Garrad, Eleni Gatsou, Francesca Gavin, Georgia Gay, Tierney Gearon, Laura Genninger, Boo George, Graeme George, Kat George, Julie Gerstein, Zoë Ghertner, Mhairi Gibb, Tom Giddins, Luke Gilford, Andy Gillette, Andy Gilmore, Samia Giobellin, Danilo Giuliani, Sean Glynn, Emma Goetz, Rosie Gogan-Keogh, Jim Goldberg, Nan Goldin, Melissa Goldstein, Paula Goldstein, Marcelo Gomes, Lauren Goodman, Mikhail Gorbachev, Isla Gordon-Crozier, Thomas Gorton, Karen Goss, Vicki Gotterson, Jess Gough, Ellie Grace Cumming, Mhairi Graham, Paul Gravett, Carmen Gray, John Gray, Darren Green, Robert Greenwald, Avi Grewal, Emily Grievson, Stuart Griffiths, Gareth Grundy, Tim Guest, Nicole Guga, Rebecca Guinness, Vincent Gutierrez, Axel Gutschenreiter, Tim Gutt, Amy Gwatkin, Julia Hackel, Nick Hackworth, Mimi Haddon, Anthony Haden-Guest, Oliver Hadlee Pearch, Gareth Hague, Daryoush Haj-Najafi, Phil Hale, Ross Halfin, Louise Hall-Strutt, Annie Hall, Cheyne Hall, William Hall, Jonathan Hallam, Courtney Hamilton, Lila Hamilton, Sarah Hamilton, Duncan Hammond, Stuart Hammond, Sharif Hamza, Geoffrey Han, Flora Hanitijo, Jay Hanna, Matt Hanson, Christina Hardy, Matt Harlock, John Harris Dunning, Greg Harris, Paul Harris, Chris Hatherill, Hayley Hatton, Michael Hauptman, Laura Havlin, Sarah Hay, Martha Hayes, Matthew Hayman, Will Hayward, Kate Hazell, Claire Healy, Shona Heath, Stefan Heinrichs, Fabian Heisig, Desiree Heiss, Oliver Helbig, David Hellqvist, Frederike Helwig, Nathan Henry, Paul Herbst, Tony Hero, Hannes Hetta, Julia Hetta, Ruth Hickman, Adam Higginbotham, Barbara Hilton-Staun, Tatsuo Hino, Sasha Hirschfeld, Phil Hoad, Georgie Hobbs, Jaimie Hodgson, Axel Hoedt, Ruth Hogben, Guy Holden, Michael Holden, Matt Holyoak, Holger Homann, Alicia Hood, Emma Hope Allwood, Bethany Hopper, Helena Horton, Amy Hoskins, Saorla Houston, James Howard Kunstler, Bella Howard, Kim Howells, Nick Howells, David Hughes, Caitlin Hume, Philipp Humm, Jessica Hundley, Hannah Hunter, Tabya Hussain, Jack Hutchinson, Kate Hutchinson, Carys Huws, Wendy Ide, Tony Irvine, Matt Irwin, Guy Isherwood, Ioana Ivan, Tom J Newell, Simon Jablonski, Dan Jackson, Daniel Jackson, Sacha Jackson, Sophie Jackson, Christopher James, Clive James, David James, Emily James, Jesse Jarnow, Drew Jarrett, Antoine Jarrier, Ewa Jedrzejczyk, Heather Jemetta, Emma Johnson, Leigh Johnson, Rashid Johnson, Charlie Jones, Claire Jones, Kim Jones, Matt Jones, Geetha Joseph, Paul Joseph, Jason Jules, Sebastian Junger, Lauren Juska, Martin Justesen, Jacob K, Peter Kaaden, Hannah Kadah, Rasha Kahil, Nell Kalonji, Barry Kamen, Jonny Kanagasoorium, Ashleigh Kane, Mattias Karlsson, Tom Kavanagh, Bruna Kazinoti, Mark Kean, Ben Keegan, Liam Kelly, John Kennedy, Olga Kenny, Leo Kent, Jesi Khadavi, Imran Khan, Jason Kibbler, Luke Kiley Jules Kim, Sandy Kim, Andrew King, Luke Kirwan, Alexey Kiselef, Jói Kjartans, Immo Klink, Marcela Klitzke, Sam Knapp, Gemma Knox, Pedro Koechlin, Rachel Korine, Mikel Koven, Hans Kristian Riise, Fabien Kruszelnicki, Johan Kugelberg, Johanna Lacey, Hannah Lack, Jessica Lack, Caroline Lambie, Dean Landley, Karen Langley, Andreas Larsson, Kris Latocha, Cynthia Lawrence-John, Kristen Lazaric, Anna Leach, Ronny Leach, Serge Leblon, Suzie Lechtenberg, Stephen Ledger-Lomas, Sanghee Lee, Sehoon Lee, Jonathan Leggett, Jan Lehner, Marcel Lelienhof, Youri Lenquette, Jean-François Lepage, Nick Levine, Danielle Levitt, Rory Lewarne, Rebecca Lewis, Hanna Liden, Jeremy Liebman, Ture Lillegraven, James Lin, Hugh Lippe, Chloe Little, Brett Lloyd, Isaac Lock, Christopher Lockwood, Elaine Lodge, Katy Louis, Phoebe Lovatt, Chico Lowndes, Andrew Lowry, Rebecca Lowthorpe, Lydia Lunch, Andreas Lux, Michael Lves, Sarah Lynch, Emma Lyon, Siska Lyssens, Kyp Lyttleton, Thanh Ma, Christian MacDonald, Cosmo Macdonald, Marc Macdonald, Richard MacFarlane, Alasdair MacGregor, Usha Machado, Fiona Mackay, Carmen MacKenzie, Ella MacKinnon, Susanne Madsen, Fanny Maduchere, Natasha Maidment, Peghah Maleknejad, Harry Malt, Marcus Mam, Carlotta Manaigo, David Manders, Eva Manticova, Alex Marashian, Jacqueline Marcus, Lucy Maria Wren, Marlene Marino, Leon Mark, Tim Marlow, Amanda Marsalis, Annie Marsh, Clancy Martin, Colin Martin, Eddy Martin, Rob Mathieson, Camilla Mathis, Zoe Maughan, Anthony Maule, Lilli Maunuula, Katja Mayer, Sebastian Mayer, Dean Mayo Davies, Ginny McAllister, Simon McAuslane, Craig McCarthy, Jamie McCartney, John McCarty, Gareth McConnell, Callum McCullough, Glynnis McDaris, John McFarlane, Callum McGeoch, Ryan McGinley, Leila McGlew, Paul McGuinness, Salma McHugh, Noel McLaughlin, Alasdair McLellan, Swax McIver, Bryan McMahon, Alexander McQueen, Anna McQueen, James Meek, Kieran Meeke, Shannon Mendes, Kati Mennett, Natasha Meradji, Siouxzi Mernagh, James Merry, China Miéville, Yusuke Miyagawa, Ali Mobasser, Brian Molloy, Stephen Monaghan, Kate Monro, Matteo Montanari, Graeme Montgomery, Paul Moody, Sara Moonves, Chad Moore, Zoe More O'Ferrall, Eleanor Morgan, Jon Morgan, Adrian Morris, Becki Morris, Octavia Morris, Shawn Mortensen, Hannah Moth, Benjamin Moulder, Joe Muggs, Al Mulhall, Matthew Mumford, Jamie Munton, Aaro Murphy, Thom Murphy, Samantha Murray-Greenway, David Mushegain, Owen Myers, Fumi Nagasaka, Tempe Nakiska, Mauricio Nardi, Alex Needham, Huw Nesbitt, Tom Newell, Rachel Newsome, Rebecca Nicholson, Tessa Nicholson, Tracey Nicholson, Stefan Nickum, Brigitte Nicole Grice, Sarah Nicole Prickett, Jennifer Nies, Tim Noakes, Jason Nocito, Simon Norfolk, Jérémie Nuel, A.J. Numan, Cristina Nunziata, Yousif Nur, Lee Nutland, Gerry O' Kane, Glenn O'Brien, Niall O'Brien, Deirdre O'Callaghan, Sean O'Hagan, Daniel O'Kane, Sam O'Shaughnessy, Tara O'Shea, Artour Ogannissian, Nathalie Olah, Alexandra Olenska, Josh Olins, William Oliver, Gary Ombler, Harriet Orman, Max Ortega Govela, David Ortega, Joseph Ortenzi, Karen Orton, Melissa Osborne, Takao Oshima, Lucas Ossendrijver, Michael Otero, Mel Ottenberg, Briar Pacey, Fergus Padel, Greg Palast, Shelley Palmer, Laura Pannack, Rémi Paringaux, Eloise Parry, Jenny Pashkova, Laurence Passera, Hetal Patel, Emma Paterson, Pani Paul, Salam Pax, Mark Paytress, Harry Pearce, James Pearson-Howes, Bjørnar Pedersen, Ashley Pegg, Russel Pegrum, Ananda Pellerin, Jenna Pelletier, Jonas Pelli, Jorge Peniche, Laurie Penny, Ben Perdue, Rafael Perez Evans, Thomas Persson, Daren Peter Ellis, Celia Peterson, Soula Petrou, Elizabeth Peyton, Walter Pfeiffer, Hardeep Phull, Sarah Piantadosi, Jack Pierson, Jason Pietra, Mark Pillai, Daniel Pinchbeck, Greta Pistaceci, Alexandra Plesner, Katharina Poblotzki, Avan Podhajsky, Fritz Polzer, Amy Poole, Jose Porroche, Charlie Post, Geraldine Postel, Alex Poulson, Gareth Powell, Pietro Pravettoni, Markus Prizti, Caroline Prothero, Leonie Purchas, Sue-Wen Q, Myles Quin, Natalia Rachlin, Errol Rainey, Lee Ramsay, Martina Randles, Atlanta Rascher, Mazdak Rassi, Jo Ratcliffe, Philip Ratcliffe, Becky Rawlinson, Alex Rayner, Ben Rayner, Peter Rayner, Ben Reardon, Monica Rebella, Shawn Records, Jeremy Reed, Simon Renaud, David Renshaw, Marcia Resnick, Simon Reynolds, Helen Rhodes, Owen Richards,Claire Richardson, Calum Richardson, John Richardson, Rickie Richardson, Tim Richardson, Mischa Richter, Charlotte Rickwood, Ola Rindal, Alex Ritman, Olivier Rizzo, Scott Robert Clark, Charlie Robin Jones, Simon Robins, Miranda Robson, Wendy Roby, Robi Rodriguez, Nancy Rohde, Shari Roman, Michael Rook, Ana Rosado, Claudia Rose Shaw, Alex Rose, Dan Ross, Millie Ross, Tom Roswell, Paolo Roversi, Lucyann Rowbotham, Sian Rowe, Mary Rozzi, Vanessa Rubio, Laura Rule, Stephanie Rushton, Susie Rushton, Jo Russell, Mat Ryalls, Caroline Ryder, Christopher Sabin, Karim Sadli, Joanna Sadowska, Nick Sagan, Alex Sainsbury, Jean-Robert Saintil, Sadia Salam, Limara Salt, Steve Salter,Francisco Salvador Weiss, Patrik Sandberg, Neil Sankey, Daniel Sannwald, Johnny Sapong, Mari Sarai, Lise Sarfati, Viviane Sassen, Jon Savage, Steven Savigear, Simon Savory, Ruth Saxelby, Maurice Scheltens, Joanna Schlenzka, Michael Schmelling, Letty Schmiterlow, Christian Schoeler, Norbert Schoerner, Ben Schofield, Collier Schorr, Aaron Schuman, Niels Schumm, Bjorn Schutrumpf, Laura Sciacovelli, Karley Sciortino, Kate Sclater, Cath Scott, Ellis Scott, Emily Scott, Venetia Scott, Mark Segal, Todd Selby, Milena Selkirk, Luke Seomore, Tommy Seres, Johnnie Shand Kydd, Payam Sharifi, Alix Sharkey, Noah Shelley, David Sherry, Skye Sherwin, Sarah Shillaker, Katie Shillingford, Akiko Shishido, Luke Shumard, Saga Sigurðardóttir, Maurits Sillem, Christopher Silvester, Christopher Simmonds, Tabitha Simmons, Alessandro Simonetti, Leigh Singer, Nina Singer, Bridgitte Sire, Dominique Sisley, Petek Sketcher, Thomas Skou Nielsen, Jenny Slapper, Natasha Slee, Olena Slyesarenko, Andrew Smith, Mark Smith, Natalie Smith, Nicholas Smith, Raven Smith, Rupert Smyth, Wendy Smyth, Ravi Somaiya, Stuart Spalding, Gregory Spencer, Robbie Spencer, Luke Spice, Andrea Spotorno, Katherine Squier, David St. John-James, Valerie Stahl von Stromberg, Carl Stanley, Rod Stanley, Ted Stansfield, Chrysanne Stathacos, Ana Steiner, Joanna Stella-Sawicka, Brad Stevens, Jack Stevenson, Bronia Stewart, Peter Stitson, Charlotte Stockdale, Samuel Strang, Joe Stretch, Chris Sullivan, Sølve Sundsbø, Paolo Sutch, Peter Sutherland, Abigail Sutton, Emma Sutton, Sergei Sviatchenko, Lee Swillingham, Hayden Syers, William T. Vollmann, Danna Takako Hawley, Edward Tang, Nobuko Tannawa, Roger Tatley, Roberto Tatti, Adam Taylor, Nik Taylor, Sam Taylor, Trey Taylor, Sam Taylor-Johnson, Maria Tedemalm, Terence Teh, Esther Teichmann, Alex Teighi-Walker, Tom Teodorczuk, Matthew Thibault, Tai Thittichai, Errol Thomas, Henry Thomas, Paul Thomas, Henrietta Thompson, Melissa Thompson, Sam Thorne, Paul Tierney, Karen Tillotson, Andrew Tingle, Dan Tobin Smith, Gail Tolley, Clarke Tolton, Ben Toms, Kevin Trageser, Scott Treleaven, Anna Trevelyan, Scott Trindle, Toby Triumph, Amy Troost, Jonny Trunk, Zing Tseng, Terry Tsiolis, Lilya Turki, Chadwick Tyler, Tyler Udall, Körner Union, Magnus Unnar, Va Va Ribeiro, Mika Vaajoki, Mathias Vagni, Carla Valdivia, Benni Valsson, Vincent van de Wijngaard, Willy Vanderperre, Hannah Vasdekys, Eva Vermandel, Francesso Vezzoli, Joanna Vieira, Marco Villalobos, Javier Villegas, Kate Villevoye, Thomas Viney, Jennifer Vineyard, Issy Virden, Natasha Vita-More, Mariano Vivanco, Pete Voelker, India Volkers, Lotta Volkova, Sam Voltage, Ellen von Unwerth, Jan von Holleben, Steven von Shultzler, Billy Vong, Matthias Vriens, Calum Waddell, Joseph Wade, Alexander Wagner, Bruce Wagner, Genevieve Waites, Olivia Wakefield, Danielle Waldman, Glenn Waldron, Ben Walker, Florence Walker, Harriet Walker, Gary Wallis, Corey Walters, Rachel Ward, Gary Warnett, Rachel Warrilow, Lucy Warwick, Nadya Wasylko, Nancy Waters, Albert Watson, Gavin Weale, Adrian Webb, Gwen Webber, Sophie Wedgewood, Indigo Weeks, Kirsti Weir, Tamsin Weir, Markus Weisbeck, Adam Welch, Hannah Welling, Bruno Werzinski, James West, Will Westall, Stevie Westgarth, Paul Wetherell, Stephen Whelan, Ed White, Logan White, Lucy White, Stephen White, Stuart White, Chris Wiegand, Moses Wiener, James Wignall, Abi Williams, Greg Williams, Adam Winder, Nicky Wise, Rosamund Witcher, Zoë Wolff, Haley Wollens, Courtney Wong, Flora Wong, Kin Woo, Suzy Wood, Joshua Woodford, Matthew Woodson, Daisy Woodward, Matthew Worthington, Magda Wosinska, Ianthe Wright, Stuart Wright, Tish Wrigley, Agata Wycichowska, Emma Wyman, Junsuke Yamasaki, Yoonjung Yang, Phillipe & Césarie Yard, Kieran Yates, Panos Yiapanis, Mayuko Yoshida, Victoria Young, Lin Yung-Chieh, Kai Z Feng, Corina Zappia, Xixi Zheng, Sonia Zhuravlyova, Philip Zimbardo, Slavoj Žižek.

Credits

All slogan posters artwork devised by Jefferson Hack and Ferdinando Verderi

All re-shot magazines photographed by David Abrahams at MBK London Ltd

Typeface designer: Isar Display by Chi-Long Trieu

Cover design by Ferdinando Verderi

p21 **TILDA SWINTON: STATES OF BEING** Tilda Swinton in *Dazed & Confused*, Volume II, Issue 85, 2010, Photography by: Glen Luchford / *Courtesy Art Partner,* Styling by: Katy England, Creative Direction by: Jerry Stafford, Hair by: Sam McKnight, Make-up by: Lisa Houghton at Jed Root, Nails by: Nicola Joss at Premier, Prop Styling by: Michael Howell, Lighting Technician: Jack Webb, Photographic Assistant: Jared Price, Styling Assistants: Ellie Cumming, Louise Hall-Strutt, Max Ortega, Tailoring by: Sarah Giubilini

CHAPTER ONE

p37 **DAZED & CONFUSED ISSUE ONE** *Dazed & Confused,* Volume I, Issue I, 1990 • p41 **FOAM** Foam Fotografiemuseum, *What's Next? The Future of Photography* exhibition, Amsterdam, 2011, Curated by: Jefferson Hack, Alison Nordström, Erik Kessels, and Lauren Cornell, Photography by: Christian van der Kooy • p47 **THOM YORKE** Thom Yorke in *Dazed & Confused*, Volume I, Issue 19, 1995, Photography by: Rankin • p55 **FELDMAN** *AnOther Magazine*, Issue 16, 2009, Questions: Hans-Ulrich Obrist, Answers: Hans-Peter Feldman © DACS 2015 • p63 **NOWNESS** Quentin Jones, *Paint Test No. 1*, NOWNESS, 2012, Artwork and Direction by: Quentin Jones, Photography by: Alex Franco, Music and Sound Design by: William Skeaping, Animation Assistance: Kamila Maslowska | Jacob Sutton, *L.E.D Surfer*, NOWNESS, 2012, Directed by: Jacob Sutton, Snowboarder: Will Hughes, Executive Producer: Grace Holbrook, On Set Producer: Katrina More-Molyneux, Focus Puller: Warren Buckingham, Snowboarding Camera Operator: James Sweet, Second Camera Operator: Mike McDuffie, DIT: Mike McDuffie, Set Design and SFX by: Flatcat Consultancies and Jake Sutton, Offline Editor: Julian Fletcher, Colour Grade and Frame Work by: Rushes, Music Composition by: Shervin Shaeri at Mutant Jukebox | Matthew Donaldson, *Getting There*, NOWNESS, 2014. Directed by: Matthew Donaldson, Music Performed by: Yohji Yamamoto, Edited by: Alice Fisher, Journalist: Shiraz Randeria, Director of Photography: Koho Katake, Camera Assistant: Aito Kodama, Sound Recording by: Takashi Kaneko at SC Alliance, Driver: Toshio Isaki | Saam Farahmand, *Les Fleurs*, NOWNESS, 2014, Directed by: Saam Farahmand, Starring: Kirsty McQuade at Storm Models, Laura Holmes Production, Rogue Films, Executive Producer: Laura Holmes, Producer: Shion Hayasaka, Visual Effects: Absolute Post and Blind Pig, "Les Fleurs" performed by Minnie Riperton / *Courtesy of Capitol Records Inc. , Under license from Universal Music Operations Ltd,* Sound Design by: Deewee for Studio Deewee, Lighting Cameraman: Tom Townend, Edited by: Tom Lindsay, Production Designer: Marie Lanna, Hair by: Karin Bigler, Make-up by: Niamh Quinn, Nails by: Michelle Humphrey at LMC Worldwide | Ben Murphy, *Mishkin's: Salt Beef and Sours*, NOWNESS, 2011, Photography by: Ben Murphy | Albert Moya, *Trees Company: Cotubín*, NOWNESS, 2014, Directed by: Albert Moya, Producer: Emi Fort, Director of Photography: Claudia Mallart, Music by: Elsa de Alfonso, Editor and Colourist: Octavio Roes, Sound Design by: Marc Bech, Production Assistant: Cristina Moreno, Camera Assistant: Leo Calzoni, Title Credits by: Atlas | Linda Brownlee, *Edie Campbell: In the Arena*, NOWNESS, Directed by: Linda Brownlee, Edit and Grade by: Dave Slade, Audio Mix and Sound Design by: Fonic, Titles by: Ciara Leaf Meaney, Interview Conducted by: Rebecca Guinness • p67 **MANTRA** Joaquin Phoenix in *Another Man*, Issue 1, 2005, Photography by: Craig McDean / *Courtesy Art + Commerce,* Styling by: Beat Bolliger, Grooming by: Catherine Furniss, Photographic Assistants: Andrew Eliot, Sebastian Lucrecio and Huan Nguyen, Styling Assistant: Alex Slavycz, Printing by: Pascal Dangin for Box Ltd

CHAPTER TWO

p75 **DOLLAR BILL** *AnOther Magazine*, Issue 4, 2003, Curated by: Mark Sanders, Emma Reeves and Neville Wakefield, Artwork by: Dario Robleto, Bill Saylor, Jim Shaw, Chris Johanson, Richard Louderback, Banks Violette / *Courtesy: Maureen Paley, London,* Brian Degraw, Brad Kahlhamer, Tara Donovan / *Courtesy Pace Gallery,* Tom Friedman, Hanna von Goeler, Christopher Taggart, Jason Rhoades / *The Estate of Jason Rhoades / Courtesy Hauser & Wirth and David Zwirner, New York / London.* José Parlá, Peter Coffin, John Baldessari, Jason Meadows, KAWS, Carrie Moyer, Jeremy Blake, Meg Cranston, T. Kelly Mason, Barry McGee / *Courtesy of the artist and Ratio 3, San Francisco. With thanks to: Ace Gallery (LA), Acme (LA), Casey Kaplan (NYC), China Arts Objects (LA), Deitch Projects (NYC) , Feature Inc (NYC), Marc Foxx Gallery (LA), The Happy Lion (LA), Nicole Klagsbrun Gallery (NYC), Leo Koenig inc (NYC), Andrew Kreps Gallery (NYC), Modern Art Inc (London), Regen Projects (LA), Team Gallery (NYC), Emily Tsingou Gallery (London), Works on paper (LA), David Zwirner (NYC).* • p85 **CORINNE DAY** *Dazed & Confused*, Volume I, Issue 34, 1997, Photography by: Corinne Day / *Courtesy Trunk Archive* • p91 **NATURAL BEAUTY** Lernert & Sander, *Natural Beauty*, NOWNESS, 2011, Directed by: Lernert & Sander, Starring: Hannelore Knuts, Produced by: Blinkart, Make-up and Consultancy: Ferry van der Nat at Unit c.m.a, Assistant: Vanessa Chan at House of Orange, All Make-up by: Ellis Faas Cosmetics, Director of Photography: Ram van Meel at Umsjatka, Edited by: Mathijs Kok, Music by: All Shall Be Well, Set Dressers: Hadewieg & Egbert Steenwinkel, Assistant: Derek van Egmond, Producer: Jennifer Byrne, Post Production: Condor Brussel • p95 **THE DIGITAL EDITION** Rihanna in *AnOther Magazine,* Volume II, Issue 1, 2015, Film and Photography by: Inez van Lamsweerde & Vinnodh Matadin / *Courtesy Trunk Archive,* Promotional Film Stills by: George Harvey, Styling by: Katy England, Hair by: Peter Gray at Home Agency, Make-up by: Yadim at Art Partner, Creative, Movement Director: Stephen Galloway, Nails by: Maria Salandra for Gelish, Photographic Assistant: Joe Hume, Digital Tech: Brian Anderson, Lighting by: Jodokus Driessen, Styling Assistants: James Campbell, David Casavant, Cristina Firpo, Alex Beattie, Hair Assistant: Takayuki Shibata, Make-up Assistant: Kanako Takase, Production by: The Collective Shift, Soundtrack by: John Gosling, Fashion: Alexander McQueen, Technology by: Liam Casey / PCH International, Dimensions: 30mm x 230mm x 300mm

CHAPTER THREE

p103 **SCARLETT JOHANSSON**   Scarlett Johansson in *AnOther Magazine*, Issue 15, 2008, Photography by: Craig McDean / *Courtesy Art+Commerce*, Text by: A.M. Homes / *AnOther Magazine interview with Scarlett, Johannson by AM Homes. Copyright © AM Homes, 2008, used by permission of The Wylie Agency (UK) Limited,* Styling by: Tabitha Simmons, Hair by: Oribe For Oribe Hair Care, Make-Up by: Lucia Pieroni for Clé De Peau Beauté, Set Design by: Piers Hanmer, Photographic Assistants: Chris Ferretti, Huan Duong Nguyen, Teppei Maruoka, and Quinton Jones, Styling Assistants: Tracey Nicholson and Gabriel Balestra, Hair assistant: Judy Erickson, Make-up assistant: Enrique de La Paz, Set Design Assistants: Andy Myers and Karle Francke, Nails by: Myrdith Leon McCormack at Pure Management, Casting by: Starworks, Production by: Katie Collings-Post at North Six   •   p111 **NICK WAPLINGTON** *Safety in Numbers*, Booth-Clibborn Editions, 2002 | *Nothing*, 1999, Directed by: Nick Waplington, Producer: Jefferson Hack, Original Music Compilation by: Orbital, Online Editor: Marc Eskenazi, Dubbing Mixer: Bob Jackson, Camera: Nick Waplington & Nick Clegg, Production Manager: Seb Grant, Edited by: David Richards, An Illuminations Production for BBC Television in association with Dazed TV, 1999 © *BBC, MCMXCIX*   •   p117 **KM3D-1**   Kate Moss in *KM3D-1*, 2011, Directed by: Baillie Walsh, Director of Photography: John Mathieson, Creative Direction by: Jerry Stafford, Styling by: Alister Mackie, Hair by: Sam McKnight, Make-up by: Petros Petrohilos, Produced by: Première Heure, Paris, Paris Production by: Première Heure, Producer: Patrice Haddad, Executive Producer: Jerome Ruchi, London, Production by: Gainsbury and Whiting, Executive Producer: Sam Gainsbury, Producer: Stefania Farah, Production: Kat Davey, Visual Effects Supervisor: Sylvery Bolotte, James Senade, Production Designer: Alan MacDonald, Art Directed: Patrick Rolfe, Construction Manager: Dan Crandon, Carpenter: Dan Marsden, Nails by: Marian Newman, Stylist Assistant: Ellie Cumming, Hair Stylist Assistant: Koji, Make-up Assistant: Sofia Bermudez, Seamstress: Caroline Thorpe, Post Production Executive: Louis Arcelin, Post Producers: Jean Marc Raygade, Bastien Harispe, Edited by: Mario Battistel, Lead Flame Artist: James Senade, Flame Artist: Damien Peiro, Lead CGI Artist: Sylvery Bolotte, CGI Artists: Thomas Lefevre, François Xavier Broussard. Technical Support: Sylvain Canaux, Post Production Coordinator: Rachel Hue, Production by: Department Video PH, Sound Design by: Sylvain Rety, Sound Production by: Schmooze / Mathieu Sibony, Credit Design by: Francisco Salvado, Focus Puller: Keith MacNamara, Grip: Paul Hatchman, Phantom Technician: Michael Gans, 3D Stereographer: Melissa Byers, 3D Rig Technician: Gavin Overstall, 3D Playback Operator: Simon Hargreaves, 3D Post Production Consultant: Angus Cameron, 3D Production Coordinator: Richard Shepper, Camera Assistance: Jaime Feliu, Ross MacNamara, Rigger: Micky Seymour, Gaffer: Alan Martin, Electrician: Dave Moore, Electrician: James Nesbitt, Special Effects Supervisor: Neal Champion, Runners: Harry Flinder, Susie Mashford, Charlie Mather, Location: Park Royal Studios London   •   p121 **SX70**   Jefferson Hack's mix CD *SX70*, released in collaboration with Colette, 2011, Featuring: Junip, Marianne Faithfull, Boys Noize, Erol Alkan, and Bauhaus, Creative Direction, Art Direction, Design, Photography and Illustration by M/M (Paris), 2011   •   p125 **MAKING IT UP AS WE GO ALONG** Somerset House, *20 Years of Dazed & Confused Magazine: Making It Up As We Go Along* exhibition, London, 2011, Exhibition Images by: Rankin Studio, Curated by: Jefferson Hack and Emma Reeves, Creative Direction by: Jack Flanagan, Produced by: Genevieve Waites, Production Assistants: Felicity Shaw and Daniel O'Kane, Design by: James West and Carla Valdivia, Marketing and Events Coordination by: Abby Bennett and Johanna Lacey, Thanks to: A.Bliss Mounting, Myles Ashby at Art+Commerce, Daniel Brown at Play-Create Ltd, Nathalie Burgun at Juergen Teller, Natalia Christina, Stephen Doherty, Gwyn Miles, Christopher Mills and Jonathan Powell at Somerset House, Paula Ekenger at Sølve Sundsbø Ltd, Ruby Gaba at Box Studios, Katherine Gardner at Mr Reason and Mr Squalor, Nick and Charlotte Knight, Sophie Liardet at Rizzoli, Josh Love at Devise London, All at Rankin photography, Josephine Rodrigues, Georg Ruffles, Mark Sanders, Louise Stern at Sam Taylor-Wood, Fanni Szokoli at Management Artists, Dionne Thornton at Jed Root, Jan Trädgårdh at Förstoringsateljén, Rainer Usselmann at Happy Finish, The White Wall Company | Yves Saint Laurent in *Dazed & Confused*, Volume I, Issue 63, 2000, Photography by: Juergen Teller / *Courtesy clm* | Kristen Stewart in *Dazed & Confused*, Volume II, Issue 77 / 2009, Photography by: David Benjamin Sherry | *Dazed & Confused*, Volume I, Issue 7, 1994, Photography by: Rankin

CHAPTER FOUR

p135 **U2 SONGS OF INNOCENCE**   U2, *Songs of Innocence*, 2014, Creative Direction: Jefferson Hack, Album Cover Photography by: Glen Luchford / *Courtesy Art Partner*, Production: MAD Agency, London   •   p139 **SKATEISTAN**   *Skateistan*, in collaboration with Diesel New Voices for *Dazeddigital.com*, 2010, Filmed on location in Kabul, Afganistan, January 2010, Produced and Directed by: Orlando von Einsiedel, Producer: Louis Figgis, Executive Producers: Rod Stanley, Robert Montgomery, Thanh Ma, Executive Producers for Grain Media: Jon Drever, Orlando Von Einsiedel, Original Music: Patrick Jonsson, Hiatus, Director of Photography: Franklin Dow, Film Editor: Peta Ridley, Telecine Supervisors: Nigel Horn, Russell Rowe, Telecine Facility: iLab, Colourists: Ben Rogers, Peta Ridley, Grade Facility: Glassworks, Graphic Design: Damien Attenborough, Audio Mix: Patrick Jonsson / Ignition Studios, Production Coordinator: Amelia Franklin, Researchers: Tom Dearden, Patrick Vernon, For Partizan Films: Jordan McGarry, Translators: Wallid Azizi, Mariam Azizi, Fixers: Shams Razi, Mirwais Mohsen, Ahmad Razi, Camera Equipment: SLV, Lens Hire: Ice, Music: "All Things To all Men" Composed by: Barry / Leigh / France / Swinscoe / Smith, Performed by: The Cinematic Orchestra, Published by: Just Isn't Music / *Courtesy Ninja Tunes / Chrysalis / Warner Chappell © Diesel New Voices*, 2009   •   p143 **STUDIO AFRICA**   Diesel+Edun Studio Africa Spring / Summer Campaign, 2013, Diesel+Edun Studio Africa Behind the Scenes Photography by: Jasper Clarke, Creative Direction by: Jefferson Hack, Art Direction by: Sara Hemming at DJA, Campaign Photography by: Alasdair McLellan, Cast: Sy Alassane, Flaviana Matata, Uviwe Mangweni, Baloji, Yannick Illunga, I See A Different You, Tanya Mushayi, Adbellah Taia, Laurence Chauvin Buthaud, Production: MAD Agency, London | *Dazed & Confused*, The South Africa Issue, Volume II, Issue 15, 2004, Photography by: Rankin   •   p147 **BARBARA KRUGER / DAMIEN HIRST** *Dazed & Confused*, The Freedom Issue: Know Your Rights, Volume II, Issue 39, 2006, Artwork: Barbara Kruger; Damien Hirst, designed by Jason Beard   •   p151 **PATTI SMITH** Patti Smith in *AnOther Magazine*, Issue 10, 2006, Photography by: Melodie McDaniel / *Courtesy Trunk Archive,* Polaroid Photography by: Patti Smith, Text by: Jefferson Hack , Handwriting excerpt from Patti Smith's notebook   •   p159 **PROJECT RED**   *Dazed & Confused*, Volume II, Issue 36, 2006 | INSPI(RED), Photography by: David Sims | BA(RED), Artwork by: Peter Blake | (RED)EMPTION, Photography by: Yelena Yemchuk | RESTO(RED), Photography by: Martina Hoogland Ivanow | (RED) ECORATE, Photography by: Laurence Passera | EMPOWE(RED), Photography by: Rankin | RETI(RED), Photography by: William Selden | SCO(RED), Photography by: Gillian Wearing | COVE(RED), Photography by: Jenny van Sommers | IGNO(RED), Photography by: Ola Bergengren | SO TI(RED), Photography by: Ed Templeton | (RED)UCED, Photography by: Nadav Kander / *Courtesy Trunk Archive* | AMI(RED), Photography by: Richard Bush | FI(RED), Photography by: Terry Richardson / *Courtesy Art Partner* | PINK AND (RED), Artwork by: Barry McGee / *Courtesy Stuart Shave / Modern Art, LLP, London* | INC(RED)IBLE, Photography by: Horst Diekgerdes

CHAPTER FIVE

p169 **AI WEIWEI**   Ai Weiwei in *AnOther Magazine*, Issue 24, 2013, Photography by: Jamie Hawkesworth / *Courtesy M.A.P*, Text by: Jefferson Hack   •   p179 **BARBARA KRUGER**   Artwork by: Barbara Kruger, *Dazed & Confused*, Volume I, Issue 21, 1996   •   p185 **DAZED VS. WARHOL**   Baltic Gallery, *Dazed Vs. Warhol* exhibition, Newcastle, 2007, Curated by: *Dazed & Confused* and Jerome Sans, Featuring Artwork by: David Fryer, Cyprien Gaillard, Trevor Jackson, The Kills, M+M (Paris), Miltos Manetas, Robert Montgomery, Gareth Pugh, Rankin, Rafaël Rozendaal, Peter Stitson, Henry Holland and Matthew Stone | Artwork by Matthew Stone, *Reaching the Mountaintop*, 2007 | Photography by: Matthew Stone   •   p189 **MOVEMENT**   Designer: Prada, Choreographers: Dancers of Tanztheater Wuppertal, Director: Kevin Frillet, Photography by: Albrecht Fuchs | Designer: Iris Van Herpen, Choreographer: Russell Maliphant, Directors: Warren Du Preez & Nick Thornton Jones, Photography by: Rory van Millingen | Designer: Calvin Klein Collection, Choreographer: Jonah Bokaer, Dancer: Julie Kent, Director: Daniel Arsham, Photography by: Hart + Lëshkina | Designer: Gareth Pugh, Choreographer: Wayne McGregor, Director: Ruth Hogben, Photography by: Timo Wirsching | Designer: Alexander McQueen, Choreographer and Dancer: Marie-Agnes Gillot, Director: Daniel Askill, Photography by: Sam Rock | Designer: Chalayan, Choreographers: Aya Sato and Ryan Heffington, Director and Photography by: Jacob Sutton | Designer: Stephen Jones Millinery, Choreographer: Jasmin Vardimon, Director: Matthew Donaldson, Photography by: Lena Emery   •   p193 **DRESS ART**   Dress Art, *AnOther Magazine*, Issue 12, 2006 | Designer: Bernhard Willhelm, Artist: Olaf Breuning, Materials: Vinyl flooring, Model: Lucie Marzin, Marie Valot and Devin Blair | Designer: Dolce & Gabbana, Artist: Ahn Duong, Materials: Silk faille, cotton tulle, duchesse satin, black satin, velvet ribbons, black chantilly lace., Model: Ahn Doung | Designer: Christopher Bailey, Artist: Annie Morris, Materials: Silk faille and 25,000 British clothes pegs, Model: Anouck Lepère at IMG | Designer: Stella McCartney, Artist: Jeff Koons, Materials: Metallic cotton satin, platinum chain, white gold rabbits, Model: Jessica Stam at IMG | Designer: Sophia Kokosalaki, Artist: John Isaacs, Materials: Silk organza, steel, plaster, electric light fitting, shoes by Sophia Kokosalaki, Model: Bette Franke at Viva | Designer: Maison Martin Margiela, Artist: Gotscho, Materials: Stockman, silk satin, leather shoes | Designer: Francisco Costa for Calvin Klein Collection, Artist: Ghada Amer, Materials: Lace, Model: Missy Rayder at DNA | Designer: Jean-Charles de Castelbajac, Artist:

Meredyth Sparks, Materials: 100% silk with glitter and photographic work by the artist, Model: Irina at Marilyn | Designer: Ann-Sofie Back, Artist: Annika Von Hausswolff, Materials: Black sheer elastic, Model: James | Designer: Rifat Ozbek for Pollini, Artist: Manfredi Beninati, Materials: Ink, acrylic gesso, tic tacs, cotton thread, Model: Stella Schnabel | Designer: Agnès B, Artist: Ryan McGinness, Materials: Acrylic on cotton fabric, Models: Zuzana at Karin and Darla at Marilyn | Designer: Rick Owens, Artist: Ian Kaier, Materials: Muslin, watercolour paints, paper, Model: Maria at Women | Designer: Giles Deacon, Artist: Simon Periton, Materials: Anodised aluminium, wicker cane, plastic, nylon, cardboard, hessian, polythene, bamboo, mylar, felt, steel, brass, acetate, shellac, paint, calico, gloss paint, poster paint, emulsion, plastic, Model: Jess | Designer: Riccardo Tisci, Artist: Paolo Canevari, Materials: Rubber from inner tube, Model: Leandro Cerezo | Designer: Issey Miyake by Naomi Takizawa, Artist: Yoshitomo Nara, Materials: Paper, Model: Brea at Ford | Photography by: Richard Burbridge / *Courtesy Art+Commerce,* Text by: Penny Martin, Curated and produced by: Emma Reeves, Photographic Assistants: Amy Troost, Tim Zargoza, and Jerome Hunt, Digital: Christian Hovarth and Nicholas Lemery at DTouch, Retouching by: Pascal Dangin at Box Studios • p197 **FILMS OF INNOCENCE** Artworks created for U2's *Songs of Innocence* album, 2014 | Vhils, *(Raised By Wolves)* | ROA, *Sleep Like a Baby Tonight* | Todd James, *The Troubles* | Chloe Early in collaboration with Robert Francis Muller, *Iris (Hold Me Close)* | D*Face, *California (There Is No End To Love)* | DALeast, *This is Where You Can Reach Me Now* Production: Fly on the Wall | Mode 2, *Song for Someone,* Director: Marcus Lynam, Producer: Hoop-la, Director of Photography: Richard Donnelly, Editor: Hoop-la / Richard Donnelly, Colourist: Eugene McCrystal (EMC), Camera Assistant: Richard Twomey, Animator: Jam Media | Oliver Jeffers, *The Miracle (Of Joey Ramone)* | Robin Rhode, *Every Breaking Wave* | Ganzeer, *(Volcano)* | Maser, *(Cedarwood Road)*, Director: Marcus Lynam Maser, Producer: Hoop-la, Director of Photography: Richard Twomey, Editor: Mick Mahon, MAD Colourist: Gary Curran (EMC), Camera Assistant: Zia Pfeiffer, Production Assistant: Anna Clark, Animator: Scott Wallace (Tomorrow is Closed), Technology: Bit Banger (Pixelstick)

CHAPTER SIX

p205 **ANOTHER MAGAZINE** *AnOther Magazine,* Issue 1, 2001, Photography by: Nick Knight / *Courtesy Trunk Archive,* Styling by: Katy England, Retouched by: Allan Finamore, Models: Zora and Olivier | *AnOther Magazine,* Issue 1, 2001, Photography by: David Sims | *AnOther Magazine,* Issue 1, 2001, Photography by: Nick Knight / *Courtesy Trunk Archive* | *AnOther Magazine,* Issue 1, 2001, Photography by: Mario Sorrenti / *Courtesy Art Partner* | *AnOther Magazine,* Issue 1, 2001, Photography by: Richard Burbridge / *Courtesy Art + Commerce* | *AnOther Magazine,* Issue 1, 2001, Photography by: Alberto Korda • p209 **ANOTHER 13 PERFUME** Le Labo Another 13, produced in collaboration with Le Labo, exclusively stocked in Colette, Paris, launched in 2010, Campaign Photography by: Lina Scheynius, 2010, Artist Interpretation by: Wayne Liu, 2010 • p213 **BLOW UP** Photography by: Rankin • p217 **THE FIRST COVER STAR** Björk in *Dazed & Confused,* Volume I, Issue 16, 1995, Photography by: Rankin, Text by: Jefferson Hack • p223 **DECADE IN STYLE** Decade in Style, *AnOther Magazine,* Issue 17, 2011, Photography by Craig McDean / *Courtesy Art + Commerce* | Kate Moss in John Galliano, Spring/Summer, 2003, Charlotte Gainsbourg in Balenciaga by Nicola Ghesquière, Spring/Summer, 2003, Milla Jovovich in Prada, Autumn / Winter, 2002, Sophia Coppola in Chloé, Autumn/Winter, 2009, Courtney Love in Givenchy Haute Couture by Riccardo Tisci, Spring / Summer 2009, Winona Ryder in Marc Jacobs, Autumn / Winter, 2009, Christina Ricci in Gucci, Autumn / Winter, 2008, Michelle Williams in Louis Vuitton, Spring / Summer, 2007 | Kate Moss and Charlotte Gainsbourg, Styling by: Panos Yiapanis, Hair by: Luigi Murenu for John Frieda, Makeup by: Peter Philips for Chanel, Photographic assistants: Chris Ferretti, Huan Nguyen, Styling assistants: John McCarty, Rich Aybar, Hair assistant: Akki Shirikawa, Makeup assistant: Valérie Joudelat, Nails by: Typhane at Jed Root, Production: Brachfeld | Milla Jovovich and Sofia Coppola, Styling by: Tabitha Simmons, Hair by: Orlando Pita at Art + Commerce, Makeup by: Virginia Young at Streeters NY, Set design by: Piers Hanmer, Photographic assistants: Chris Ferretti, Huan Nguyen, Styling assistants: Tracey Nicholson, Gabriel Balestra, Hair assistant: Christian Miller, Makeup assistant: Kumiko, Nails by: Meg Yamamoto at Susan Price | Winona Ryder, Christina Ricci and Courtney Love, Styling by: Panos Yiapanis, Hair by: David Babaii for David Babaii for WildAid, Makeup by: Diane Kendall at Art + Commerce, Nails by: April Foreman, Set design by: Bill Doig, Photographic assistants: Chris Ferretti and Huan Nguyen, Styling assistants: John McCarty and Serafima Sama, Hair assistant: Adam Campbell, Makeup assistant: Gia Harris, Set design assistant: Jason Kisvarday, Production: Kate Collings-Post at North Six | Michelle Williams, Styling by: Nicola Formichetti, Hair by: Orlando Pita at Art + Commerce, Makeup by: Diane Kendall at Art + Commerce, Nails by: Yuna Park at Streeters NY, Set design by: Piers Hanmer, Photographic assistants: Chris Ferretti and Huan Nguyen, Styling assistant: Emily Eisen, Hair assistant: Christian Miller, Makeup assistant: Karan Franjola | Casting *AnOther Magazine* and Greg Krelenstein / Starworks • p231 **DROP DEAD LETTER CLUB** Photography by: Philip Andelman, Featuring: Jack White, Alison Mosshart, Garance Doré, Philip Andelman, Sarah Andelman, Mike D, Paul Yauch, Dead Fertita, and Jack Lawrence, Location: Ritz Hemmingway Bar, Paris • p235 **CHANEL** Chanel, *31 Rue Cambon,* Autumn / Winter 2011 and Spring / Summer, 2012, Photography by: Richard Burbridge / *Courtesy Art + Commerce,* Katja Rahlwes, and Kacper Kasprzyk • p239 **RAG & BONE** Rag & Bone campaign featuring Michael Pitt and Léa Seydoux, Fall/Winter 2014, Photographer and Director: Glen Luchford / *Courtesy Art Partner,* Creative Direction by: Jefferson Hack, Art Direction by: Sara Hemming, Production by: MAD Agency, London | Kate Moss in Glen Luchford's "Damaged Negatives" series, 1993, *Glen Luchford / Courtesy Art Partner*

CHAPTER SEVEN

p247 **MCQUEEN / BOWIE** Alexander McQueen & David Bowie, *Dazed & Confused,* Issue 26, 1996, David Bowie Portrait, Photography by: Nina Schultz, Alexander McQueen Portrait, Photography by: Ann Ray • p253 **RENEGADE TV** Devised by: Jefferson Hack and Rankin, Aired 17th September 1998, 11.30pm on Channel 4 *Video Portraits,* Directed by: Rankin, Styling by: Miranda Robson, Camera: Adam Rodgers, Sound by: Nick Robertson | *Interview Highlights with Paul Kaye* | *Modern Minimalists,* Directed by: Christopher Walker, Camera: Marcus Birsel, Sound by: Alex Thompson | *Nish,* Directed by: Wiz | *Men Woman Homeless,* Directed by: Big TV, Producer: Cathy Hood, Music by: Artificial | *The End,* Written by: Kathy Burke, Directed by: Joe Wright, Producer: Christopher Simon, Director of Photography: Seamus McGarvey, Production Designer: Eve Stewart, Edited by: Melanie Oliver, Executive Producer: Stephanie Faugier | *Doorstep Challenge,* Directed by: Andy Brewer, Producer: Suzie Morton, Camera: Paul Robinson, Edited by: Sue Moles, *A Brewers Production* | *Fish Tank,* Written by: Irvine Welsh, Directed by: Nick Waplington, Camera: William Churchill | *Dial H.I.S.T.O.R.Y,* Directed by: Johan Grimonprez, Producer: Rony Vissers | *Kill The Day,* Written & Directed by: Lynne Ramsay, Producer: Gavin Emerson, Director of Photography: Alwin Kuchler, Sound by: Cath Patton, Procution Designer: Jane Morton, Edited by: Lucia Zucchetti | *Colin Tries New York,* Created by: Paul Davies & Paul, Sound Design & Music by: Brick, *A Simple Production* | Edited by: Darren Jonusas, Michael Harrowes, Melanie Oliver, Rodney Sims, Dubbing Mixer: Bob Jackson, Sound Design & Music by: Howie B, Graphics by: Form, Production Assistants: Guillaume Ruette, Jessie Economakis, Production Manager: Alison Grade, Assistant Producer: Catherine Peters, Executive Producer: Michael Proudfoot, Produced by: Laura Hastings-Smith, *An Uden Associates / Dazed TV Production for Channel Four © Channel Four Television Corporation MCMXCVII* • p257 **MASQUERADE** *AnOther Magazine,* Issue 2, 2002 | Bernhard Willhelm / Philip Treacy / Vivienne Westwood / Olivier Theyskens / Raf Simons / Hussein Chalayan / Jeremy Scott / Naomi Filmer / A. F. Vandevorst / Alexander McQueen, Photography by: Richard Burbridge / *Courtesy Art + Commerce,* Styling by: Sabina Schreder at Walter Schupfer Management, Coordinated by: Susannah Frankel and Sofia De Romarate, Hair by: Sally Hershberger and Philippe Baligan, Make-Up by: Sergio Corbacho, Models: Anna E, Jana and Olaf at DNA, Danielle Smit at Next, Christina Jacklein, Leanne Knight and YFKE at Elite, Osana at Supreme, Omahyra at Boss, Nadine and Derrick at Karin, Agola, Damian Pierce and Travis Cambern at Ford, Anthony, Diane M and Ryan Curry at IMG, Photographic Assistants: Stefan Kochs and Richard Lee, Casting by: Jennifer Baptista, Retouching by: Scott Norkin at Norkin Digital Art • p261 **GWYNETH PALTROW** Gwyneth Paltrow in *AnOther Magazine,* Issue 5, 2003, Photography by: Mario Sorrenti / *Courtesy Art Partner,* Text by: Jefferson Hack, Styling by: Katy England, Hair by: Recine, Make-Up by: Gucci Westman, Nails by: Yuna Park at Streeters, Photographic Assistants: Lars Beaulieu and Kenny Jossick, Styling Assistant: Mhairi Gibb, Set Designer: Jack Flanagan at Magnet NY, Production by: Steve Sutton, Printing by: Pascal Dangin for Box Ltd • p267 **FASHION-ABLE** Fashion-Able, *Dazed & Confused,* Volume I, Issue 46, Concept by: Alexander McQueen, Photography by: Nick Knight / *Courtesy Trunk Archive,* Styling by: Katy England, Styling Assistant: Rini Kundu, Research and Production: Zoe Bradley, Models: Alison Lapper, Aimee Mullens, Sue Bramley, David Toole, Mat Fraser, Helen McIntosh, Catherine Long, Jo Paul, Make-Up by: Val Garland for Nars, Hair by: Malcolm Edwards for Toni and Guy and Sam McKnight, Nails by: Marian Newman at Amalgamated Talent

p272 **BJÖRK: JUST LIKE A MUSICAL** Björk outtake from *Dazed & Confused,* Volume I, Issue 65, 2000, Photography by: David Sims | The Lymphatic System / *Courtesy Anita Impagliazzo / UVA Health System.* | Left lateral view of Einstein's brain, prior to sectioning / *Courtesy Harvey Collection. Otis Historical Archives. National Museum of Health and Medicine.* | Bismuth Crystal / *Courtesy Ken Keray, www.bismuthcrystal.com*

Slogan Poster Overview

We Can't Do This Alone

Hack The System

Nostalgia Of Now

A Cultural Resistance Movement

Everything, Always, Everywhere, Forever, Now

If You Can't Afford It, Steal It

A Conspiracy of Ideas

Protest Against Indifference

The Best Way To Make Money Is Not To Make Any

Optimism As Cultural Rebellion

Delusions of Grandeur

Don't Read It, Feel It

We Can't Do This Alone

Own Your Own Voice

Ask Unanswered Questions

 Drop Dead Letter Club

 If You Stand For Nothing You Will Fall For Anything

 An Independent State Of Mind

 The Opposte Is Also True

 Caught In The Slipstream Of The Extreme

 Another Point Of Intervention

 Death Of The Cover Star

 Been There Seen It Done It

 100 % Individual

 What Remains Is Future

 Making It Up As We Go Along

Its is designed to reinforce stereotypes

It is closed to those who think differently or who oppose its value systems

Hackers re-route systems

To Hack the system is to pose a threat to its security

Through media intervention in culture

We change perceptions

And offer new routes and possibilities

Hacking is never a short cut

It is not a cheat

It's not a backdoor

It is a thirst for enquiry

A responsibility

To steer the culture

Together

Through continuous, positive

And unparalleled

Generational change.

Hack the system

The system is a methodology,

A way of thinking and doing

The system is something we are all in collusion with

Media, manufacturers, governments and society

Reflects our cultural fears

A fear of change

A fear of extinction

Yet we live in an age of extremes

Never before have so few of the world's population been so wealthy

And so many lived in poverty

So many been connected

And so many live helpless

The system is the pervasive cultural attitude of our time

It is the information architecture that maintains the status quo

It is designed to maximise profit

It is designed to negate change